ALSO BY MAGGIE & NIGEL PERCY

LEARN DOWSING

YOUR NATURAL PSYCHIC POWER

MAGGIE PERCY

NIGEL PERCY

ISBN: 978-1-946014-41-2 (Ebook version)

ISBN: 978-1-946014-42-9 (Paperback version)

ISBN: 978-1-946014-44-3 (Hardcover version)

Sixth Sense Books

150 Buck Run E

Dahlonega, GA 30533

Email address: discoveringdowsing@gmail.com

I know very well that many scientists consider dowsing as a type of ancient superstition. According to my conviction this is, however, unjustified. The dowsing rod is a simple instrument which shows the reaction of the human nervous system to certain factors which are unknown to us at this time.

~Albert Einstein

CONTENTS

FOREWORD

Maggie and Nigel Percy have been exploring, practicing, sharing and teaching dowsing for over thirty years, and in this book bring all of the accumulated knowledge, skills and experience into a comprehensive training program and handbook for both beginner and experienced dowsers alike.

Their engaging writing style, richly laced with examples, anecdotes and personal stories, makes this book a delight to read and re-read as we become increasingly aware and familiar with the world that they so generously share with us.

Many fellow dowsers and clients around the world have benefitted from their extensive working career, and we are grateful that they have finally brought all of their material into one volume for us to enjoy, share and use as a reference.

We wish them great joy in their retirement and can be sure that a pendulum will always be close to their hands…

Dr. Patrick MacManaway, MB ChB

Past President, British Society of Dowsers

PREFACE

In the late 1990s, we weren't looking for dowsing. Nigel in the UK and I in the US were busy exploring the world of energy healing modalities, invisible energies, techniques like yoga and t'ai chi, and methods of divination and personal growth such as astrology and tarot readings, all new and shiny subjects for us.

We had each reached a point in our lives where the conventional view of reality just didn't fit. We found ourselves restless to discover purpose for ourselves beyond just a job. The world seemed shallow and lackluster until we began to delve beneath what we could see. What we discovered when we opened ourselves to a new way of seeing was that there is so much more to the Universe and to life than we ever imagined.

Filled with enthusiasm, we committed to becoming certified in healing techniques and began to practice moving energy through our systems with t'ai chi and other methods. We consulted with experts who offered insights via astrology and tarot readings.

Dowsing wasn't on our radar. It came out of the blue. Yet it became the most powerful tool in our kit, and more importantly, it was the thing that brought us together.

An online dowsing forum introduced me to Nigel, and the rest, as they say, is history. I crossed an ocean to meet him, we married and returned to the US to work together as dowsers.

My life blossomed and the future seemed filled with potential. Over the years, our passion for dowsing led us to create many presentations, books, courses, events and websites that allowed us to share what we loved.

This year we decided to fully retire, which meant shutting down our websites and our online dowsing course. We had never written a book on how to dowse, preferring instead to interact with students to mentor them as they learned. But full retirement did not offer us that option. So we created this book to be the best dowsing course you can find in book format.

We realize the limitations of this format, but we felt it was important to continue to tutor people in such a valuable skill, because opportunities for in-person and online dowsing training are severely limited. This book is our effort at distilling the key things you need to know to become a confident and accurate dowser and to learn many ways to use it to improve your life and have fun while doing it.

The big upside to this format is its affordability. You won't find a good course anywhere for so little investment. So in the end, it was a no-brainer for us to write this book.

Our goal in this course is to show you how natural and straightforward dowsing is, and to include everything you need to know in order to master dowsing rather quickly. We want to help you avoid the 'hard knocks' school of learning; we hope to offer you a platform that allows you to begin at a higher level than we did by standing on our shoulders.

Dowsing is a skill that can improve many areas of your life, and each application can contribute such benefit that it is worth exploring all of them. We invite you to read this book and then get dowsing in as many ways as possible. We're certain that once you start, you will see the incredible value of dowsing.

We all start our journey as beginners. You will probably never have more enthusiasm for learning dowsing than you do as a beginner, because as a newbie, you can imagine the potential for changing your life, and it's all shiny and fresh, and a door is opening, revealing dazzling possibilities. Ride the wave of that excitement as you read this book. Never let it become a chore to dowse.

Your intuition is telling you that dowsing could be the key to a happier, healthier and more prosperous life experience. Your intuition is right.

Maggie Percy

March 2022

1

YOU ARE ALREADY 'PSYCHIC'

Story: X-ray Vision

Nigel was not 'psychic' in any way until later in life, when he opened himself to his intuition via dowsing. He shares a remarkable story of how perception can change when you choose to allow yourself to be intuitive.

I was teaching at the time the story I'm about to tell happened. I was also just getting really interested in dowsing but had no real idea what to do with it. All I knew was that it showed me that what I could see and touch wasn't the whole of what was around me. I suppose that it had allowed my mind to begin to think in different ways.

What happened was that I was at lunch, as usual. As far as I can recall, it had been a normal sort of morning and my usual practice was to relax over lunch while I ran over what I was going to be teaching in the afternoon. I wasn't paying a great deal of attention to what others at my table were talking about. I knew them only in passing, really. There was a large teaching staff and sometimes the administrative people lunched with us as well. It was one of those support people who was sitting near me. I was vaguely aware of her name, but that was about as much as I knew about her.

I was satisfied with how my afternoon was looking, so, with nothing pressing to do, I sat back after finishing my meal and let my mind drift a little. You should know that I am a very visual person. In other words I think in pictures. I see snapshots of events in my mind. If someone asks me if I have seen something they have misplaced, I see the area and can tell if it was there or not. It's just the way my mind has always worked. If I watch a film, I'll be looking at the background and picking out items such as books on a shelf or trying to identify what type of stove they have in their kitchen. (Especially true if the film isn't that entertaining in some places.) In other words, pictures, not words, are predominant for me.

So there I was, wondering whether to get up and leave or just let the time pass a little more when I heard this woman talk about a pain she was having in her knee. She said that it has been getting worse recently. There were murmurs of condolences from the others. Then she said that she thought that it was probably due to an old injury she had had when she was still in school. She said that it had happened when she was playing netball and she had damaged her knee then.

I still wince a little when I think about what I did next. Without meaning to, I got a very clear picture of the internal structure of her knee in my mind and I just knew, without any doubt, what the injury was. So, not thinking at all, I piped up and said, "Oh, you tore the anterior cruciate ligament in your left knee."

She had not said which knee was giving her pain and had given no other detail, and yet here I was letting her know that, somehow, I knew the precise details of what had happened. I knew I was right in what I had said, because she turned to me with a very strange expression on her face (Angry? Upset? Annoyed? Astonished? I don't know, maybe a mix of all of them.)

She asked (demanded, actually), how I knew that, and I, only then realizing what I had said, couldn't find the words. I mean, really? Would saying I saw it in my mind have done any good? I mumbled something about having to leave and get ready to teach and made a hasty and embarrassed exit.

She never showed up again when I was eating lunch. Not surprising, really.

But the point is, I somehow allowed my mind to tap into information from 'somewhere.' Would that have happened if I hadn't begun to take an interest in dowsing? Maybe. Maybe not. But I went into that lunch with the belief that the world was not as I had always thought of it and, being relaxed and receptive, I allowed my mind to do something I would not have thought possible, would have stopped it from doing, if I hadn't begun to see the world differently.

WHAT DOES 'PSYCHIC' MEAN TO YOU?

Being Fully Human Means Accepting What We Cannot See

Do you sometimes feel that there is more to life than what you can see, smell, taste, hear or feel? Does the conventional view of life seem incomplete and colorless to you? If so, that's because you are naturally tuned to your intuitive senses, which tell you there are many things in this world that cannot be physically sensed, measured or known.

When you hear a story like the one about Nigel 'seeing' the damage to a colleague's knee, you may believe it's true, but say something like, "But I can't do that; he has a special ability." We'd like to convince you that that belief is not only disempowering; it's wrong. You have the same ability, but it's latent.

If reality has a nonphysical as well as a physical aspect, it makes biological sense that humans have dedicated senses that make them aware of those nonphysical things, just as humans have senses that inform them about the physical world in particular ways. Why is that? Because you **need** the ability to sense all aspects of your environment so you can navigate it safely and find what you need in order to live.

What kind of design would leave you blind to a vast array of things in your environment that have an impact on you? Whether you believe in creation or evolution, neither one makes mistakes. Our human body is optimized for perfect performance in a natural setting. So it's simply logical that you have sensing abilities for both physical and nonphysical things.

Your intuition and your intuitive senses help you gather information on the invisible aspects of life and interpret that information, just as your rational mind and physical senses help you deal with the physical realm.

When you engage both the physical/rational and the nonphysical/intuitive parts of yourself, you expand your ability to live happily, safely and abundantly; you are accepting your full human potential. Yet where do you turn to learn to use those 'psychic' senses? And what happens when you choose to explore them?

Before we go farther, we want to dispel misconceptions about what 'psychic' means. The word 'psychic' is defined as:

Lying outside the sphere of physical science, or… spiritual in origin or force

To disparage the word 'psychic' is to deny the existence of anything outside the physical realm. Which means denying some of the most important and satisfying aspects of life.

Embracing Your Psychic Side Enriches Your Life

The fact that you are reading this book indicates you are interested in exploring a new viewpoint that goes beyond the conventional. Maybe you are simply curious. Perhaps you are strongly attracted to anything psychic. Or possibly you thirst for a more satisfying and complete view of reality than that offered conventionally.

Whatever your motivation, by opening yourself to seeing things in new ways, you are accepting the potential for change and growth. You are stepping into your power, the power to create the life you want.

Dowsing: A Simple Way to Explore & Express the Psychic

We believe dowsing is the most accessible way to step into the power your intuitive/psychic side offers. We also believe that anyone can learn to dowse well.

This is not true of other intuitive methods like tarot, which rely more heavily on excellent interpretive ability and an immediate strong connection to your intuition/inner voice.

You only need to learn a few simple steps to start dowsing and begin to get answers. There are ample tips and techniques for avoiding pitfalls. Thus, the learning curve in dowsing can be far more rapid than in most intuitive methods, and it doesn't involve expensive seminars, apprenticing with a master or arduous and boring practice.

Dowsing is uniquely positioned to quickly open the door to your psychic side. Your psychic side is rich with meaning about love and joy and spirituality and all kinds of things your rational mind cannot navigate. By learning to dowse, you are empowering yourself to experience a life that is richer and more fulfilling.

Become Your True Self

Your intuition has been waiting for you to find a way to expand your viewpoint and tap into a this richer, more empowered Self. This book is a map for guiding you on your journey. The trip is safe, fun, and most of all, you reap rewards right from the start, and they keep getting better.

Welcome to the Dowsing Tribe, where you embrace your natural psychic power and change your life for the better.

TUNE IN TO YOUR INNER VOICE

Before we show you how to dowse, we want to give you a valuable tip on how to improve your connection to your intuition. This will help you learn dowsing faster, but it will also significantly change your life experience, because the skills that make a good dowser also make for a happier, more fulfilling life.

Fear Blocks Intuition

We have found that fear is the most common and biggest block to using intuition successfully. Removing fear is like taking earplugs out so you can hear your inner voice.

It may seem to be sidetracking to address this subject before you even learn to dowse, but it is important to keep this fact uppermost in your mind. We advise you to use whatever method you like for removing fear so you can tune in to your intuition. And use it regularly.

Removing fear is a vital part of creating detachment about answers, which comes into play when you start dowsing important questions. This will give you a head start so you don't run into a wall when you need dowsing most.

How to Remove Fear

There are many effective ways for removing fear. You may need to try several before you find the right one for you. It may also be helpful to use more than one method. These are a variety of simple, effective and inexpensive techniques that have worked for us.

EFT

We like EFT (Emotional Freedom Technique) for clearing any negative emotion. It is simple and can be learned fairly easily, often for free, by doing a search online.

You can measure results with EFT by assigning a 0-10 intensity to the negative feeling you want to clear. If you are successful, you will perceive that number go down to a 2 or less after one or two tapping sessions.

The Emotion Code

The Emotion Code uses kinesiology or muscle testing, a form of dowsing, as part of its process. We have had some success with this technique, and we know many people swear by it. You can start by getting the book and giving the method a try before investing in further training. Dr. Bradley Nelson, the originator of this method, was a speaker at our online Dowsing World Summit event in 2013.

Mindfulness Practices

Meditation, guided visualization, yoga nidra, and self-hypnosis are all methods of stilling the mind and helping you to get a grip on what you focus on. Stilling the mind can be very useful in releasing fear, because fear is not a negative intuition; it's your mind loudly throwing scary 'what ifs' at you.

These methods are very simple and inexpensive to apply and require little training. We have found all of them to help us connect better to our intuition.

Dr. Patrick MacManaway, who wrote the Foreword for this book, offers a number of very simple and affordable but effective techniques for harmonizing your energy that will also support removing fear. See the link to his site in the Resources.

Jin Shin Jyutsu

Another very easy method for releasing fear is a jin shin jyutsu finger hold. Hold your index finger by wrapping the fingers of your other hand around it. As you hold your finger, empty your mind and focus on slow, deep breathing. When something stimulates fear, do this simple activity and you will see quick reduction in your level of fear when you revisit it afterwards.

Unplug from Fear in Your Environment

Another very simple action step is to unplug from the media. Get off social media, network news and stop hanging out with folks who talk about the latest crisis. Negative thinking stirs up fear. The media is a propaganda machine, and it controls you with fear. Unplug from that, and you will find it easier to create a peaceful mind.

Choose Your Tribe

Find like-minded people to spend time with. Talk about your goals and support others in the pursuit of theirs. Try to avoid talking about victimhood or powerlessness. Avoid thinking about negative subjects as much as you can. Talk and think instead about what you intend to create.

Be Patient

Not all methods are equally appealing or effective for all people. That's why there are so many of them. Give several a try and find what works for you.

Calming the mind and removing fear go together. When you begin to dowse, you'll need to get into a dowsing state, and any of these methods will make that easier to do. Plus they have wonderful benefits for your life in general.

APPLY WHAT YOU'VE LEARNED

It's time to prepare to dowse. First, let's set the stage for success in your dowsing by applying what you learned in this chapter.

Remove Fear

Which method we suggested for removing fear resonates most with you? Spend some time researching and using that method. Evaluate how it makes you feel.

Expand Your Viewpoint: Rewire Your Perception

As they say, if your only tool is a hammer, everything looks like a nail. For most of us, we've only had our brains to rely on for making decisions, and if you start dowsing, your brain will elbow its way into the process, because that's the way you're used to living.

You may or may not be aware of this, but this habit will become obvious when you start dowsing. Your brain will not want to be still; it will inject doubt; it will give you an answer like it always does.

You don't have to tell your mind to shut up and sit down. You can be polite and thank your brain for its hard work over the years, but explain that you are going to play to its strengths from now on. Your brain excels at logic and analysis, and you need it. But it is crap at nonlinear thinking or making choices without hard data.

From this point forward, when faced with a choice or apparent problem, consciously ask yourself which will serve you best at that moment, the rational or the intuitive. Examine the situation for whether gathering physical data and linear thinking is best, or tuning in to intuition and using nonlinear processes appear best. Sometimes, you need a little of both along the way.

If your brain can't show you a way to your goal or you simply lack data and cannot think of a rational way to get it, then practice putting the rational on hold and turn to the intuitive. By becoming aware of your ability to make this choice, you increase your connection to your intuitive senses and choose where to focus your power.

Master the Mindset of Dowsing

Dowsing is a natural skill, and mastering it is so much easier if you adopt a proper mindset. If you apply the above suggestions with good intention, it is our belief that you will succeed at becoming an excellent dowser.

2

FOCUS YOUR INTUITION WITH DOWSING

Story: Finding a Needle in a Haystack

F inding lost objects is one of the most valuable applications in dowsing. What follows is the story of how Maggie used dowsing to find a small lost object on a vast farm. The degree of difficulty was much like finding a needle in a haystack, but dowsing was a success.

Years ago, Nigel and I went to Tennessee to visit some friends. They owned a lovely house on a hilltop with about 100 acres of rolling, partially wooded land, a stream and a lovely stable for their horses at the foot of the hill.

The weather was beautiful, and they took us on a walking tour of their property, through meadows, woods and into the stable to visit their horses, then back up the hill through tall grass to the house. I had carried my L-rod on the journey, checking energies as we went, because we had promised to report on the energies and do a space clearing for them.

On arriving back at the house, I noticed that the small bronze ball that screws onto the end of the long arm of the L-rod had somehow fallen off. The gold metal ball was about 1/4 inch in diameter and had no function other than to look nice on the end of the rod, but it bothered me to have lost it.

We decided to retrace our steps, as daunting as it sounded, and dowse to find the tiny ball. As I walked along, I visualized the ball and asked to get a strong 'yes' when we got to where it was currently located. Long story short, I found it easily, almost miraculously, in a grassy area between the stable and the house.

Finding lost objects is not my specialty in dowsing. I do not have a good average in finding lost objects for others. But when I lose something I really want to find, it does seem my dowsing tends to be accurate and I find the object. This has taught me that a heartfelt desire to find something does seem to help if you are using proper dowsing technique.

But it is important to distinguish between a need/desire to know something and an attachment to results. I intended to give the search my best effort to finding the brass ball, but since we were visiting, I had no intention to make a crusade out of it; if I couldn't find it on one sweep, I had planned to give up.

I'll never be good enough to make a fortune finding lost objects for others, but for me, dowsing has been a very helpful tool in finding things I have lost and really wanted back.

DEVICELESS DOWSING TECHNIQUES

Your Body is the Tool

When you dowse, you are asking a yes/no question and getting an answer. The answer comes through your body's response to the question, whether you are using a tool or not.

We like to teach deviceless dowsing first, because it is probably the way people dowsed thousands of years ago. We want you to understand you don't need a tool to dowse. Your body *is* the tool.

What's the Answer?

Your body indicates a 'yes' or 'no' answer by how it moves. Therefore, learning your body's response will help you in many ways. Not everyone's body gives the same movement for 'yes' or 'no,' but certain movements are more common. So go through these exercises to learn your body's 'yes' and 'no' for each method.

Just Ask Your Body: Three Simple Techniques

What follows are instructions for three deviceless dowsing techniques. Have fun giving each one a try. If you don't find one among them that works easily for you, check out the Appendix, where we have instructions for lots of other deviceless methods.

Method 1: Body Sway

The Body Sway is the easiest, most reliable deviceless dowsing technique. This method has the advantage of being hard to overpower (unconsciously, you sometimes try to get the answer you want). It is easy to learn, and most people find that it works for them.

Stand with your feet shoulder width apart. Relax. Stand straight. Close your eyes, as that will accentuate the feeling of motion, at least at first.

Focus on the following question while in a calm and curious frame of mind.

Was I born in _____(fill in your birthplace) in this lifetime?

Note how your body moves, or how it tries to move. For most people, it will move forward. Forward is generally 'yes,' 'true,' and 'healthy,' while backward is 'no,' 'false,' and 'unhealthy.'

You can word your dowsing question as a statement if you like (*I was born in ____in this lifetime*), and in that case, your response will be 'true' or 'false.' It doesn't matter which approach you use.

Wasn't that easy? Now, using the same question, insert a location that is far from your birthplace, one you have never visited and don't particularly want to ever visit.

What did your body do this time? For most people, a 'no' answer is a backward sway. But don't worry. The important thing is that you can differentiate between your 'yes' and 'no' responses. What you got is your yes/no response for this technique.

The amount of motion may be very slight or slow at first. Later on, you may find that a strong 'yes' pulls you forward very fast, while a weak 'yes' is slow and slight.

Method 2: Finger Dowsing

There are a bunch of techniques for dowsing with your fingers or hands. They can be seen in the Appendix. This one is called the finger rub. Instead of depending on your body moving forward or backward, this method uses a change in the texture of your skin to signal 'yes' and 'no.'

This type of dowsing is practically invisible, and we like to call it 'stealth' dowsing. When dowsing in public, it's great to have a method like this, because no one will know you are dowsing.

In order to get good results, your skin needs to have a normal amount of skin oil, but should not be heavily lotioned or dirty. You might find closing your eyes makes sensing the answer easier, at least at first.

Using the same question about your birthplace as for the last example, dowse using the correct location and gently rub your index finger on a desktop, your pants leg or the back of your other hand. Test and see which medium feels best to you. In most cases, a 'yes' response is indicated by a rough or sticky feeling.

Dowse the birthplace question, inserting the wrong answer, and see how the texture of whatever you are rubbing changes. Usually, 'no' is indicated by a feeling of smoothness.

The difference in the answers is subtle, but should be clear. You can experiment with different surfaces until you find one you like.

Did you feel amazed when you got a 'yes' and a 'no' that way? It never ceases to amaze us. Isn't it fun?

Method 3: Blink Dowsing

Hands down, blink dowsing is our favorite deviceless method. Besides being a stealth method that can be practiced anywhere invisibly, it is also great when you are on the phone or doing something with your hands. Of course, don't try to do this when you are driving a car!

The yes/no response in this method can manifest in a variety of ways. You are using your eyelids to get your answer, and all you need is to be able to see a difference between your 'yes' and your 'no.'

For most people, a 'yes' is one blink. 'No' can be either no blink or two blinks or a series of blinks. As long as you get two different responses, that is what matters.

Try the birthplace question from the body sway section and see what your yes/no response is. When you first do this, just stare into empty space and relax.

Who would have thought getting answers would be so easy?

Summary

Which method felt most natural to you? Not everyone is equally comfortable or competent with all three of the above methods, but you should be able to get at least one to work for you.

If you'd like to sample other methods, we have compiled instructions for about 20 different methods in the Appendix.

Having problems or have questions? Check out the *When Things Go Wrong* section later in this chapter for tips.

HOW TO DOWSE: 4 SIMPLE STEPS

Now that you know how to dowse with your body, and that it is a simple, straightforward process, let's look at the few steps necessary to complete the dowsing process. At first, it will take time to 'do it right,' but in the long run, short cuts will cost you more time and also discourage you by giving you wrong answers. So we encourage you to learn these four steps and take your time mastering them. We promise that you will become noticeably quicker in a reasonably short time.

Step 1: Why are You Dowsing? (Make it a Positive Reason!)

What Do You Want and Why?

Think about why you are asking this dowsing question. What is your goal? Be very clear to have a positive goal, that is, one which states what you want, not what you don't want.

Example: Maybe you think you need to lose a few pounds. If you decide to dowse about how to accomplish that, don't dowse about how to lose weight. That is a negative subject.

Ask yourself what positive outcome are you aiming at? Being able to run a mile in 9 minutes? Having more energy? Feeling more fit? Fitting your clothes better? This is the subject of your dowsing.

Is This a Good Subject for Dowsing?

Don't dowse about a subject when you can use your brain or get the answer any other way. Dowsing is meant for times when your rational mind and conventional activities won't give you the answer. Don't dowse when you can google, but consider dowsing a way to google things that cannot be found rationally.

Example: Don't dowse a person's phone number. Look it up. Don't dowse how your partner feels about something you want to do. Ask.

There Must Be an Element of Need and/or Desire

When dowsing, you will find that having an element of need and/or desire makes you more accurate. That's why we don't recommend dowsing coin tosses. You don't need to know them, and you don't really care.

This element of need and desire ties into Step 4 about taking action on your answer. If you dowse when you really want to know something that will change your life for the better, then you want to take action when you believe you know what to do. Dowsing and not taking action afterwards is a vote for the status quo.

Start with Something Simple

You are able to be more detached and curious when you dowse topics that are not life or death. Getting into a dowsing state will thus be easier. And when you get an answer, even though you may doubt it, you'll be willing to go with what your dowsing said, because after all, what have you got to lose?

When you see how accurate you are, that will inspire confidence in your dowsing, and that will encourage you to use it more and on bigger topics.

The bottom line is, although it is best to take appropriate action after dowsing, showing that you will trust your intuition and really want to get what you asked about, you will not be penalized if you don't take action. We just encourage you to do so as often as possible.

When you are clear about your positive reason for wanting to dowse about the subject, go to Step 2.

Step 2: Ask a Good Question (Make it Complete!)

Form a good dowsing question based on your goal.

Make it Comprehensive and Specific

- Include *who, what, where, when, how and why* as appropriate.
- Don't use vague words like 'good'; describe specifically what you want.
- Avoid words implying obligation, such as 'should.' When you imply that only one answer is morally right, you give preference to that answer, which impedes detachment.

Compare the following dowsing questions:

Is this truck good for me?

Or:

If I buy a new Tacoma pickup truck from the Bell Road Toyota within the next 60 days using their financing, will I be completely happy with my purchase a year from now?

Can you find at least one who, what, where, when, how and why in the above questions? Can you see how leaving any of those out makes it a less specific inquiry? Do you understand that 'good' is undefined in the first question, and thus, your answer might not be useful?

For good dowsing results, take your time when forming a question and find a way to include all of the six parts of the question as appropriate. 'Where' is sometimes not relevant. The 'who' is often you, unless you are asking for a friend. The 'what, how, and why' are generally required. Necessity of saying 'when' depends on the subject matter, but is often a vital factor.

In this question, the 'why' is a little bit vague. 'Completely happy' is not defined specifically. You can ask yourself what that phrase means to you. For example, if the car broke down three times during the year, even though it was still under warranty and cost nothing to fix, would you consider yourself 'completely happy'? If you can define a word or phrase more specifically, either replace it or set your intention for it to mean the specific definition when you dowse.

Your Question is Unique to You

Not everyone has the same goals. Someone might be a perfectionist, and he won't be 'completely happy' if anything at all goes wrong in that year. On the other hand, another person might think it's fine if there is one warranty repair or recall in that time period.

Do you see how dowsing helps you to make a better decision for your specific goals? When you dowse, you can dictate what you want to accomplish and find out if a particular action, purchase or choice will help you reach your goal.

A Long Question is Better

A good dowsing question is usually rather long, because including all of the above adds quite a few words. Writing your final question down helps you remember it for later evaluation of your answer.

This step usually takes a while, but **only at first**. You'll get much quicker as you go along. So take whatever time is needed, because that will help you progress more quickly.

After you settle on a question, write it down and look at it and say it to yourself a few times slowly, as if you are putting it into your mind. When you feel you have incorporated the whole question and have a good mental grip on it, go on to Step 3.

Step 3: Get into the Dowsing State & Dowse

Get into a dowsing state and ask the question.

An Altered Brain State

The dowsing state is a combination of laser focus on your question and nothing else. Create a clear, empty space in your mind and then focus on the question and only the question. Say it to yourself slowly and clearly. Don't allow other thoughts to intrude. Keep space open for the answer.

Cultivate a sense of curiosity. The only feeling that supports an accurate answer is curiosity, as in, "I wonder what the answer will be?" Wanting or fearing a particular answer puts energy into that answer and will skew results by keeping you from getting into a dowsing state. You need the open space for the answer to come in.

This step is where many people go wrong. If you don't get into this altered brain state, you are simply getting whatever answer you expect, which is the same as guessing. This is why we say it can be an excellent sign to be surprised about your answer. Only when you are surprised can you be sure you didn't supply the answer yourself.

Support the Process

It takes practice to achieve a dowsing state. At first, it is wise to avoid distractions like a noisy environment and having other people around while dowsing. Having a safe, happy place to dowse supports the process. And practicing meditation or guided visualization is helpful for learning to quiet the mind so the answer comes through more readily. As we said in the previous chapter, learn to release fear, as it is a block to intuition.

When you become more confident, then you can dowse in public or around other people or with distractions and still get an accurate response. Be patient and do what feels best to you.

Now you have an answer to your question? What's next?

Step 4: Take Appropriate Action

You absolutely do **not** have to take action based on dowsing. However, taking action helps dispel doubt and encourages you to dowse. Success breeds success. Keeping a dowsing journal can be supportive of the process.

Just remember not to dowse above your level of competence at any time. Dowsing is not 100% accurate for anyone, but guessing is only 50% accurate, and you always improve your overall odds of success by engaging your intuition, and it will only improve with time.

Keep These Things in Mind to Improve Results

- Don't dowse if you are upset or attached to a particular answer.
- Avoid vague, incomplete or poorly worded questions. The more clear you are about your goals, the better your question will be. Words that imply judgment or obligation are not helpful. 'Good' and 'should' are two words to absolutely avoid.
- A good dowsing question is usually long. Don't be afraid of long questions. Short questions are often incomplete and lead to wrong answers.
- Don't be afraid of getting a 'wrong' answer. You learn a lot from mistakes. Look at them as opportunities to improve technique.
- Do not approach dowsing as some kind of cosmic test of you, your abilities or your skill level, as that brings fear into play.
- Avoid using terms or phrases you can't clearly define when asking a question. A common one to avoid is 'my highest good.' Your subconscious might define this phrase in a way that you wouldn't like. And you don't know what your subconscious thinks unless you can dowse well.

Dowsing in 4 Simple Steps

Now you know how to dowse. Remember, it's always just four steps, no matter what subject you are dowsing.

- Step 1: Set Your Goal
- Step 2: Create the Question
- Step 3: Dowse
- Step 4: Act

PERMISSION TO DOWSE: IS IT NEEDED?

What is Permission?

Many beginning dowsing courses teach about the importance of asking permission before you dowse. We believe strongly that when exercising a power like dowsing, you must do so ethically.

Being ethical acknowledges that there are going to be times when dowsing may be technically possible, but inappropriate for some reason. Asking permission is meant to help you identify when you should refrain from dowsing.

What Do "Can I?" "May I?" and "Should I?" Mean?

Many conventional dowsing courses address the subject of permission with the "Can I? May I? Should I?" trio of dowsing questions.

If you ask 'Can I?', you are supposedly asking about your ability to dowse accurately. But if you are not an accurate dowser, how can you be sure your dowsing answer to this question will be correct?

'May I?' is aimed at finding if the subject you are dowsing is permissible from an ethical point of view. This isn't an issue when dowsing for yourself, obviously, but comes into question if you are dowsing about someone else or a location you don't own. We believe in those cases, an accurate answer is more likely to come from verbally asking permission.

When someone asks 'Should I?' it is a little less clear why, but first, remember we said when dowsing not to use words implying obligation like 'should'? This is a prime example. Words like 'should,' that imply judgment, put a burden on you without explaining whom you are obeying or why. Unwitting obedience like this is a form of giving your power away. It's never wise to do anything because of 'should.'

Then What *is* the Best Way to Get Permission?

You don't need to ask permission to dowse about yourself, your animals and children, or your property, although it is always good to inform a child or pet of your intention and give them a chance to refuse.

An ethical dowser always asks verbal permission before dowsing for or about another person, a location or property they don't own, or a child or animal in someone else's care. Speak to the appropriate person, give them your reasons for wanting to dowse and ask if it's OK with them. If they say no, don't dowse. Then, if your subject is a child or pet, ask the subject directly or via dowsing/animal communication to verify permission. It's really that simple.

Don't insert yourself into a crisis situation like a kidnapping or lost pet without being asked unless the situation directly involves you.

You can probably see the pattern. When dowsing is about or for your health or well-being or to achieve your goals, you don't need to ask permission. For anyone or anyplace else, ask verbal permission from the appropriate authority. In the case of locations that are more public, the same rule applies.

Can't You Ask Someone's High Self for Permission Instead?

The thought is that if you use dowsing to ask their High Self for permission, you are asking a higher, purer authority. But in reality, the rationalization is that you will always get a 'yes' from someone's High Self, because, of course, your motives are so good.

We've never heard of anyone getting turned down by someone's High Self. That alone should tell you something.

We've only seen people use this technique because **they knew they'd be turned down if they asked directly.** By the way, Maggie used this technique once when she was a newbie, so don't feel bad if you have fallen into this trap.

Be brave. Ask directly. Accept whatever answer comes. This is also a good lesson in detachment, an important dowsing skill. If you're so fired up about dowsing without permission, you will have skipped over Step 3 and probably will not be in the dowsing state, because you are attached to a particular answer.

The Purpose of Permission

The goal of asking permission is to become an ethical dowser. We believe you do that by acknowledging the free will of other humans to choose their path, by acknowledging property rights and by not dowsing when it is an infringement on free will or property rights. This is one way dowsing empowers you. It teaches you to turn inward instead of outward when seeking change.

> *"As human beings, our greatness lies not so much in being able to remake the world – that is the myth of the atomic age – as in being able to remake ourselves."*
> *"You must be the change you want to see in the world."*
> *-Gandhi*

In other words… if you wouldn't like some stranger dowsing about you or your property, don't do it to anyone else.

WHEN THINGS GO WRONG: AVOID COMMON PITFALLS

Let's examine a few common pitfalls that might happen when you dowse and show you how to avoid and remedy them.

Slow Response

It is very common for newbies to have a slow (sometimes very slow) or small response when they dowse and to wonder if that's a bad sign. Be patient, stay curious but unattached, and let the answer come through. Your response will get faster and stronger with time.

Wrong Response

A wrong response to your birthplace question indicates you have reversed polarity. When the body's polarity is reversed, your yes/no response will be backwards.

It is wise to start each dowsing session with your birthplace question to check your polarity. If you get a 'wrong' answer, use the technique described later in this section for restoring your polarity. Then check the birthplace question again.

If you find that you often have reversed polarity, this is a sign of something not being relaxed and balanced. See below where the the causes are discussed and do your best to resolve them so that your polarity is appropriate when you dowse.

None of the Deviceless Methods Work for You

So you've tried all three deviceless dowsing methods, and none of them works for you? Don't be discouraged. There are about 20 others in the Appendix. Try them until you find at least one that works for you.

Most people are able to get a couple of deviceless methods that work reliably. If problems persist, see the *When Things Go Wrong* section in Chapter 4 for other possible causes.

Doubt: How Can You Be Sure You're Not Making Up the Answer?

Trusting your dowsing can be really hard at first. You're not used to getting answers intuitively. It feels like you just made them up, because they seem to come out of the blue. This feeling is natural, and it can be confirmation that you are tuning in to your intuition.

A rational answer, one you make up, will come from your mind in a linear way. You will be able to 'feel' the process when it is rational. An intuitive response is just the opposite. It's as if it were injected into your brain.

Everyone feels doubt at first. Give yourself time to build confidence by dowsing simple subjects and succeeding. But don't attempt to prove to yourself that dowsing works by dowsing coin tosses or card suits. Pointless exercises which ignore the four steps will not make you trust dowsing.

The Most Common Dowsing Problem: Polarity Reversal

Your body has a polarity that contributes to your dowsing response. Under certain conditions, your body's polarity flips, and north becomes south. When that happens, your dowsing response gets reversed, and 'yes' becomes 'no' and 'no' becomes 'yes.'

Using your polarity question (about your birthplace) before each dowsing session allows you to see that your polarity is right, so you can trust your answers. If your polarity is reversed, either one of these techniques usually restores it:

#1: Thymus thump: *Gently* tap your sternum (breastbone) with either fist a number of times while intending to restore your polarity to right and perfect function.

#2: Take the first two fingers of your right hand and sweep them across your forehead from right to left three times while intending to restore your polarity to right and perfect function. Warning: if you are reversed, this will feel clumsy, and you will probably do it backwards.

After you have applied either of the above techniques, test your polarity question again. The answer should be correct. If not, apply the other method.

If your polarity simply will not fix, then you have a more fundamental issue that could benefit from research. However, you can still dowse if your polarity is reversed. You just need to remember that 'yes' is 'no' and vice versa. We do advise you to do whatever it takes to keep your polarity balanced.

Other symptoms of polarity reversal are a tendency to clumsiness, right/left dyslexic symptoms, or a feeling of not wanting others too close to you.

Many factors contribute to the reversal of polarity. Among the most common are:

- Dehydration
- Mineral deficiencies
- Toxicity in the body
- EMFs or other noxious energies in the environment
- Strong negative emotions

Attending to these factors will reduce polarity reversal. Longstanding polarity reversal, if not due to environmental energies, can also be caused by beliefs and/or emotional trauma that makes a person always feel at risk from the world.

The good news is that most polarity reversal is brief and easily fixed. We have rarely met people who are constantly reversed.

APPLY WHAT YOU'VE LEARNED

Congratulations! You've learned basic dowsing technique. When it comes down to it, dowsing is really pretty simple:

Four Steps to Dowsing:

1. Determine your specific goal.
2. Make a comprehensive question.
3. Get into a dowsing state and ask the question; get the answer.
4. Take appropriate action.

Right now, though, you're probably eager to get dowsing. First, we suggest you do the following from this chapter to make sure you understand the 'language' of dowsing:

- Be sure to find one or two deviceless dowsing methods that feel good to you, that are easy for you to do, and that give you a clear yes/no response.
- Use the Appendix if necessary to find one that works for you.
- Then proceed to the next chapter, where you'll start dowsing.

3

DOWSE EVERY DAY

Dowsing Every Day Builds Confidence

The reason most people don't use dowsing is that they don't use dowsing. That sounds circular, but it's true. In order to have confidence in your dowsing, you need to dowse and get positive results. If you don't dowse, you cannot become confident.

But so many people have told us, "I don't know what to dowse. What can I use dowsing for? I dowse my vitamins, and that's it." They also say they don't dowse because they mistrust their ability.

To overcome doubt and learn to trust your natural ability, you must face your fear. And to do that, you dowse simple, everyday subjects that your brain can't know, but knowing them will improve your life.

Often these subjects are small, but they add stress to your life. And each time you successfully dowse, you lower stress. And even if you get one or two wrong, they are not life-threatening, meaning you are no worse off, so there's no risk involved.

What Can You Dowse About?

There are so many questions you have each day that your brain cannot answer, questions that add incremental stress to your life. By dowsing and getting answers, you eliminate that stress. Life becomes happier, and you gain confidence and build trust in yourself. Here are some examples:

- You have multiple ways to get to work, and you never know which one is going to have a traffic backup or accident, so you aren't sure which one to choose.
- The weather is unpredictable, and you're concerned about wearing the right clothes for optimal comfort.
- You need a gift for your Mom, but you just aren't sure what she would like, and it's really important to you that you wow her.
- You are going out to eat at a new restaurant, and it's expensive, and you probably won't be back to it anytime soon, and you really want to choose something you'll love to eat that will be memorable.

Every day is filled with little choices that all add up to creating a smooth, happy day or a day that is filled with frustration or anxiety. Dowsing is a powerful tool for smoothing out life. And daily dowsing of everyday topics like the ones above is the best way to hone your skill.

Download Our Free Ebook for Ideas

Our book *101 Amazing Things You Can Do With Dowsing* is free in digital format. We urge you to download this book online and use it as a source book for dowsing topics. You'll find a link in the Resources section.

In the book, we include good dowsing questions and interpretation of results for each subject. It will give you countless things to dowse about. Some are more advanced; just follow the above guidelines and you'll be fine.

Overcome Doubt

Dowsing subjects that are not life and death, but which matter to you, is the key to building confidence and accuracy. There's no additional risk involved in dowsing these subjects; you don't know the answers anyway. Isn't dowsing preferable to rolling dice, which is what you usually do? And let's not overlook the fact that doing this can be fun.

Simple Tips for Success

We're going to give you just a few ground rules to apply as you begin your dowsing journey. Whether you are a complete newbie or you've been dowsing for a while, follow these guidelines for best results.

- **Use dowsing only to ask questions about things your rational mind cannot answer.** For example, don't dowse someone's phone number; look it up. If you dowse about things your rational mind can answer, you may get a wrong answer.
- **Dowse about subjects that you feel a need/desire to get an answer about.** Dowsing coin tosses has no element of need or desire; it's more like a test. If you dowse things you don't care about or are only testing your skill, your answers may be wrong, plus you'll get bored and you'll never gain confidence.
- **Never dowse above your level of competence.** Going too far, too fast is self-sabotage. You can tell you're out of your depth if you are attached to a particular answer. Such dowsing often yields a wrong answer.

So with nothing to lose, you begin to use dowsing in your life and watch how it improves things. The same four steps you learned in the previous chapter apply to all dowsing situations. So let's get dowsing.

LET'S GET DOWSING: 2 SIMPLE EXERCISES

Let's get started. Do either or both of the following exercises to experience what we mean when we say dowsing can improve your life in situations your brain can't resolve.

Check Your Polarity

Before dowsing, always check your polarity with your birthplace question to make sure your polarity is not reversed and to demonstrate your yes/no response.

Dowse This: Choosing the Perfect Gift

The practical experience we've chosen is one that most people face multiple times a year. This exercise is for you if:

- You really want to give gifts that wow the recipient.
- You don't want to duplicate something the person already has.
- It would disappoint you to have the person not use the gift.
- Although you know what the person likes, you aren't sure

exactly what to get, and you realize that in the end, you will be guessing if you rely on your rational mind.

So those are your goals, and your brain can't get you all the way there. We'll give an example, and you can adapt it to your specific situation. Say you have to buy your Dad a gift, and you know he likes a good single malt scotch, and you even know the brand he usually buys, but you want to get him something he'd like even better, something special. So you head out to the liquor store.

When you arrive at the liquor store, you are overwhelmed at the variety in the scotch section. You simply are not knowledgeable enough about scotch to choose. You could ask the attendant, but he looks too young to drink (even though you figure he must be at least 21). Time to dowse! (Please note this same process applies if you are shopping online for a gift.)

Your dowsing questions will reflect the answers that will help you reach your goal, which is to buy a wonderful gift for your Dad that he will use and doesn't already have. (Or whatever your version of the goal is.)

Question 1: Will He Like This?

Is there any brand of scotch on this shelf (in this row) that my Dad would think is absolutely spectacular? If yes, continue. If no, find a new store. (It might be good to dowse a list of stores rather than drive to each one.) Hint: make sure you have defined 'spectacular' to mean a brand that exists, that you are able to find in your location and that you can afford at this time.

Is the brand he would most like at this time on the top shelf? The second shelf? The bottom shelf? You should only get one 'yes.'

Point your index finger at the bottle on the end of the shelf that gave you a 'yes.'

Please give me a 'yes' when my finger is pointing at the brand my Dad would most like. Walk slowly along, keeping your finger pointed at the bottles, repeating the question in your mind as needed.

When you get a 'yes,' you can verify the answer.

Is this the best brand in the store to buy overall for my goals at this time?

But wait, don't buy it yet! You can do more!

Question 2: Will He Use This?

If you've ever bought a nice present that never got used, you don't want to repeat that. Sometimes a gift is too nice, and your recipient puts it on display but won't use it. If that matters to you, ask this question:

If I buy Dad a bottle of this scotch for his birthday, will he drink it?

Probably, you will get a 'yes.' However, if you get 'no,' it could mean a number of things. Maybe his doctor just told him he had to quit drinking. You'd hate to invest in something that would only cause him longing or harm his health.

Question 3: Does He Already Have This?

It's frustrating to buy the same gift someone else does or to buy a duplicate of what the recipient already has. So ask this question:

Does Dad currently have a bottle of this brand of scotch, or is anyone buying him one for his birthday this year?

If you get 'yes,' make other plans.

Dowse This: What to Eat at a New Restaurant

Eating out is fun, but for most of us, going to a new restaurant, while exciting, poses challenges. You want to have a great experience, but the menu is complex, and you're not sure what to order. Plus, for those with allergies, it can be tricky, as many ingredients are not listed, and sometimes your waiter doesn't know the answer. This exercise is for you if any or all of the following apply:

- You want to have a truly wonderful experience eating out.

- You'd like to have your food be digestible for your system, not giving you unpleasant symptoms.
- You want to avoid allergens.
- You have a budget and want to stay on it.
- You know the kind of food you like, but there are too many choices that look good, and you know you'll just be guessing if you rely on your brain.

In this case, your dowsing questions aim to give you information your brain can't provide so you can make a good choice for your goals. Select the ones that apply from the above list and add any others you can think of that matter to you.

Question 1: Does What I Want/Need Exist?

Don't assume just because the restaurant is expensive that you will find the perfect '10' meal here. Find out if your expectations are realistic.

Is there a dinner item on this menu tonight for a price I am willing to pay that will satisfy my goals for this meal?

If you get a 'yes,' keep dowsing. If you get a 'no,' it could be your budget is too low or your expectations are too high or this menu just doesn't suit you. If you are allergic to things, it might mean there isn't a dish on the menu you won't react to (a friend who was allergic to garlic had this experience at an Indian restaurant). You can ask about each individual goal before you proceed to the next question if you wish to see why you got a 'no.'

Question 2: What to Order?

Since you have not learned list dowsing yet, let's take advantage of the usual design of a menu. First, find the page that has the best entree for your goals. Look at a page or point at it and ask (it's OK to ask silently):

Is the best dinner entree for my goals on this page?

Go through each page until you get a 'yes.'

Look at the selected page. If there are columns, ask:

Is the best choice for me in this column?

Keep asking until you get a 'yes.'

Then point your index finger at the item at the top of that column/page and say:

Please give me a 'yes' when I point at the best choice for my goals.

When you get a 'yes,' you can verify it by asking:

Is this the best dinner item for my goals tonight?

Checking Your Dowsing Builds Confidence

These are two examples of how dowsing can improve your life, and they are ways that you get fairly quick feedback on whether your dowsing was correct. Getting confirmation of your dowsing will encourage you to dowse more often. Plus, it's fun to see how powerful dowsing is.

KEEP A JOURNAL

Over the years, we've found it very helpful for new dowsers to keep a dowsing journal. This is a diary of your dowsing activities, and you can progress more quickly if you keep one.

What Goes into a Dowsing Journal?

You can put anything you want into a dowsing journal. At the very least, we suggest you note the following:

- Date and time
- Your mental/emotional state about this dowsing topic
- The conditions under which you dowsed, like in a quiet room or out in a public location; note the level of distractions
- The exact dowsing question
- How you felt as you dowsed
- Any other sensations you had while dowsing
- The answer you got and how solid it felt

You can include any other additional information you wish. This may look like a lot of info, but it is not. It will only take you a few moments to write this down. You'll be glad you did.

Why Keep a Journal?

We have found that confirming your results is the best way to gain confidence. A lot of the time, that will happen without keeping a record of what you did. When you get a correct answer, you cheer and move on.

However, when you don't get an answer that appears to be right, it can be demoralizing. Our experience has shown us that especially for new dowsers, **wrong answers are not always wrong**. How can that be? Because if your technique is proper, your dowsing answer is usually correct for the question you asked. But that doesn't mean you asked the right question.

In other words, even when you are 'wrong,' your dowsing response is often appropriate, if not useful. By writing down the question you asked, you can go back and examine it. How good was the question? Did you include how, what, where, when, who and why as appropriate? Did you use a vague word? Was the question worded in a way that it could be misinterpreted?

Ask yourself how the answer you got could be correct for that question while still being wrong for what you wanted to know. Here's an example:

Years ago, when home loan modifications were being offered by banks in the US, we were eager to be considered for one. We went through a laborious application process and were turned down. Our dowsing had consistently said we'd get the loan. Yet we did not.

Less than a year later, our mortgage was sold to a new company. Within a few weeks, the new company reached out to us and asked us if we wanted to apply for a home loan modification. We did so, and we got accepted. As it turned out, 'when' had been missing from our dowsing question. We were both so focused on the present, it hadn't occurred to us that 'when' was needed. But it was crucial.

The moral of the story is, if you keep a journal, you can go back and often figure out how to improve your results. Things you might discover that can improve your dowsing:

- Maybe you will notice you dowse better at a certain time of day.
- Perhaps you need to improve your questions, removing vague words, making them more specific or assuring you include how, what, why, when, where and who.
- You'll see patterns that need correcting: you can't dowse in noisy areas, you can't dowse well if you're tired or upset, you can't get good results with an audience.

You are an individual, and we can't tell you what exactly to watch out for, but you are intelligent and can see the patterns if you keep a journal and go back and look at it.

Another advantage of keeping a journal is if you have a dowsing buddy, you will be able to give your buddy the exact same question you dowsed, which is vital if you want someone to confirm your results.

When Can I Stop Journaling?

You don't have to journal forever. Just give it a try, and when the time comes that you are getting consistently accurate results, you will probably only want to record dowsing activity when you start dowsing at a more challenging level.

Eventually, you will find that your results are so good that you don't feel a need to continue journaling. Of course, that doesn't mean you have to stop. Do whatever feels best to you.

HOW ACCURATE CAN YOU BE?

How Accurate Do You Want to Be?

One of the common questions new dowsers have is, "How good can I get with dowsing?" It's a fair question, but we can make no promises. Everyone is unique, so as with any skill, your progress will have its own path and proceed at its own pace and arrive at whatever destination aligns with your energy. And how far you take dowsing will depend on a number of factors.

So here's the short answer. How good do you want to be with dowsing? The answer you give is the biggest factor in how good a dowser you will become.

The number one factor is not how much intuitive talent you have. It isn't how hard you work to learn. It isn't even how much you practice or study. The most important factor in fulfilling your dowsing potential is how good a dowser you want to be.

It May Sound Counterintuitive

We live in a culture that values work and talent, and there's nothing wrong with either of them. And it's true that if you have natural talent in intuition and/or you work hard to learn dowsing, you will proceed at a faster pace than if you are not gifted or are unwilling to practice.

But a good outcome starts with being committed to a goal. If you choose to become a good dowser, you will. It's that simple.

95% is a Reasonable Goal

When you were in school, 95% was a very good grade on a test. As a dowser, you can aspire to being accurate 95% of the time with your dowsing. That means that when asking questions your brain cannot answer, you can expect to be right 95% of the time. Isn't it nice to think there's one subject everyone can get an A in?

It might sound like an incredible promise, but it's been shown to be true of water dowsers by statistical analysis of their success at finding water for clients. Anecdotally, we have seen that a 95%+ accuracy seems to be true for any dowser within their area of expertise.

A Small Caveat

When we say 'within their area of expertise,' we mean that a good water dowser tends to be at least 95% accurate on water dowsing. The same person might only be 60% accurate on health dowsing if they rarely dowse for health.

Each application of dowsing has its own skill set and learning curve. You will find a few applications of dowsing that you love, that you turn to often, and for those applications, you will eventually become quite accurate. On other dowsing topics, you might not have the same level of accuracy, but then again, you might.

The Bottom Line: With Dowsing, You're Always Ahead

In the end, even if your accuracy for dowsing is only 70%, then that means instead of guessing, which has a 50/50 chance of being right, your dowsing will guide you to the correct answer far more often. No matter what your level of accuracy, even from the start, by choosing to dowse, you are improving your odds over random chance or guessing, which is what everyone does when their brain doesn't know the answer to their question.

APPLY WHAT YOU'VE LEARNED

To make dowsing easier and get better results, do the following things:

- Get a dowsing journal and use it.
- Download our free ebook *101 Amazing Things You Can Do With Dowsing* (a link is in Resources). In it there are many simple things to dowse with excellent questions and interpretation provided.
- Make a point of dowsing at least once a day about a simple subject your brain can't help you with that you need or want an answer to, or that having an answer will improve your life in some way. Record the process in your journal.
- Intend to spend 80% or more of your time on dowsing things that at some point can be verified. Tangible target dowsing (as it is called) is usually about things that happen in the physical world. Intangible target dowsing is about invisible things. It's easier to look back and measure results for tangible targets, so focus on doing mostly that. We don't mean coin tosses. We mean activities like which item to choose on the restaurant menu, what jacket to wear for greatest comfort or what route to take to work.

These things eventually give you feedback in most cases. That contributes to confidence.

- When you appear to have made a mistake, go back to your journal and try to see what might have caused the problem, whether it was a vague dowsing question or a distraction or attachment while dowsing. Learn from your mistakes.

In the next chapter, we add some tools to your tool kit (literally) and some techniques that will expand your horizons and help you take on bigger dowsing subjects. Mastering the basics and everyday dowsing will make your learning curve quicker.

4

TAKE YOUR DOWSING TO THE NEXT LEVEL

Story: Real-life Romance

This story from Maggie tells how trusting your intuition and dowsing can help you find your life partner, even if they live on another continent.

I discovered dowsing in 1999 in my Karuna Reiki Master Teacher class. The teacher took out a pendulum at one point and began dowsing the chakras of one of the students, who was lying on a massage table.

I watched the different movements of the pendulum when held over each chakra, and it was like a revelation. You didn't have to see the chakras or sense the chakras to know what was going on. The implications were astounding.

I immediately bought one of the teacher's handmade pendulums when she offered it. As fun as it was to play with, I soon realized I didn't have any idea how to use it. And I really wanted to learn.

So when I went back home, I joined the local dowsing chapter, went to every meeting, enrolled in every course and bought every book I could find about dowsing. I'd been dowsing for several months when the summer arrived and dowsing meetings were suspended until fall, and I couldn't find any resources to continue my education.

The internet was quite new then, but I was able to find a dowsing group online called the Digital Dowsers. I loved participating, but I was frustrated that so little was posted about dowsing. I noticed one member who posted thoughtful and intelligent things about dowsing, so I reached out and asked him if we could email one another directly about dowsing, and he said yes. His name was Nigel Percy, and I had no information about his location, age, marital status, or anything about him, because the forum provided no information about members. I had no idea that by reaching out to him, I'd changed my life forever.

We soon struck up a correspondence about dowsing, and the thing that grabbed my attention was that I got the strongest intuitive feeling when I read his emails that he was supposed to be important in my life. Bear in mind I had no details about him and we only spoke about dowsing, so it was a pretty strange way to feel.

After going back and forth a few times about dowsing, I finally asked Nigel if he'd mind sharing some personal details. When I found out he was currently not married and my age, I got scared, because that only made me feel more compelled to figure out this strange attraction.

I really needed to know what this feeling was about. So I used dowsing to ask what role Nigel had in my life: dowsing friend, dowsing teacher, lover or life partner. I think I had a couple other roles in the list. When I dowsed he was my life partner, I was floored.

Seeking confirmation, I went to a psychic whom I regarded highly and had consulted a couple of times. When I explained my situation and said I was looking for guidance, she wouldn't tell me what I should do, but gave an evasive answer about no choice being wrong in the long run.

I then turned to my friend who had taken the Reiki class with me and who had also taken up pendulum dowsing, as she was my dowsing buddy. I wanted her to say my dowsing was accurate, that Nigel was meant to be my life partner. She told me that she had dowsed I was going to the UK, not that it was the right thing for me to do.

Notice the pattern of how I was looking for a guru to tell me what choice to make; I didn't really trust my dowsing. In the end, I had to decide for myself whether to trust my dowsing and the intuitive pull I felt from Nigel. It was my first step on a long journey of self-empowerment with dowsing. Dowsing had begun to teach me to be my own guru.

My family and friends advised me not to go to the UK, pointing to the cost, the risk, the disruption in my career, and the lack of certainty about the outcome. But in spite of that, I quit my job, put my Reiki practice on hold, stored my belongings and bought a round trip ticket to the UK. By no means was I comfortable or certain about my choice; I had never done anything so rash and risky. I just knew I had to do it, no matter what the outcome. So I did.

While it was wonderful that a mutual interest in dowsing brought Nigel and me together, the main thing to understand is that without dowsing, I probably would not have had the courage to follow a strong but inexplicable, irrational attraction to a man who lived on another continent. And thanks to dowsing, we lived happily ever after…

DOWSING WITH TOOLS

Dowsing with Tools

Deviceless dowsing is a natural method that costs nothing, and it appears from one scientific study that dowsing without a tool is more effective at creating the complex altered brain state for accurate dowsing. This is one reason we start newbies with deviceless techniques and encourage them not to use a tool unless they have a particular reason to do so.

Another reason we start with deviceless techniques is that tool use makes you regard the tool as if it gives you the answer, which is not only incorrect; it's disempowering. A tool should only be seen as an indicator.

However, there are times when a tool is indispensable. When a tool will indicate an answer more effectively than a deviceless method, then you will want to use a tool. In this chapter, you will learn how to use all three of the most common dowsing tools.

Pendulum

The pendulum is now the most popular dowsing tool. You will find a pendulum particularly handy for dowsing charts. Charts present you with a lot of possible answers beyond 'yes' and 'no,' and a pendulum can point at the right choice on a fan chart.

We've found it helpful to use a pendulum with a distinctly pointy end when chart dowsing. Especially when there are many blades in the fan chart, a sharply pointed end makes it easier to see the answer.

To find the location in the aura or body for the cause of a particular symptom, a pendulum can be very handy. You could just take your hand or point your index finger and scan, but many people find it easier to use a pendulum while scanning with the index finger of the other hand, waiting for a 'yes' to their question, such as, *Where is the root cause of _____(name the symptom)?*

Rods

Dowsing outside in the weather, walking over rough land, can be done without a tool. Certainly, there are stories of people finding water by fainting over it. Maggie found herself getting weak when she stood in lines of noxious energy. But not everyone has a body that is physically sensitive to energies, and a tool can be helpful in amplifying the response.

The dowsing response outdoors is complicated by the distractions of trying to walk without tripping over things and keeping your question in your mind while staying in a dowsing state and tuning in to your body. When moving, most deviceless methods are unhelpful (the exception being blink dowsing). Rods are your go-to tool when dowsing on-site outdoors.

With either the L-rod or Y-rod, you are not terribly affected by weather, nor are you as affected by body movements that stem from walking the land. The tool enhances the yes/no indication and helps you overcome the other factors.

Bobber

The bobber is a versatile tool that combines many of the benefits of both rod and pendulum. The movements of the bobber are like your pendulum answers translated from the vertical to the horizontal. It isn't useful for chart dowsing, but it can be used on most other types of indoor dowsing activities for which you use a pendulum.

Outdoors, the bobber has the benefits of rods, because it isn't as sensitive to wind as a pendulum would be, and it will handle your walking the land in search of something without confusing your yes/no response.

Which Tool is Best?

The best tool for the job is the one that works best for you and is comfortable in your hand. It doesn't matter what the tool is made of. There are no magic materials that improve dowsing, and there are no materials that detract from your results.

We have found a lightweight pendulum, like those made of wood, didn't respond as well for us, but you may disagree. Try one and see. We prefer heavier pendulums made of metal. Some people love crystals, but do keep in mind that clearing the energies from the crystal is wise if it is a type of crystal that requires clearing.

Don't ever buy a tool for a high price based on the claim that it will work better than a cheap one. A tool is only an indicator and has no effect on your dowsing.

Care of Tools

We've heard some folks say you can't share your pendulum with a friend. As with some of the rules we hear about energy healing, this doesn't strike us as accurate. Since there is no magic in the tool, there is no harm in someone else using it. A tool is just a tool. You'd lend a hammer to a friend and not feel you had to clear it afterwards. Don't build rituals around dowsing. It isn't necessary, and they only restrict you and cause you to give your power away.

In case this sounds unbelievable, many times we've had clients and students tell us they could not dowse, because they didn't have their pendulum. That is a faulty belief inculcated by teaching dowsing only with tools. People draw the conclusion that the tool does the work, so they need it. Nothing is further from the truth. Keep your attitudes about tools simple and practical.

Summary

While tools are not required for most dowsing, and indeed deviceless methods are more natural and probably more successful at helping you reach the dowsing state, there are some times when a tool is going to be more effective for your dowsing. We suggest you learn the basics of using all the tools and then do whatever seems best for you.

PENDULUM

Years ago, dowsing was mostly about finding something underground, like water, minerals or underground services. In the latter part of the last century, people began to expand dowsing to other applications which were mostly done while seated and indoors. Thus the rod became replaced with the pendulum.

The pendulum is great for dowsing applications that are done indoors, whether the subject is physical or nonphysical. Pendulums have the advantage of being easy to carry in your pocket or purse. They are particularly useful when dowsing charts or evaluating chakras.

Considerations When Choosing Your Pendulum

Anything can be a pendulum as long as it is a weight on a length of chain or string. The cheapest pendulum we know of is a metal nut on a several inch length of dental floss.

A pendant on a chain is handy, as you can wear it everywhere. Your car keys on a chain or piece of string can be a good pendulum. Of course, you can buy nice ones online or in New Age stores. If you have jewelry supplies, you can make yourself a beautiful one.

We have found for our purposes that metal pendulums work best and require the least care and maintenance. They have a nice weight, aren't delicate and don't accumulate energies like crystals do.

Pendulums made out of wood might be a bit light for ease of use. Test before buying.

Crystal pendulums may require regular cleansing of energies (as almost all crystals do), and semi-precious gemstones of certain types seem to also require regular clearing.

Some pendulums have a place for a 'witness,' a small sample of what you are looking for.

When using charts, a pendulum with a pointed end is most effective at indicating the answer.

As you can see, you can end up with more than one pendulum, depending on the different things you dowse.

Your pendulum can give you 'yes' or 'no' in answer to your question; it can indicate an answer on a fan chart or other type of diagram; it can trace the path of energy on a map or diagram; it can point to the cause or source on a map, body, or diagram. Grab your pendulum and let's go through some basic training.

How to Hold the Pendulum

Hold the pendulum chain or string at the most comfortable distance from the pendulum. If you have it too long, the answers will come very slowly, as it will take more time for the direction to change. If you have the chain or string very short, the answers will come faster, as the pendulum can change direction faster.

You will be able to determine what works best for you by trial and error, but start with a middle sort of length, curling the extra up in the palm of your hand or letting it hang to the side while you pinch the string/chain between your fingers.

Do NOT loop the chain over your finger. Rather, let the chain or string be suspended directly downward, allowing the pendulum to move freely.

The Neutral Swing

One of the challenges some people have with a pendulum comes from wanting it to move all by itself. All tools are basically showing you a change in your body when you ask a question. They amplify that change. The energy of that change is subtle most of the time. It won't be enough to move a pendulum from a standstill to a 'yes' response. So we use the neutral swing to enhance results.

The neutral swing is simply having the pendulum in motion before you dowse, so that it has momentum and can more easily indicate an answer. By 'neutral,' we mean you set your pendulum moving in a non-yes/no direction. Then it will move to indicate 'yes' or 'no' when you dowse.

For example, if your yes/no response is to/fro and left/right, set your pendulum in a circle as its neutral swing. Or you can set it to move back and forth at a 45 degree angle to the vertical. If your yes/no response is clockwise/counterclockwise circles, have a to/fro motion or a left/right motion be your neutral swing.

Having momentum before you dowse and using a motion that is neither 'yes' nor 'no' makes it much easier to get an answer with the pendulum.

Getting "Yes" and "No" Answers

For most people, 'yes' being an up and down motion and 'no' being left to right (like nodding and shaking yes/no with your head) is the easiest way. But some people get a clockwise circle for one and a counterclockwise circle for the other. Use whichever works best for you.

You can 'program' yourself to have a particular 'yes' or 'no' response by just telling yourself, *This is my 'yes' response*, and doing it. *This is my 'no' response*, and show that response.

Then, you can ask a question for which you know the answer is 'yes,' like your birthplace: *Was I born in _____ in this lifetime?*, inserting the right place in the blank. Your pendulum should give a 'yes' response.

When first starting, the answers often come slowly. Be patient. They will get much quicker over time.

Next, test a question that has a 'no' answer, like substituting the wrong place for your birthplace.

The most important thing is that you get a different answer for 'yes' and 'no,' so you can easily tell which is which.

Now that you can get 'yes' and 'no' answers, you can begin dowsing! Just use the simple steps laid out in Chapter 2.

RODS

The two most commonly-used types of dowsing rods are L-rods and Y-rods. While a pendulum isn't reliable in a high wind, rods are less affected by wind or the jarring of your body as you walk on uneven ground.

Some typical applications for rods include:

- Finding a site for a well (water, oil, etc)
- Locating underground pipes and services before digging
- Finding the exact location of your septic tank so it can be pumped
- Dowsing gravesites
- Dowsing energy lines at sacred sites
- Archaeological dowsing
- Treasure dowsing
- Dowsing the location of anything with respect to your current location
- Finding lost objects and pets
- Following a line of energy or pointing in the direction of some target with one L-rod

Rods are indispensable for on-site dowsing purposes. There are even some that are telescoping, so they can easily be carried when traveling. Both types of rods are fine for any of the above applications. Let's look first at L-rods, as they are the most popular.

L-ROD

L-rods are the second most popular tool for dowsing after the pendulum. With a pendulum, pretty much everyone can hold one so that it dangles below their hand. However, L-rods require a little more sophistication in the way they are held.

You can make your own L-rods using a metal hanger bent into an L shape. If you like adding sensitivity to the rod, you can take the empty body of a ballpoint pen and slip the short end of the L through it and secure it by bending the metal end to keep the sleeve in place. You hold the rod by the shorter end. If using a sleeve, hold only the sleeve to allow the rod to move freely within it. If not using a sleeve, hold the shorter end of the rod with a loose enough grip to allow movement.

Of course, you can purchase readymade L-rods in a variety of materials and designs. All that matters is they are comfortable in your hands. Don't buy expensive rods that are advertised to be more accurate because of some material or design feature. That type of advertising is a scam.

Because L-rods have handles, they have to be held in such a way that they can move easily to one side or the other, or cross over in front of the dowser. That means they cannot be pointed too high above the horizontal, or they will fall back on the dowser, nor can they be held too low, as they will only dangle uselessly.

Holding L-rods

The ideal orientation for holding the L-rods is with the longer part of the L close to horizontal, pointing straight ahead; test to find your most comfortable position for keeping the rods pointing forward in neutral position. Your hands and arms should be as relaxed as possible and still hold the rods easily in that position. If your thumbs are on top of the rods, they simply won't move, so make sure that the rods can swing by making small movements with your arms or hands. When you're happy with that, get the rods back to the start position and hold them steady there.

Most rods come in pairs, but you don't actually need two for most dowsing purposes. So, if you find that one hand is more sensitive, go with just that one to begin with.

The same four steps apply to dowsing with rods as without a tool. The only difference is how the answer presents.

Determine Your Yes/No Responses

For most dowsers, a 'yes' is when the rod swings inwards toward the body. Conversely, a 'no' is when it swings outwards. Of course, your response might be different. Practice with your birthplace question and see.

Decide Exactly When You Want Your 'Yes'

When outside, if you fail to decide when you want your 'yes' response to show before beginning dowsing, you may end up being inaccurate by several inches or more, and that can be critical when dowsing underground features. So decide exactly when you want to get your response.

It could be when your leading foot is over the target, when your hands are over it, or even when the tips of the rods are over it. As long as you know what will be the trigger of the response to move the rods, you will be able to locate exactly what you are looking for.

Y-ROD

The Y-rod is a very old type of dowsing tool. One of the earliest pictures of someone dowsing shows them using this type of y-shaped dowsing rod.

When such tools were more popular than they are today, they would be cut fresh from a tree or bush on site. After a few days, the wood would dry out and the rod would crack or split, so having a fresh rod was essential.

This type of rod was used mostly in water dowsing, or water witching as it's sometimes known, although that first picture available was showing its use for dowsing for metal ores.

Various dowsers have proclaimed that certain types of wood-based rods work better than others for finding water. Some dowsers have even said that the rod should be cut at certain times of the month. The truth is that if you look at what successful dowsers have used, there is a huge variety of woods mentioned and the time of the month, the phase of the moon, or time of day are disregarded. All those dowsers were looking for was a tool they could cut and use straight away while it was still supple.

The length of the rod is very much down to personal preference. Some people use a shorter length than others. Some use a very long length indeed.

Modern dowsers tend not to use fresh-cut wooden rods so much. Instead there are plenty of rods made out of a variety of materials which do not decay, dry out or snap easily. These tend to be made of metal or plastic. It's usually easier to buy a Y-rod than to be sure you can find an appropriate branch where you are going to dowse.

Holding the Y-rod

No matter what material the rod is made of, how it is used remains basically the same. The most usual method of holding the Y-rod is to have your hands palm up. Sometimes you see it being held palms down, but that's a more difficult method.

Grip the handles of the Y-rod with your hands palms up, thumbs outward, and apply tension so that the long part of the Y, which is pointing in front of you, balances at about a horizontal level. Holding it properly causes the heels of your hands to press towards each other to maintain proper tension. Get the rod to balance in the neutral position. At first, this can take a bit of practice. Then follow the usual steps in dowsing, and as you walk, you are focused on allowing the answer to come through.

The Y-rod works because of the amount of tension it is being held under. If you simply held it out in front of you by the ends, it probably wouldn't do a thing for you. But, held under tension, the rod can move up or down very easily. In fact, if you're not careful, you can get a nasty smack in the mouth from a longer rod while you are learning!

Get Your Yes/No Responses

The most common 'yes' is when the point of the rod is pulled toward the ground. 'No' tends to be pointing upward. So you would get into a dowsing state and ask your carefully worded dowsing question and walk whatever grid you have set out, waiting for a 'yes' response. Don't be afraid to stop, get your bearings, and start again.

When you are new to using a Y-rod, watch out for unexpectedly strong 'no' answers, which can cause the tip of the rod to smack you in the face.

Most people find the Y-rod a bit trickier to use than L-rods, but go ahead and try it and see how it feels to you.

BOBBER

AN UNDERUSED TOOL

When it comes to tools, the bobber is the cinderella of the family. Not many people use bobbers regularly, but it's very simple to use and has the benefits of a rod and the flexibility and ease of use of a pendulum. If you are mainly familiar with the pendulum, you should find it very easy to learn how to use a bobber.

Make Your Own Bobber

There are many different designs for bobbers. Mostly, they have a length of metal with a bit of a weight on the end. The best design we've seen is one you can make yourself for almost nothing. It consists of a length of speedometer cable, which is quite flexible, inserted into a simple wooden tool handle, like you have for a rasp or file. You can put a plastic cap on the end.

Most bobber designs have long parts that do not bend, so like L- and Y-rods, they are clumsy to carry. If you make a bobber with speedometer cable, you can actually fold it up and carry it in a purse or pocket without harming it.

Your Yes/No Relates to Your Pendulum Response

The bobber is used in dowsing just as any other tool. You follow the basic dowsing steps and then wait for the answer to be amplified by the bobber. The movements of the answers tend to mirror your pendulum yes/no response. If your pendulum 'yes' is up and down, the bobber will probably be the same. If your pendulum 'no' is to and fro, that will be your bobber 'no'.

If on the other hand, you use clockwise and counterclockwise circles for your pendulum responses, the bobber will probably mirror them.

All that matters is you know what your yes/no response is. The only difference between a bobber and a pendulum is that pendulum dangles down and the bobber is held horizontally.

While rods tend to be clumsy except for outdoor dowsing, a bobber can easily be used when dowsing subjects indoors. For some people, a bobber is their go-to all around tool for dowsing.

SCALES, LISTS, CHARTS & MAPS

Give Your Dowsing Depth

Learning basic dowsing technique opens a door to an expanded viewpoint of the world. It empowers you to know more and to make better choices for creating the life you want.

What you will find when you begin to feel confident about your dowsing response is that you aren't really comfortable using dowsing for serious choices yet. While everyday situations are fairly simple to dowse about, such as which route to take to work for the quickest journey, many situations are more complex. And that gives you pause. You are doubtful about your ability to 'know' exactly what to do in more serious situations.

When you start taking your dowsing to a more advanced level to dowse about things that really matter, a simple 'yes' or 'no' feels inadequate. You want more detail. Or, you trust that doing something like taking supplements or doing exercise will help you reach your goals, but you aren't sure exactly how to move forward, as you aren't an expert in those subjects.

You can certainly turn to an 'expert' when this happens, if you wish, but that is always rather costly. You can even dowse which expert will be most able to help you reach your goals. However, if you want to move forward on your own, dowsing can help.

That's where scales, lists, charts and maps come in. They help you to expand your dowsing to topics that have a greater impact on your life. You want to dowse subjects that can make a big difference, and you need more tools in your dowsing kit to build your confidence and get useful answers.

Learning these techniques will definitely take your dowsing to a more advanced level and help you to get even more benefits from your intuition. And they're really quite simple to learn!

Scales

When making a big decision, you'll feel more confident of success when you are certain the choice you make is highly likely to give you the outcome you desire.

For example, it might improve your health to take that vitamin C supplement, but given the fact that you are on a budget, is it worth the investment? Or, even if it is 'good' for you, how does that translate into your actual physical health? Will it help you attain your health goals in the desired time frame?

In order to gauge the intensity of your 'yes' or 'no,' you can use scales. A weak 'yes' is not usually worth acting on. You want to invest in things that can make a big difference, right? Scales will help you make the right choices.

The two most common scales are 0 to 10 and +10 to -10. The former shows you the level of intensity of whatever you are dowsing, like how positive the change or how strong the side effect. The latter is useful when you don't know the outcome at all, and you want to know not only whether it will be good, bad, or neutral, but how good or bad it will be.

Dowsing with scales can be done in a number of ways. You can draw a scale on a piece of paper and point at each number, asking to get a 'yes' when you point at the one that is correct for your question. The 0-10 scale would be a line, while the +10 to -10 scale looks like a protractor.

If you are using a deviceless technique, just imagine the scale or say the numbers in your head and wait for your response. If you are using a pendulum, you can have the scale on the table in front of you and allow the pendulum to point to the right number. Or you can visualize it in your head and ask for a 'yes' when you focus on the correct number.

For us, anything over an 8 is significant and worth taking action on. When you get a 3 or less, the effect is marginal. Any number in between obviously requires a judgment call. We have gotten good results using 8 this way. Experiment with it and see. It really expands your intelligence to be able to feel confident in your choices when you use scales.

You can also incorporate scales into your questions easily. You can ask if that supplement is an 8 or higher for your goals on a scale of 0-10. Or you can ask if the geopathic stress in your bedroom is -8 or worse for your health on a scale of +10 to -10. This allows you to bypass having the scale and goes straight to what you really want to know.

Lists

There are many decisions in life that are multiple choice rather than yes/no. Some of those decisions involve many options, and if you are dowsing a topic about which you are not an expert, you may find yourself overwhelmed when trying to move forward. How can you possibly know all the options about places to move or remedies for a symptom?

Lists made by experienced people (or even made by you) are a solution. You can easily find lists of remedies online, whether it is lists of crystals you might use for space clearing or lists of vitamins for your immune system. You don't personally know complete lists of things like this, but the internet or a good book will provide them.

If you are dowsing something about which you can't easily find a list of options, you can make your own list. Bear in mind that all lists are potentially incomplete. Before you begin to dowse a list, dowse if the answer you seek is included in that list. Doing that will save you lots of trouble. Another way of doing this is to always include 'other' as a choice in your lists.

There are many ways to list dowse. Find one that works for you. The goal is to find the one choice that is the best answer to your dowsing question.

Depending on the size of the list, after you have formed your proper dowsing question, you might just go down the list pointing at each option and asking, *Is this the best answer to my dowsing question?* When you get an item that gives you a 'yes,' confirm it by asking your original dowsing question to check if this item is the correct choice.

If your list is very long, break it down into groups of potential answers, and dowse to see which group the item that gives a 'yes' answer is in, then go down that group item by item. The idea is to make this a simple and quick task and dowse as few times as possible.

An expanded use of this technique allows you to dowse a reference book for the answer to your question. Say you have a book on homeopathic that is like an encyclopedia with pages on each remedy, and you want to find the best remedy for your situation. You can dowse a list, certainly, and dowsing the index of the book would be an example of that.

On the other hand, you can dowse the entire book; maybe your book doesn't have an index. Open the book roughly at the middle and ask which half contains the remedy that will give you the 'yes' answer to your dowsing question. Then take that section and split it roughly in half and ask again. Keep doing this until you are down to several pages, and then dowse each page until you get to the right one.

You can use various deviceless dowsing techniques to dowse lists. Finger dowsing and blink dowsing excel at that. Or use a pendulum or bobber. Lists allow you to select the perfect answer from many options when you don't have all the options in your head. How cool is that?

Charts

Most dowsers love charts. It's so fun to pendulum dowse over a fan chart and have your pendulum point to an answer. It's like magic. But it's really not magic. By using a chart, you've basically taken a list and turned it into a visual representation of a list that is easily dowsed using a pendulum.

Chart dowsing with fan charts is one dowsing technique that requires a pendulum. We recommend using a pendulum with a point on the end for ease of interpreting your answers.

There are many books and online resources for chart dowsing. From health and finance to spiritual topics, charts can be a wonderful resource for dowsers. See the Resources for a link to our favorite provider of charts, Nita Ott at Mirrorwaters. She offers individual charts and groups of charts at an affordable price.

We became certified in SRT (Spiritual Response Therapy) years ago, which uses fan chart dowsing in its process for finding causes of problems and solutions. If you want to combine chart dowsing with a healing method, SRT is a good option.

We created a type of charts we call Whole Brain Charts that are designed like branching trees. You can dowse our charts with or without a tool, as they simply require a 'yes' or 'no' for each question and proceed in different directions based on your answer.

Our Whole Brain Charts help answer complex questions that usually require many dowsing questions to get to the desired answer by giving you all the possible combinations with appropriate questions. They are a good resource for you to see how to craft a series of questions on complex topics and how to analyze your results. You can find them in Chapter 5.

While charts can be a very useful tool in dowsing, we prefer to use lists and dowse them devicelessly in most cases. Sample the various techniques and use what works best for you. Chapter 5 contains a mini-training on chart dowsing.

Maps

When you are dowsing a location to find a lost object or to clear space, it would be tedious and time-consuming to make a list of all the questions you'd need to ask to get the information you want. That's where maps come in.

Whenever 'where' is an important part of your dowsing answer, maps and sketches shine. Depending on what you are looking for and how big an area you want to cover, maps of different scales can be used. But they don't have to be professional or to scale most of the time. A hand-drawn sketch of a floor plan makes a useful map for a space clearing. It can also be adequate for helping you find your lost ring.

There are different ways to dowse using a map, and in Chapter 5, we have a comprehensive article on how to map dowse, because this is a very popular and useful technique for dowsers. Map dowsing takes a little more practice than using charts, lists, and scales, but the techniques are very intuitive and easy to learn.

Summary

Your dowsing can become a superpower if you expand the detail you get by using scales, charts, lists, and maps. Instead of a simple yes/no answer, you can get intuitive guidance that has the capability of solving even the most complex problems using these techniques. These rational organizational tools will ramp your dowsing to the next level. All you have to do is use them. They are easy and fun to master. You'll be truly amazed at how empowering they are.

PROGRAMMING A QUESTION

Programming a question is of the greatest benefit when dowsing for health. The health dowsing question that we have used most often with the greatest benefit is, *Do I need a doctor?* (or a vet, if this is a pet problem).

Why program the question? Because *Do I need a doctor?*, as you now know, is not an adequate question to get the answer that is most useful to you. There are many factors that contribute to your choice, and emergency situations don't lend themselves to taking the time to consider goals and formulate a good dowsing question. So by taking the time when you are relaxed and can think straight, you will form the best possible dowsing question (which is long and detailed), and then program a shorter version to substitute when dowsing.

Make a List of Your Priorities

You'll be dowsing this question when a health challenge comes up that you aren't certain how to handle. You need dowsing for those in-between situations that aren't obviously emergencies, but don't appear to be something you can easily handle at home. Your answer will be based on your unique goals.

Some or all of the following factors may apply:

- Can you afford what it is going to cost to consult with a professional in this situation? This is especially true these days for vet visits, or for seeing a holistic doctor, which often aren't covered by insurance.
- Is going to a doctor going to yield the outcome you want?
- Is going to the doctor going to give you faster, better results than trying to take care of this yourself using what you know?
- Will there be significant negative side effects to consulting a doctor?
- Is this health situation so serious that you really would be wiser to see a professional as soon as possible?

You might have different factors that matter to you, such as the time you will have to take off from work to visit the doctor or vet. The above are just examples. Think about what matters most to you in a situation like this.

Programming Your Question

For emergency situations with complex factors, having programmed a short question to mean something complex and more detailed allows you to ask the short question and get the answer to a longer one, which is very helpful in times of stress.

You can make the short form anything you like. You can even include words you normally wouldn't use, because you will have programmed their meaning in advance. So the key is to think about this carefully while you aren't in an emergency situation, define your goals and preferences, and then program the question.

The question should be simple, like *Do I need a doctor/vet for this issue?* or *Should I see a doctor about this?* Use words that seem right to you.

Do you have your list? Here is an example of what one person's program could look like:

*I want to get a 'yes' to the question 'Do I need a doctor for this issue?' if **any** of the following apply:*

- *I don't have the knowledge or tools to resolve the issue myself, or to resolve it in a reasonable time frame for my goals.*
- *Consulting a doctor is the only way this issue will be resolved to my satisfaction.*
- *Consulting with the doctor will significantly improve results over handling it myself or significantly ease the healing process or significantly speed the healing process over what I can do myself.*

*And if **none** of the following apply:*

- *Consulting a doctor will have significant negative side effects.*
- *Consulting a doctor won't resolve my issue or will create significant new issues.*
- *Consulting a doctor won't resolve my issue within the budget I have for this problem.*

Note how specific this program is. Each person will have a different list. Including your 'deal-breakers' in the second half of the program can really help you avoid regrets. You can be pretty flexible with how you set this up in terms of wording. Just spend time thinking about when you really want to get a 'yes' and when you really want to get a 'no.' It's that simple.

You program the question using a simple statement of intention with good focus. You have made your program statement that includes all the factors that matter to you, then you make a statement out loud that is something like this:

When I ask the question "Should I see a doctor about this?", a 'yes' response means _____(insert your program statement here).

Always seek a second or third opinion whenever you have an important decision to make, and when in doubt, get professional assistance. Do not use this technique on life or death issues until you

feel competent and accurate, and even then, get a second or third opinion. Never let ego put you in danger.

Programming is a method you can use with any dowsing situation that involves a complex question or one that you intend to use often. An example would be a water dowser using a brief question like, *Where's the best well site for this property?* after programming a very long and detailed question with all the variables he wants to have met. (You can read more about this in the article on water dowsing in Chapter 5.

It is good to revisit your original list and program from time to time to allow yourself to grow and to change factors to suit your needs.

PROTECTION

What is Protection?

People ask us if dowsing is dangerous. When you dowse for yourself, there are virtually no dangers to dowsing. Looking inward or asking about the environmental energy in your house is just shining a light on your everyday life. It doesn't expose you to new 'dangers.'

However, when you dowse about or for other people or places, then you are exposing yourself to new, potentially noxious energies, entities and situations that can bring you harm. The degree of harm depends on your own energy and the energy of what you have contacted.

Everyone and every situation is unique, so there isn't one form of protection that will protect every dowser from every negative situation.

If you never protect yourself and you do a lot of dowsing about entities or do space clearing for friends or dowse to help your friends with personal problems, you may find yourself getting sick more often, having mental or emotional challenges, or experiencing unexplained physical symptoms.

The good news is you don't need to worry if you protect yourself as appropriate and avoid dowsing things that are beyond your level of competence.

When You Need Protection and How to Get It

If you become a professional dowser involved in activities like space clearing, you need to use protection before each session and do an energy clearing on yourself afterwards. The same is true for practitioners of energy healing methods and therapists who counsel troubled people.

Dowsing is the perfect tool for finding out whether you need protection, how to get it, and what level of protection you have. It's simple to include protection in your dowsing. There are a few simple steps:

Step 1: Is It Safe?

Whenever you dowse for or about someone or someplace else, especially when dowsing the invisible realm, the first thing to do is to make sure it's safe for you to do so. Most of the time, this question will give you a 'yes.' If you get a 'no,' absolutely do not dowse.

Can I achieve and maintain a protection level of a 10 on a scale of 0 to 10 throughout this entire session, where 10 means I am fully protected from any negative energies or harm of any kind?

If the answer is 'yes,' go to Step 2. If the answer is 'no,' stop. This can be very frustrating, we know. Nigel has rarely gotten a 'no' answer to this question. In the many years of working with lots of clients, Maggie has gotten a 'no' several times. She believes that her tendency to over-empathize was a great strength when working with clients, but also a liability when there were dangerous entities or energies present. When that happened, she turned things over to Nigel.

If you have weak boundaries, tend to empathize a lot or have a lot of 'victim' or 'powerless' energy, you are more at risk when dowsing dangerous things. Be aware of your strengths and weaknesses and stay in the safe zone.

Don't let your ego lead you into danger. Your health is your greatest asset. Don't risk it for anything.

Step 2: How to Get Fully Protected

Your intention is most important. Your energy vibrates a message. What message are you broadcasting?

Fear and judgment are dangerous energies. The first makes you a victim, while the other makes you a caped crusader looking for demons to vanquish. In both cases, you will get what you ask for.

There are many things out there which are stronger than you, and some of them wish you harm. Your first line of defense is to avoid them. But if you encounter them while dowsing, protection will allow you to leave the encounter unscathed.

You need to have a toolkit with a variety of things that work as protection. Everything has a vibration, and many things can be used for protection. Crystals and symbols are commonly used. They are inexpensive and you can even create your own symbols if you like. Spiritual helpers can be included in your protection. Your guides or guardian angel want to help keep you safe. Ask them for help, but also for guidance when not to dowse or do something. Don't assume it will always be OK to dowse even if you have some form of guides. Be flexible in your thinking and acquire a variety of objects or methods of protection.

To choose what to use, dowse this:

Which of these methods/objects will protect me at a level of 10 on a scale of 0 to 10 during this entire session?

Then dowse among your options. Always make sure you use a method that is a 10. Never less.

Be aware that what you use will vary. Don't get in a rut and think one object or method will work every time. As you change, you will probably need to add new methods, or let go of some of the old ones.

Finding protection and applying it is easy. Your intention will always be to stay safe throughout the dowsing session, and your crystal or symbol will help power that intention.

Step 3: Keep Checking

Listen to your intuition, to how you feel as you work. If you do a lot of work with others, on rare occasions you may feel your protection 'drop out' during the session. Stop and restore it immediately. Until you are able to sense this, it is wise to occasionally check your level of protection during a long session to make sure you are still protected.

Go Beyond Protection

Protection is powerful, but as you can see, sometimes you cannot get full protection. Sometimes you just have to avoid contact with something for your own good.

The reason everyone needs protection is that no matter how much self-work you do, you still have some energetic mechanisms within you that can attract trouble or resonate with making you a victim in some way. Fear, powerlessness and judgment are the most likely to create problems for you. This is one of many reasons we urge you to use methods to remove these energies from yourself and replace them with love and empowerment.

The more loving, nonjudgmental and empowered you are, the less protection you will need when dowsing. And you will also have a happier life experience.

DETACHMENT & WHY YOU NEED IT

What is Detachment?

Detachment doesn't mean you don't care. Remember, we've said there must be an element of need and/or desire about your dowsing subject, and it's hard not to care when you need or want something.

However, you must set your emotions aside when you do the actual dowsing; this is called detachment. An accurate dowsing response depends on your being merely curious about the answer while you dowse, so that whatever it is, the answer can flow to you easily. This is why we suggest you regularly use a method to eliminate fear, as fear is the biggest challenge to detachment.

Tune in when you dowse. How do you feel? Are you simply wondering what the answer will be? Perfect! That is detachment.

Fear is Not Intuition

It's true that sometimes, intuition acts to save you from bad things. Sometimes it is totally subconscious, as when people missed the sailing of the Titanic. Other times, you get a feeling not to go down that particular road at this time. Intuition never guides you to harmful outcomes.

Fear feels different from intuition. Fear does not guide you from danger, nor does it guide you to positive outcomes. Fear comes from your mind wanting to know the outcome and also from the need to control. When you cannot know or cannot control, fear comes in. Fear is not pre-knowledge, and focusing on fear puts energy into an outcome you don't want to create.

Fear is always about the future. In reality, you never can be sure of the future, nor can you ever control outcomes. Accepting that and trusting your intuition to guide you towards your goals allows you to become detached.

You can tell when you are more detached, because you don't feel as much fear. When you are detached, you are able to be curious about the answer you will receive when dowsing.

Challenges to Detachment: Conscious and Subconscious

Detachment is hardest in situations that you feel are potentially dangerous **on any level.** We are all consciously afraid of certain things, and we have plenty of subconscious fears as well. Possible fears include:

- Fear of death (physical, emotional, or spiritual)
- Fear of physical harm
- Fear of harm to our loved ones
- Fear of change
- Fear of rejection
- Fear of disapproval
- Fear of poverty
- Fear of uncertainty

The list goes on, but you get the idea. When dowsing, you are tempting your system to be fearful, because you are usually trying to make some change. You may be intending to be more successful, or more happy or healthy, or more prosperous.

Your subconscious has only one goal: to keep you alive. It doesn't care whether you are happy, healthy, wealthy or fulfilled. It only cares that you survive. Most of us have subconscious beliefs based on fear that are activated when we make changes.

The fear keeps you locked into the same rut, even though you consciously want to change, because your subconscious feels the devil you know is preferable to the devil you don't know; at least you're alive now. But you need to help your system focus on what you want, not what is feared. (We have a training on dowsing the subconscious in Chapter 5 if this topic interests you.)

Detachment Takes Practice

You can see how fear can lead to attachment to certain answers and a tendency to block change. But fear not! Detachment can be cultivated over time. It helps to maintain a conscious awareness of your emotions and guide them to a more trusting and curious attitude.

This aspect of dowsing is probably one of the hardest to teach, and yet it is so vital for good results. Don't expect to acquire detachment overnight. You've spent years letting your fears guide you; now you're choosing to turn away from them. You know this is going to make life a lot better, but it may take some conscious effort to create a new habit.

Summary

Don't give up and don't judge yourself. Avoid dowsing about a subject if you know you cannot be detached. If you really feel you must dowse and you are fearful, use the blind dowsing technique we describe in the next section or have a dowsing buddy dowse your question.

BLIND DOWSING

Distance is Detachment

Blind dowsing is an excellent way of removing yourself from the answer. It teaches you emotional distance, which is very important. When dowsing blind, you don't know what the question is, or you don't know which answer you've chosen until later.

Hiding the Question

Use this type of blind dowsing when you want confirmation from your dowsing buddy or when you know you are too emotionally involved to dowse accurately. To do this, you simply hold the question (or problem) as clearly as possible in your head as you ask another dowser to get the answer to it without telling them the question. Note: This technique is more accurate if you ask a good question.

Why Not Try It?

With a partner, take turns in blind dowsing the other person's question. For the person asking the question, **do not tell your partner what the**

question is. Simply have it as clearly in your mind as possible.

Suggestions for the person doing the dowsing: Wait until your partner is ready, then calm your mind. You can ask a question such as, 'Is the question held clearly enough for me to answer it?' If so, then dowse whether the answer is either 'yes' or 'no.'

Hiding the Answer

Use this version of blind dowsing when you are on your own and you know that you will be too emotionally involved to dowse accurately yourself. You might think having one card or bit of paper for 'yes' and one for 'no' would work fine, but it's better to have more than two of each.

It can even be useful to have different numbers of 'yes' and 'no,' as it helps you feel you can't guess which is which. Make sure that they all look alike when turned over (cards) or scrunched up (bits of paper). Your goal is to really have this as randomized as possible.

If you use the scrunched paper technique, you can put all the bits of paper in a bowl or other container for the choosing process. With cards, you can lay them out face down and point to them when focusing on the question in a dowsing state, or you can stack them like a deck of cards and focus on your question as you slowly 'deal' them out face down in front of you, waiting for a response. (We frequently used to use this method with a card deck of flower essences in order to mix the best formula for a particular goal.)

When you do this, you will often get sensations in addition to your yes/no response. You may get a buzzing or feeling of anticipation as you approach the right answer. This method is a good way to expand your intuitive senses beyond the usual dowsing response.

By getting to know how your body feels when a 'yes' is coming, you more quickly will reach the point where you don't need to dowse some things; the answer will come to you before you even pick up your tool or before the tool indicates an answer.

Give It a Try

For this experiment, make either four cards or four bits of paper with two having 'yes' on them and two having 'no.'

Before you dowse, you need to think why you are dowsing. If the following questions don't resonate with you, make up others.

Question 1: Dental Health

This is useful to dowse if you would like to get rid of pain in your mouth, want to have a whiter smile or perhaps wish you could cure an overbite. Think about your goals. Then dowse the following question and see what you get.

On a scale of -10 to +10, would it be a +8 or better for my health and well-being to have professional dental work done on me in the near future?

What did you get? Does it make sense? Did you get any physical sensations while picking the answer? Did one bit of paper or card tingle more or attract you more? Use this as an opportunity to tune into all of your intuitive senses.

It's up to you whether to take action on your dowsing answer. You are not required to, but since it's best to only ask questions about which you have a sense of need or a desire for change, when you dowse in an exercise like this, you can set your intention at the start that it be only for demonstration purposes, and then it is understood that no action is required once you get the answer.

Question 2: A Supplement Regimen

What are your basic health goals, meaning what would you like to improve about your health? Would you like to have more energy? Feel better in your physical body (meaning no pain, but remember, we only use positive wording)? Reduce a certain symptom?

Shuffle the cards or toss the scrunched bits of paper to randomize them. Always do this between questions.

If you take supplements:

On a scale of -10 to +10, does my present regime of vitamins and supplements dowse as +8 or better for my health goals at this time?

If you currently don't take supplements:

On a scale of +10 to -10, does taking a daily multivitamin with high bioavailability rate as +8 or higher for my health goals at this time?

By being specific about your health goal rather than dowsing health in general, you will get more useful information. Anyone can benefit these days from nutritional supplements that are effective. But they are expensive enough that you want to make sure you invest in a program that will give you the results you want.

You can ask this same question about your diet or exercise regimen by substituting appropriate words and phrases if those subjects are more pertinent to your situation.

How Did It Go?

While you were blind dowsing, how did you feel? What emotions did you have, and how intense were they? Being able to answer these questions will help you gauge your level of detachment during dowsing, which affects your ability to get into a dowsing state and allow the answer.

You will soon learn that your dowsing accuracy is dependent on your ability to be simply curious and wonder what the answer is. Not afraid of the answer. Not wishing for a certain answer. Simply curious.

Remember how we started out by saying fear is the enemy when using intuition in any form? Now you can see how true this is, and you can take steps to eliminate fear from your dowsing process. Have fun when blind dowsing, prepare to be amazed at how accurate you are, and take appropriate action when you get the answer.

WHEN THINGS GO WRONG: SECRETS FROM MASTERS

Tool Won't Move: Past Life Issues Can Block You

When we teach dowsing in person, sometimes a student is unable to get her tool to move. In most cases, if she is using proper technique, the problem is caused by the subconscious. If you lived a past life where you were persecuted or killed for being intuitive or using an intuitive method, it is possible that you have a subconscious belief that doing so in this life will kill you.

Since you can only know what your subconscious believes by looking around you, when your tool won't move, this can be a message from your subconscious saying, "Don't go there."

Such negative subconscious beliefs about intuition are faulty, because in this lifetime you are safe and free to choose to use your intuition. Clearing the past life using intention usually fixes this problem.

We have a detailed article on past life dowsing in the next chapter, and we encourage you to go through it if you are attracted to that subject. Right now, if you are having a problem, you can use a simple statement of intention: "Please clear the connection to any past lives of mine that are currently active. Please clear any issues that perpetuated those connections. Please clear anything that came over as a result of those connections."

These statements are like hanging up the phone energetically. It can be as simple as that.

Not Every Tool Works Equally Well for You

It's perfectly normal to find that some dowsing tools are easier and more comfortable for you to use than others. You don't have to master every tool. Remember, a tool is just for amplifying your body's response to the question. Tools are not necessary in most cases. Practice with those you think will be beneficial to you in dowsing, but you don't have to master all of them.

Odd Pendulum Movements

If you continue to dowse, you will probably at some point notice that your tool seems to have a mind of its own and starts moving in nonstandard ways. The most common reason for this is your intuition is trying to give you additional information beyond a simple yes/no reply.

There are no rules about what different nonstandard movements mean. You will have to work it out for yourself. You can even find out by dowsing the possibilities.

Some possible meanings are: 'wrong question,' 'stupid question,' 'unethical question,' 'above your level of competence,' 'maybe,' 'try another time,' or just about anything other than a 'yes' or 'no.' Learning what your particular nonstandard tool movements mean can greatly expand your dowsing success.

Pendulum Movements Change

Many newbies (including us years ago) report that one day, suddenly and without warning, their tool changes to another type of yes/no response. For example, if your tool usually goes in circles, it may switch to back and forth motions, or vice versa.

We're uncertain why this happens, but it appears to have to do with whatever is most comfortable for you as a dowser. Perhaps you were taught a certain way and the other way works better for you.

Whatever the cause, don't worry. As long as you know what is 'yes' and what is 'no,' you'll be fine. It usually doesn't happen more than one time in your dowsing career.

Sometimes a Wrong Answer is Wrong for a Reason

There are two reasons we've seen this happen. One reason has to do with improving technique, while the other is more complex and involves your bigger goals or purpose in life.

#1: Your Technique Needs Work

As a newbie, you sometimes get an answer that apparently is wrong. If you go back to your dowsing journal, you will be able to guess why. Knowing why will help you improve your technique. Mistakes can thus become valuable learning experiences if you allow them to.

Some of the possible causes for a wrong answer are:

- Your question was incomplete or used vague/inappropriate words.
- You weren't in a dowsing state.
- There were too many distractions, which prevented you from getting into a dowsing state.
- You were dowsing above your level of competence.
- You were emotionally attached to a certain answer.

All of the above are easily remedied. Accept the message the Universe is sending and make some tweaks to your technique, and you'll see progress.

#2: Your Life Purpose Takes Precedence

As a dowser, you have goals for your dowsing, and you will become more interested in creating goals for your life in general. Sometimes an action or direction you are taking is one that will lead you away from your overall life goals or purpose. In cases like that, dowsing about it then becomes detrimental to your progress. At times like that, you may get the 'wrong' answer to your question in order to prevent you from going further along that path.

This is a more subtle and complicated situation, but if you are aware that you are always being guided by your intuition overall as well as on a specific issue, you will have to agree that it is more important to stay on the path to your life's purpose than to get an accurate but distracting or misleading dowsing answer.

Usually, this realization comes after the fact, after you have blamed yourself for getting a wrong answer. This highlights the fact that you should not flagellate yourself for apparent mistakes. Consider them learning experiences, and they will become that.

When Sharing Dowsing is a Challenge

You'll be so excited about dowsing that you want to share it. Proceed with caution. Not everyone is ready to be empowered to see beyond physical reality. Let people ask you why you like dowsing rather than trying to persuade them of its value.

How Can You Tell If You are in a Dowsing State?

As we said above, not being in the dowsing state messes up your dowsing, because in that case, your brain, not your intuition, is giving you answers. Your brain has been answering your questions forever. It can be hard to get it to be quiet while you dowse.

Learning to tell when you are in a dowsing state is challenging. It just feels different. With practice, you will learn how you feel when you fall out of the dowsing state or can't get into it.

Most of all, strong emotions will let you know you aren't in a dowsing state. If you can't be simply curious, don't dowse.

Another hint that you aren't getting into a dowsing state is when you never get surprising answers. If you always get the expected answers when you dowse, you probably are not dowsing. Dowsing inevitably leads to the occasional shocking and unexpected answer, and those answers are challenging. Your brain will never give you a shocking or scary answer. So if you never get surprised, do some work on your dowsing state.

LET'S GET DOWSING: RELATIONSHIPS

Relationship Dowsing

When you reach an intermediate level of dowsing or higher, you are capable of dowsing subjects that have some emotion attached to them. Maybe you aren't yet ready for life or death dowsing; maybe you won't ever be. But at this level, you can dowse about topics that can improve or heal your life in many big ways.

Relationships are the heart of living, and most of us could use some help making healthier relationship choices for our goals. Dowsing can be the key to doing that. Dowsing about relationships will save you money, heartache and stress.

Appropriate and Inappropriate Topics

As with all dowsing, it's important not to dowse inappropriately about relationships. The most common mistake we see is when people want to use dowsing to avoid communication.

Good, honest communication is vital to the health of relationships. Dowsing is not a substitute for communication. Dowsing is useful when you cannot solve a problem using a rational method.

Don't dowse about how your boyfriend or boss feels. Ask him. You might say, "But how do I know I'm getting the truth?" Nothing is guaranteed, not dowsing, not communicating. Dowsing works better when you have exhausted rational methods. Also, when dowsing is done from fear or to avoid confrontation (which is based on fear), you are not going to get good results, because you are focusing on what you don't want. You are vibrating with fear.

Dowsing needs to be done in an empowering way. Use dowsing to empower yourself to get better results in relationships. Everyone has plenty to learn about communicating openly and honestly and diplomatically. We all make mistakes. Do it anyway, and do it with good intentions. Use dowsing when rational means cannot help you.

Here are a few examples:

- After dating for over a year, your lover asks you to marry. You've talked about your personal goals and how you see marriage and what you want out of life, and you feel good about it, but you still have doubt. You can dowse and gain confidence to make the right choice for you.
- Someone has asked to be your business partner. They've laid out a business plan and goals, and it sounds good to you. But you just aren't sure. Dowsing will help you make the right choice.
- A friend asks you to share an apartment with her to save money. It would be financially beneficial, or appears to be. You seem to have the same values, and you've talked over basic details. But you still aren't sure. Dowsing will help you make the right decision.
- After twenty rocky years of marriage, you are feeling a desire to divorce your partner, but it will be costly in many ways. You fight a lot and haven't seen progress with counseling. You think that breaking up is the right path, but you can see down sides. Dowsing will help you figure out what to do to reach your goals.

Remember, dowsing is for those times when the right choice isn't obvious. Sometimes, you just know what to do. But on the continuum of choices in various relationships, sometimes you find yourself on the gray part of the scale, uncertain which choice is best. Those are the times you need to dowse for best results.

Different Types of Partnerships: The Same Method

The main difference between beginning and intermediate dowsing is that as you progress, you dowse more challenging topics, you get quicker and you improve your accuracy. There aren't a lot of tricky new techniques to learn. Every time you dowse, you use the same four steps from Chapter 2. Every type of relationship choice can be adapted to that process. So let's look at this subject and get dowsing.

Step 1: Why are you dowsing? What do you want and why?

Whether you are contemplating acquiring or leaving a roommate, a business partner or a spouse, you need to be clear on what you want from that action. Take your time and make a list of everything that matters. The list of goals will be personal and unique to you, but might include:

- You want the freedom to grow in the relationship and express yourself without being judged.
- You desire a deep and meaningful interaction.
- You want the relationship to have longevity.
- You expect the relationship to increase your financial security/wealth.
- Having that partnership means life gets more fun and easy.
- Honesty and openness matters to you.
- Fidelity is important to you.
- You like the idea of it being fun doing things together.

Tailor your list to your goals for that particular type of relationship. Make it long and detailed.

Step 2: Form a good dowsing question

A good dowsing question is long and specific. When dowsing important subjects, the use of a scale is crucial in finding out how strong your 'yes' or 'no' response is.

Option 1: Base the question on goals

Write your finalized question based on your goals. For entering into a relationship, it could be something like:

On a scale of +10 to -10, with positive numbers being positive for me and 8 or higher meaning significant success and happiness, how would entering into a partnership with _____for the purpose of_____at this time (or state what the time frame is) be for me overall, using the list I have compiled of things that matter to me?

Or you can make it simpler still:

Is entering into a partnership with _____for the purpose of_____an 8 or higher overall at this time for all the subjects on my list?

If you are contemplating a breakup, your list will be somewhat different and your wording of the question will change slightly, but the overall format is the same.

Option 2: Base your question on compatibility

Another tack is to approach this question from the viewpoint of compatibility of that person or partnership for your goals. Sometimes you wish you could take a relationship farther, but the compatibility is not supportive of that action. Knowing in advance will save you a lot of grief. A possible question of this type is:

On a scale of 0 to 10, with 8 or higher meaning highly compatible and very likely to create significant satisfaction, how compatible is _____(person's name) for_____(name the purpose) with me?

While you can dowse the list overall, it's also possible, and sometimes a good idea, to also dowse for any single item on the list that is a dealbreaker for you.

For example, if fidelity is a must-have, dowse that item alone and see where compatibility falls on the scale. The point is, an overall rating doesn't tell you where the strengths and weaknesses of the partnership are. So go ahead and dowse them individually.

As you can see, you may need to dowse multiple questions to come to a decision that feels good for you.

Step 3: Get into a Dowsing State and Dowse

Measure your level of detachment by tuning in to your emotions and see if you can be curious about the answer, not attached to a particular one. Detachment does not mean you don't care; it means you can detach long enough to dowse with curiosity even if you do.

Step 4: Take Appropriate Action...or Don't

The thing that makes detachment hard is the concern that if you get an answer you don't like, you have to act on it. No, you don't. Of course, in terms of improving your intuition, ignoring your dowsing answer doesn't help in that regard. But as long as you know you have the right to postpone or not to take action at all, that will help you with detachment. Don't borrow trouble.

Trust is a big part of intuition. Because you cannot see the linear path to your answer, it feels like it isn't as solid. It's as if you somehow think your brain is so reliable, that if you can see how you got to this answer, it must be right, but if you can't, it's liable to be wrong.

Think about that. Your brain has led you astray often. You have rejected your intuition or your heart many times in your life and regretted it. Learning to listen to your heart and intuition will bring you greater happiness. And we don't mean infatuation is the same as love. Your heart knows when you are in lust or infatuated. It knows the difference.

Let your dowsing highlight the path that will lead you to your goals. You won't be sorry.

Our Whole Brain Dowsing chart on relationships gives you a series of yes/no questions to reach the decision on your relationship. Check it out as an alternative to forming your own questions, if you are not yet confident enough to form your own dowsing questions.

Get a Second Opinion

As with any important decision, you should always get a second opinion when dowsing about relationships. However, it does matter who you ask. And no one's opinion is more important than yours. Turn to a trusted dowsing buddy for support via blind dowsing, but don't outsource your decision to anyone else.

Taking Action on Your Dowsing

When you decide to do something, do so only after dowsing as many questions as it takes to clarify the intuition you already have about this choice. Take your time, sleep on it, and be confident.

Intermediate and advanced dowsing come with a higher degree of risk, but the thing to remember is that without dowsing, you would still be making this choice. Only you would be making it without the benefit of your intuition.

When you are deciding something your brain cannot know, you are just guessing, and guessing is always only 50/50. With dowsing, you are not guaranteeing the 'right' choice, but you are definitely improving the odds of it by including your intuitive senses in the process.

APPLY WHAT YOU'VE LEARNED

You now have all the tools you need to master dowsing. You are in a minority of self-aware people who have chosen to empower themselves. Dowsing gives you an amazing advantage for creating the life you want.

Every day, you have opportunities to use focused intuition to make choices that will create greater happiness, prosperity and health for you.

You're ready to use dowsing on just about anything. Don't let fear hold you back. Remember, to master dowsing, just keep dowsing. If you are stuck for ideas, go to our free ebook 101 Amazing Things You Can Do with Dowsing and dowse something new.

Use blind dowsing if you feel too attached to results. Choose whichever tool you like, but if a tool doesn't give an obvious advantage, stick with deviceless methods. Employ charts, lists and scales as appropriate.

The next chapter has about 30 articles that are mini-trainings on how you can use dowsing in special situations. Choose the topics that appeal to you and dive in. We promise that these trainings will give you an in-depth perspective on using dowsing and allow you to explore all kinds of ways to use dowsing meaningfully.

Most of all, have fun! You are using your natural psychic power, and few people ever do that. You've really progressed a lot since you began this book!

5

SPREAD YOUR WINGS WITH
ADVANCED APPLICATIONS

Story: If Shrimp Could Kill

W e spent a lot of years working with clients, and dowsing was a key tool for finding causes of problems and choosing solutions. Advanced dowsing applications like health dowsing can totally change your life, and we loved to help people improve their life by dowsing on health issues.

Note: We are not saying health dowsing replaces the help of an appropriate professional, but as a tool in your kit, it can enhance your results tremendously. The method used in this story clears only the energy of the allergy; it is not presented as a cure for physical allergies.

What follows is the story of a client who asked Maggie if there was a way to resolve his shellfish allergy. Among this chapter's trainings, you will find one on clearing the energy of allergies and one on dowsing past lives that give you detailed instructions on how to do this yourself. Our experience is that a certain percentage of lifelong, unexplained allergies are due to traumatic past life experiences. When this is the case, then clearing those energies can sometimes erase the allergy altogether.

A client, whom I will call Joe, had been working with me a long time and was pleased with his results. One day when I asked him what he wanted to focus on, he said he had a shellfish allergy he wanted to get rid of. My dowsing indicated that he did have an allergy or sensitivity to shellfish, and that we could succeed at clearing the energies that were the root cause, thus giving him relief. Not all allergies respond to this method, but in his case, it tested well.

We proceeded to do the usual dowsing about past lives and found two that needed clearing. We found the details of those lives and cleared them using intention. I warned Joe that there were no guarantees, but he could, if he felt like it, very cautiously eat a small amount of shellfish. I warned him to take it slow and said he didn't have to do it, just that he could if he wanted.

Joe decided to go out to eat and ordered a shrimp dish. He said it had seven large shrimp in it. He reported he was thrilled with his results. He ate the whole portion and only had slight tingling in his lips when eating it. I was a bit horrified, because I know the symptoms of anaphylactic shock. I also felt he shouldn't have had any symptoms at all if the clearing had worked.

I tried to be upbeat and said, "At least you don't have an allergy that causes an anaphylactic reaction." He asked, "What's that?" I replied that some people are so allergic that they get symptoms if someone at the next table has sizzling shrimp and they smell it. I nearly choked when he said, "Oh yeah, that's happened to me before."

Joe had just confirmed he had a potentially life-threatening shrimp allergy, and he'd eaten seven of them with almost no symptoms, certainly no ill effects. After I recovered my cool, we had a dowse together. I suspected clearing for shellfish instead of shrimp was the problem. 'Shellfish' includes shrimp, but is too general; the clearing was incomplete. We went through the process again and found another past life to clear.

After we cleared that final past life that impacted his reaction to shrimp in this life, he had no symptoms at all when eating shrimp. I advised him not to think about those past lives and never to gorge on shrimp, but otherwise, to act normal.

I would never advise anyone to assume a life-threatening allergy has been 'cured' by dowsing and energy clearing techniques. *However, the*

Universe saw fit to show us both the power of intention to shift energy and the power of dowsing to navigate the process through this situation.

Past lives are often (but not always) the root cause of unexplained allergies in this life, and past lives are fairly easy to clear. If you believe as we do that disease begins in the subtle energy body, then it makes sense to look for root causes in the energy body and heal them.

This is one shining example of how health dowsing can change your life. Nigel's lifelong cheese allergy and my dairy allergy were both eradicated in this way. In our cases, it was via a method called SRT, or Spiritual Response Therapy, which uses dowsing over charts to identify past life issues and intention to clear them.

We think our method is simpler and has the advantage of not requiring expensive training, but if you feel drawn to it, SRT is a great method. For a deep dive into our technique, have a look at the two trainings in this chapter on past lives and allergies.

TIPS FOR USING THE ADVANCED TRAININGS

What is Advanced Dowsing?

To be advanced in any topic or skill usually means that you have mastered all the basic or foundational information and techniques, and that you have had a great deal of experience and have attained a certain skill level. In dowsing, that of course means being accurate.

There's nothing wrong with peeking at these trainings when you are a beginner. And if you are particularly drawn to one, no one is going to slap your wrist for doing the training.

However, be aware that until you have mastered basic dowsing technique and gained a certain amount of confidence, these trainings could be challenging.

Use your judgment and have fun. And if you get stuck, go back to basics. Then come back and try again later.

How to Use These Trainings

Each mini-training consists of about 1500 to 3000 words of detailed instruction on a special application of dowsing. Just scan the list and pick whatever attracts you most. The techniques in these articles are not the only paths to success, but they are the methods we have used successfully over the years.

Give them a try. You'll find the techniques all follow a pattern, regardless of the subject matter.

All you have to do for success is apply the four simple dowsing steps you learned in Chapter 2.

As you begin to see the pattern repeat, you will suddenly realize how simple dowsing really is. Have fun!

ANIMAL COMMUNICATION

Sometimes you want to communicate with your pet, and words just don't work. There are two ways to cut through the silence. You can dowse **about** your pet's attitude, issue or desires, forming dowsing questions that refer to your pet in the third person. Or you can try and connect **with** them and ask them directly, using your body or tool to indicate a yes/no answer. The latter is sort of like channeling, but it offers no risks, as you are connecting with a known individual.

Take whichever approach appeals to you. The only difference is in one you ask about what the animal feels or wants, and in the other, you directly ask the animal.

Note: If you approach this subject with the view that it is some sort of power you have or that you feel 'special' in some way, don't. Instead, be humble, be curious, be respectful.

Benefits of Using Dowsing for Animal Communication

What are the benefits of dowsing to communicate with animals? Here are just a few applications we have used:

- Talking to the deva of a species in order to move or remove members of that species from your property, as in ants or gophers.
- Speaking about behavior issues in a pet.
- Discovering what is ailing a sick pet: where it hurts, how much and further details.
- Communicating your desires to your pet or animal companion.
- Finding out why a training program is not getting results.
- Determining if your animal wants to be bred or wants to compete.
- Finding out how your pet feels about its food, companions, etc.
- Tracing the location of lost pets

These are only a few practical applications of dowsing for animal communication. Even without further explanation, you can see how using dowsing in this fashion can improve your relationship with animals and Nature, save you money, help your pet, and help you avoid making costly or painful mistakes.

Avoid Pitfalls

No matter what your level of dowsing experience, you can quickly learn to communicate with animals using dowsing. There are pitfalls to avoid, as with all dowsing applications and techniques. Here are a few common ones:

Be sure the animal you want to talk with is 'talkative.' Some animals are shy and won't open up. This may cause you to feel you are doing something 'wrong.' So start by dowsing if your subject is willing to speak with you via dowsing. Respect the choice they express.

Animals can lie, no matter what you have been told. Do not expect that every answer is accurate, especially if you are talking about something involving fear or other emotions on either your part or the animal's.

As with all dowsing, how you formulate your question is vital in terms of getting accurate answers. Avoid vague, subjective or emotional words like 'good,' 'should,' and 'best.' Don't go down the path of asking about someone's highest and greatest good. That is still too vague. Be specific. Ask more questions to get more details.

All questions must be in 'yes' or 'no' format. For some people, this may pose a challenge. But most questions can be phrased to get yes/no answers. It just takes practice. Sometimes you have to put together a battery of questions that are yes/no to get where you are going.

Ask questions that your animal is likely to understand or have information or opinion on. Especially at first, you will get stronger responses with questions about food or your animal's likes and dislikes than about abstract topics. This will help reinforce your confidence in the process. With practice, you may get amazing results.

Other Considerations

You do NOT have to be physically present to communicate with an animal via dowsing. It works just as well long distance. You use the same procedures either way. We have communicated with animals we never met across thousands of miles.

At first, you might find it useful to write your questions down beforehand, and to be in a quiet place while doing your communication. Later, you will find it easier to work with distractions, but make it as calm and quiet as you can at first.

Some people find that the answers seem very clear during a session, but quickly fade away if not written down right away. Sometimes, it is helpful to have an assistant taking notes during the session, so you don't have to.

You may doubt your answers are coming from your subject. Everyone feels that way.

And you may be asking questions you think you know the answers to, so you think you are supplying them. Be open to surprises. Most people do very well using dowsing to communicate. As you become more experienced, and you ask more complex questions, you will get confirmation that you are actually talking with the animal.

An example is that of Bear, a lost Bernese Mountain Dog. Here's his story:

A Story About a Lost Dog

Bear was a show dog who escaped from a car at a rest area at Donner Pass in California during a road trip and ran away, never to return. His owner had a number of dowsers and communicators throughout the US try to locate him in that rugged wilderness, but he did not want to be found. Nigel and I both had a number of sessions communicating with him. (I wrote an article for the Journal of the American Society of Dowsers about this project.) This project covered 18 months of my life. Nigel joined it in the last year.

One of the happiest outcomes of that project was that we got independent confirmation of the validity of animal communication and dowsing. We had no contact with, or details on, the other people doing communication or dowsing on the case. Here's what happened:

Apparently another communicator talking to Bear reported that Bear had told her lots of people were 'talking' with him, but there was a man in particular who 'talked funny.' Nigel as you may know is British and has an accent. By the way, Nigel was the only man involved in the case, so there was no chance of mixing him up with another man. We heard about this indirectly from the dog's owner, who got reports from everyone on the case. Even she was unaware of Nigel's British accent. One wonders how the heck the accent came through to the dog via dowsing…

You will often get very good confirmation that what you are dowsing is indeed true. Sometimes it comes in unexpected ways, as it did in this instance.

Any animal may be communicated with. Even insects can understand what you are saying to them. As you focus on using dowsing to communicate with animals, you will begin to naturally speak to them and treat them with respect even when you are not dowsing. Dowsing can thus be a great way to have a greater harmony with all of Nature.

Give It a Try!

Here are some basic steps in an introductory communication session with a cat, dog or horse. Pick a subject (an animal) to talk to and give it a try. Record your answers. Notice this example uses the direct approach, but if it feels better to you, you can ask the same questions about the animal instead of asking directly.

Dowse whether the animal is willing to talk with you at this time. If you get 'yes,' proceed, if 'no,' choose another animal.

If the animal is not yours, be sure to get permission from the owner as well, and then tell him/her a few things about yourself before starting the dowsing session.

Animals respond better if you send them pictures about what you are asking or saying, because animals think in pictures, like autistic people do.

Avoid using negative terms like 'no,' 'never,' and 'not,' as the meaning doesn't always convey. You can end up sending the opposite message to what you intend.

Here are some simple questions that work for beginning sessions:

- Do you like your food?
- Do you like your water?
- Do you have any pain?
- If the answer is 'yes': Do you have pain all the time? Is the pain very bad?
- Is the pain in a leg? Your head? Your gut? Your chest? Your joints? All over?
- Do you like the treats you get?
- Do you like _____? (name of another pet in the family, if there is one; stallmate; rider, etc.)
- Do you feel loved by me (or the owner)?

When you end the session, be sure to thank the animal for taking the time to talk with you.

Obviously, the answers you get can lead to further questions. This will lead you to more advanced communication. The main difference between novice and advanced communication is in the questions. What follows is an example of how you can take a simple question and learn a lot by asking followup questions.

Most animals do not like city water. The chemicals offend their strong sense of smell and taste. Sometimes they are chronically dehydrated from not drinking enough of the stinky water.

Chronic dehydration can lead to health issues in animals just as it does in people. For example, we have seen horses that were prone to colic due to not drinking enough water. By asking about their reaction to the water, you may find you need to filter it. Further questions could be:

- Does the water smell bad to you?
- Does the water taste bad to you?
- Does it always smell/taste bad to you?
- Are you getting enough to drink? Are you often thirsty?
- Would you prefer water that tastes or smells better?

Then you need to dowse about what water to use, or what filter to get for the water. Then go back and ask the animal's opinion again after you have made the changes. Repeat the process until you get a thumbs up on the water.

More Complex Communication

If you create a series of yes/no questions, you can eventually get very detailed and useful practical information that will help your animal friend. It is a bit more tedious than traditional forms of animal communication, but it works and has the advantage of not requiring special training or talents.

Likewise, diagnosing the problems between pets or causes of problem behavior can take a series of questions, but it is well worth the effort. Remember that animals don't always see things the way you do. Fido may not know why he eats the couch. He doesn't have the phrase 'separation anxiety' in his vocabulary. This will challenge you to study more about animal behavior so you can formulate intelligent questions.

Here is an example on couch-eating:

- Did you chew on the couch while I was gone?
- Do you know why you did it?
- If 'yes,' then ask direct questions, if 'no,' you have to work slowly around to it. What follows are the questions if he answers 'no.'
- Do you feel relaxed while I am gone from the house?
- Does anything bad happen while I am gone?
- Are there any big noises that bother you when I am gone?
- Do people come knock on the door/ring the doorbell while I am away?
- Does it disturb you when this happens?
- Do you need to pee when I am gone?
- Is it hard to hold it in until I return?
- Are you in pain when I am gone?
- Do you feel sad when I am away?
- Are you lonely when I am gone?
- Do you feel more like chewing when I am away from home?
- Do you feel upset when I am away?
- Does chewing make you feel better?
- Does your mouth hurt, and that's why you chew? (teething dogs will chew, as will dogs bred to use their mouths in their work)
- Are you hungry when I am gone?
- Are you thirsty when I am gone?
- Are you getting enough exercise?
- Do you wish you could play/go on walks more?
- Are you aware that I am stressed?
- Does it bother you when I am stressed?
- Do you take on my 'stuff' as a way of helping me? (frequently dogs will mirror stress in their owners, becoming destructive).

For more advanced and detailed answers, dowse on a scale of 0-10 or +10 to -10 instead of just 'yes' or 'no'.

You can adapt this type of questioning to any problem. You will find it easier to ask good questions if you have an understanding of the problem, so do some reading on your pet's species, as that will give you clues to good questions.

The results of your questioning will point you in the direction of possible 'cures' to use. If there are many options, follow basic dowsing steps and dowse which one will best suit your goals.

Your use of dowsing to communicate with animals is guaranteed to give you a better relationship with your animal companions and Nature itself. It will open doors to a whole new way of looking at the world that will enrich your life. Not to mention the money, time and heartache it will save you.

ANIMALS: HOW TO HELP WITH DOWSING

Choosing a Pet

The choice of a pet is a major decision. Yet most of us make it with our hearts instead of our heads. Often, it is done on the spur of the moment. Sometimes it turns out great, and other times, it is horrible.

If you use dowsing, you will always be happy with the pets you choose. The same is true if you are buying an animal for some purpose.

You already know whether you want an animal or not. You also know how strongly you are attracted to an animal. But how can you dowse to find out if you will be happy adopting or buying that animal? You need to formulate one or more good dowsing questions based on your priorities, and then dowse them.

Everyone has their own priorities. There is no one set of questions that apply to everyone. Your finances, your lifestyle, how much time you have for pet care and why you want a pet all go into the answer. And each has different weights in that final answer.

The first question to ask is:

On a +10 to -10 scale, what is the overall level in effects on me of adding a dog/cat/horse to my life at this time?

That will give you an overall idea of how good your timing is.

Perhaps you don't realize that in two months you will be laid off from your job, divorced, or newly pregnant, and that your priorities will change radically. Dowsing can help you avoid making a badly timed decision, if only you follow your answers.

Once you get a +8 or better for adding the animal to your life, one thing you can do is to make a list of priorities and dowse each one on a scale of +10 to -10 for how it will affect you on that topic to add this particular animal to your life. If you are buying it as part of a show or breeding program, you will have other questions you ask.

If you are not sure you can be objective, use blind dowsing. We had a client who came to look at our foster kittens with the goal of adopting two, and although she held and examined each one, she used blind dowsing to pick the two to take home. She was very pleased with the results.

Training

Some animals require more training than others. Regardless of what type of animal you choose, even if it is a fish or snake, it is appropriate that you learn something about the behavior and basic physical needs of the species.

By learning the basic needs and behavior of your animal friend, you will be able to avoid making mistakes that cost both you and your pet. Many animals require training so that they can live in harmony with you.

Dogs need to learn to walk on a leash and come when called. Sit and stay are useful commands. If you have a horse, it needs to learn basic manners and commands as well. If you intend to show an animal, you will have to teach it even more commands. Sometimes you take your animal to a class, and other times you send your animal to a trainer.

How can you choose a trainer or class that is perfect for your needs and your animal? Dowse it using the steps outlined in Chapter 2. An example of a good question is:

On a scale of 0-10 overall for my goals in training _____(pet's name), with 8 or higher meaning the program/trainer is very good to excellent and 3 or less meaning it/he/she is bad, how does _____(trainer or program) rate? Take action only if you get an 8 or higher.

Before you spend time and money on a class or trainer, be sure that you dowse if your animal companion wants to be trained. Maybe your dog isn't interested in obedience trials, or your horse couldn't care less about dressage.

There are a lot of people offering training, especially in the horse world, whose techniques are questionable. Do not send an animal to training unless you have convinced yourself that the trainer does not use abusive methods. If your dowsing indicates your animal wouldn't be happy with a certain trainer or program, this could be one of the reasons. (Never, however, accuse anyone of malpractice based solely on dowsing.)

Another important issue that dowsing will shed light on is whether your animal is in proper physical condition for training. If your animal is weak, ill or has some kind of physical problem, training could be painful or even dangerous. Dowse on a scale of +10 to -10 how prepared on all levels your animal is to embark on such a program. Do not ever do anything that tests under a +8.

Breeding

The first mistake a person makes in breeding is to breed an animal without determining the animal wants to be bred and is in proper condition for breeding.

The first dowsing question is, *Does this animal want to be bred at this time?* If the answer is no, do not breed the animal. Spontaneous abortions and a mother abusing or abandoning her baby come from breeding unwilling animals.

The second question to dowse is whether your animal is in good breeding condition. He or she may be underweight, have hormonal imbalances, be infertile or be carrying a toxic load.

Dowse the overall physical condition of your animal for breeding purposes, and do not breed if it comes out less than +8. Instead, dowse what you need to do in terms of food, medicine or exercise to get the animal in good condition to breed.

Next, the choice of mate is important. Dowsing is a great way to pick a proper match and assure that the offspring are wonderful. As always, you need to list priorities to formulate a good dowsing question. Some items might be:

- Potential price of offspring from this breeding is over $X.
- All offspring are healthy.
- Offspring have certain physical traits or markings. Or certain percentage have them.
- Offspring have certain talents and abilities, or certain percentage have them.

There are excellent buyers who will provide good homes for the offspring when they are ready to be sold.

The pregnancy and delivery will be easy and safe for the mother.

A certain percentage of males or females will be in the litter.

The list goes on and on and is quite dependent on the species, but you get the picture. You then ask a dowsing question to include all of the items, and ask to get a negative number if a vital item is missing from a given match. As always, look for +8 or better as your Holy Grail.

Dowsing can be used to determine the gender and number of animals in a litter. It also is useful for making sure the mother is healthy and getting what she needs during the pregnancy. You can also dowse when the babies will be delivered.

One of our Whole Brain Charts in this chapter is on animal breeding. All you need is the ability to get a good yes/no response, and you can benefit from using that chart.

Solving Behavior Problems

No matter what type of animal companion you have, problems are bound to crop up at some point. Another article in this chapter shows you how dowsing can be used to communicate with animals, and how dowsing can be used to solve health issues. In this article, we will talk mainly about behavior problems and how dowsing can help you resolve them.

Regardless of the species of animal you have, there are certain generalities that apply to problems. Problem behavior most often stems from:

- Health problems
- Poor nutrition
- Attached entities
- Lack of exercise
- Emotional imbalance due to past abuse or negligence or interaction with other pet
- Separation anxiety
- Stress
- Poor communication
- Lack of proper training
- Environmental energies

If you feed, exercise, train, communicate with and provide safe energetic space for your animal, and if you treat any emotional issues, you are unlikely to have any serious problems to solve. Conversely, if you have problems, you can check the above list by dowsing to see which items give you the biggest 'yes.'

An example is your cat is peeing outside the litter box. You dowse if anything listed above is a significant contributing factor. You get a 'yes' for health problems and poor nutrition.

It turns out that you have been feeding your male cat grocery store food, and it has caused a blockage in the urinary tract that is both painful and very dangerous. Get him to a vet right away.

Or instead, you get a big 'yes' on emotional imbalance. You have three cats and one litter box, and the new, smaller cat is not using the box because of the territorial issues with the older cats. One box per cat is the usual rule for a happy home. Problem solved.

The same issue can have radically different causes. Dowsing allows you to sleuth out what is the cause so you can more easily find the solution.

Here's an example: we did a space clearing for a woman who had a rescue horse that was a challenge. She never was able to go out into the field and put a halter on him by herself without a lot of work; his behavior was consistently dangerous. She explained that she gave him the highest quality feed and supplements, that she had energy workers and various horse therapists treat him, but all to no avail. She had to be very careful when approaching him, as he kicked viciously.

The afternoon we did the space clearing, a huge thunderstorm came up, and she was forced to go out into the field alone to bring him in. She told us she dreaded getting injured and was amazed when the gelding stood quietly and let her slip the harness on and lead him back to the barn in spite of the thunder and lightning. He was so calm, he was like a new horse, and he stayed that way. We were able to tell her that although her feeding and therapy programs were excellent, his behavior problem was caused by attached entities, which we removed during the clearing.

If you're an animal lover as we are, you will love how dowsing expands your ability to help your furry companions.

ARCHAEOLOGICAL DOWSING

In this article, Nigel shares with you his experiences with archaeological dowsing and gives you tips on how to do it.

Imagine moving across the land which is bare of human settlement and has only grass and few trees. As you walk, you are able to describe the buildings which were once there, detailing their construction and height, the course of the walls and so on.

Or, there are just a few stones standing, a few grassy ridges showing the remains of some old settlement. You, however, can fill in the details of how long the settlement lasted for, why it died out and how many lived there at its peak.

Or, in a sheltered spot by some trees, you are able to explain clearly the religious rituals which took place there, even going to the places where the standing stones of this ancient temple had once been placed. You bring to life a scene from thousands of years ago, as if it were happening before your eyes.

All of those things are possible with the use of dowsing. In fact, I have been involved in two of those types of dowsing exercises.

It is something you can do as well, as long as you are careful and methodical in your work. This type of dowsing takes a slightly different approach and, for it to be truly successful, you tend to need to back it up with some good, old, low-tech library research.

Firstly, this type of on-site dowsing is actually quite easy to do, but it is not something which any trained archeologist I have heard of so far will put any trust into. So, a word of caution. If you are intent on exploring this aspect of dowsing and delving into the past with your pendulum, be aware that, unless you can build a solid case for your results, it is unlikely that you will be asked to make a presentation at the local historical society or take part in a symposium at a university.

None of that, of course, means that what you find with dowsing is wrong. However, bear in mind about thought-forms (explained in On-Site Dowsing) because if you are dowsing over an area previously examined in one way or another, you might also be tuning in to what other people expected to find there, which, of course, is not always what is actually there.

Equally, do not let your imagination and your wish for success sway you into making more of the site you are examining than is there. Having taken part in several archeological digs myself, as well as being trained as an historian and in library research, I can tell you that a great deal of what is uncovered doesn't look significant or has no intrinsic value or can be very mundane indeed such as bits of broken tile, odd lumps of charcoal, some pottery and so on.

Evidence is just that; evidence to help build up or break down a theory about how and where people lived, fought, worshiped and died. So be aware that we are not talking about treasure hunting here. That has a different approach and what is being searched for has a monetary value today to many people, whereas historical and archeological evidence is usually only of intellectual interest to a smaller group.

There are, of course, exceptions such as finding a hoard of Viking silver and gold at a burial site. But in general, finds made in archeological dowsing tend to make sense and to have value only for that site, that location.

There is no one hard and fast rule about this type of dowsing, so what follows is a suggested approach which you can adopt and adapt as you find necessary.

Is There a 'Past'?

This sounds almost silly, but, before investing time and effort into specific dowsing, it is important to find out if there was any significant activity in the past in the area you are interested in. How you define the word 'significant' might well not be the same as I would, because our interests might differ. You might be more interested in Native American settlements, whereas I'd be more interested in the Medieval or prehistoric periods, especially in Europe.

Therefore, finding this out is important. If the answer is 'yes,' then you might need to narrow down the subject a little to make the best use of your time. If there are numerous possible sites or events of interest, you would be advised to find out how many specific ones there are which are of greatest interest or importance to you.

Of course, if you are going to be dowsing over a previously explored and documented area with a view to getting more detail, then you need to ask questions which would help you in locating the precise area or areas most helpful to you. At that time, you would be well-advised to check on any thought-forms which might be interfering with you and get rid of them.

The importance of this can be illustrated by the story of a client of ours who came to us with an unusual problem. He found he could not study in his home. Outside, it was easy, but indoors, he could not retain any information.

Investigating the problem revealed that his house had been built over the site of a Native American secret society for males. The thought forms associated with that said, effectively, that no knowledge could be taken from that site. After clearing, he found it easy to study. Now, those thought forms had been placed very carefully as a protection against outside snooping, and they were still effective. There is no reason to suppose that other, equally effective thought forms have not been placed by earlier peoples for differing reasons, or that people today are not equally capable of doing the same.

Never assume that a site is just a plain site with no other energy affecting it. Always check and re-check.

Dowsing Underground Structures

This exercise is to help you with dowsing vanished or buried buildings.

Once on site and assured that you are in the correct area, you can begin to locate structures beneath the ground. To do this, choose any starting point, or, if you have some idea of the possible layout, choose an appropriate point away from any assumed structures.

Begin walking in a straight line. If you are just beginning this type of dowsing, you don't have to do anything else in preparation. If you are experienced in this type, then locate your starting point on a map and use a tape or other measure to lay out your first path. All subsequent paths can then be measured with reference to this first track.

You are just exploring and not getting too technical in this exercise, so continue walking for a specified distance, say 25 paces. Do make sure that not only is your tool ready for dowsing, but that your mind is as well. (Remember the steps in dowsing covered in Chapter 2). Be focused on what you are looking for; lost underground structures of the 15th Century, the walls of the old village, the old fortifications.....whatever it is you are focused on.

Whenever you get a positive response, mark it in some fashion. Spray paint, marking flags, bits of wood, whatever is appropriate. Then, repeat the track on a path parallel to the first one, say 5 paces apart or whatever seems right for the site, and mark any more hits.

You can repeat this process any number of times. At the end, you then can look at what you've marked out and see if there is a pattern to the markings. This is where your intuition, your insight or knowledge come into play. Choose a marker for further investigation. Dowse around it for things like width or depth. Find out where it runs underground. It might be you are dowsing a sewer or a wall of a building. It might be you are dowsing a pathway or a stockyard. Whatever it is will determine the shape of the building.

This is where you have to go carefully. You have to be focused on the time period you are interested in. Never assume, for example, that because a building is shaped like a cross, that it was church. It could be it was an old barn and over the years parts fell down and other parts were added giving you the shape of a cross. You have to dowse which parts were erected and used at the same time.

Once you have found the layout, sketch it out for later use; how long it was in use, over what period of time. Also, while on site, you can dowse the height of the buildings, even what materials they were made of or what they were used for and when (always remember things can change over time, so make sure you know which time you are investigating).

Dowsing for Events

It could be that you are less interested in structures but more interested in specific events. Sometimes, the energies of a place are strong enough to make themselves known to you even when you aren't looking specifically for them.

This happened to me several times. One of the most memorable was in a cathedral in the UK. I was approaching the steps to the crypt when I had a sudden flash, a picture of flames and screaming. I was later talking with one of the cathedral guides who mentioned that the crypt was where some prisoners had been kept during Elizabeth I's time (in the middle of the 16th Century). The place had been set fire to deliberately and they had all died. The energy of that event was still strong enough to make itself known.

With dowsing, the energy does not have to be anywhere as strong. You can still pick up on locations where events happened. Sadly, it seems to be the case that the easiest ones to identify and locate are those associated with death in one form or another. This is not to say that you cannot identify other types of events, merely that, to begin with, it is probably going to be easier for you to find such places.

Of course, finding them is the merely the first part. After that you have to dowse the time and the rough area of the event. If it was a small battle, then how many were involved, where were they, where did they die and what weapons were used?

The Advantages of Working On-Site

Although such things can, in all likelihood, be dowsed for in the comfort of your own home using a map of some kind, there really is nothing like being able to walk the area yourself. In this way you get to know the country far better than any pictures can give you. You get to feel the way the land rises and falls, sense the residual energies of the place which would be far more difficult to understand or sense if you were not there.

You might make more sense of the data by being present, by seeing where roads and paths are now, by looking at how they meander or come to seeming dead ends, by looking at trees and crops for signs of older or younger growth. Although you are always dowsing, always open to whatever it is that your dowsing brings to you, never ignore or devalue the many visual clues all around you which give depth to your understanding, illuminate the bare results and help to develop the picture you are piecing together.

For it should be said that it is rare that you can fully flesh out a picture of the past in one or two visits. It often takes careful and precise dowsing over time to reveal what happened in the past at any one location.

Backing Up Your Dowsing

With archeological dowsing, the one resource you should never overlook is the conventional historical records themselves.

For example, I once took a group out dowsing on a fairly empty heath area just as practice for on-site dowsing and looking at various sorts of energies. In fact, we accidentally came across a series of structures. They were about 50 feet away from the present road and dowsed as being a sort of inn dating to around the 16th century. There were absolutely no physical clues at all, such as mounds or stones lying around.

Anyway, after making careful note of the location, I did some research and found that the present road did not follow the old road bed. It used to be about 50 feet further over and there was a report of a place where horses could be changed not far outside the town. The directions all pointed to the place we had found which no one else had located. In other words, we had found something that no one else knew about and had it verified by map and other reports. Of course, to prove it conclusively, we would have needed to have excavated the site. But we didn't.

So it is important for you to follow up your on-site work by doing the standard research. Look at old maps, read the old newspaper reports, dig out the local histories in your local library and see how what you dowsed fits into the bigger picture. In so doing, you can often find other information which helps you.

Object Dowsing

The last type of archeological dowsing is where you are not looking for either structures or events, but specific items of an historical period. For example, you might be collecting arrowheads or cannonballs or old clay pipes. In this case, you are less interested in building a picture but in precise locations.

The first thing you need to do is make sure you have the legal right to take things from the land, things which you have discovered.

Once you have that sorted out, then there is the problem of finding what are usually small objects hidden in large areas.

It is usually easiest to take one small area at a time for this type of dowsing. This can either be marked out visually or by using trees or rocks or other natural landmarks. Inside this area, simply start by asking if there are any objects of your search present. If no, move on to the next area.

If your dowsing says there are, then proceed to search carefully over the area. Ask in which direction you should move to find the object and then ask to be shown when you are over the object. Then ask how deep the object is before digging!

Possible Pitfalls to Avoid

One of the dangers of archeological dowsing is to make assumptions about what you have found. Or you simply put your own interpretation on the results.

This is easier and easier to do the farther back in time you are working on. Stone circles and monuments of all kinds are very inviting places to dowse, but they are also very tricky things to interpret easily. There are many people who have dowsed extensively around such places and then, on the basis of their imagination, have constructed scenarios as to what they were used for, how they were built and other assorted conjectures.

In effect, when building such visions up, there would have been little need for dowsing at all, as the imagination filled in every small gap. As you are probably aware by now, if you believe something to exist or to have existed strongly enough, the chances are very high that you will find evidence to support your beliefs, whether that evidence can be discovered independently by someone else or not.

Archeological dowsing requires careful, methodical, precise and detailed dowsing over a period of time. It is not something you can do in an afternoon. To be taken seriously, you need to be well-versed in the background of the period, have an understanding of what it is you are actually dowsing over and be prepared to go back again and again to check and re-check what you found. Then you need to fit those finds into the existing knowledge of the subject. If your finds and your research show that it does not fit in, then you have to do even more background research in order to find out why the existing ideas are wrong.

In other words, this form of dowsing is far more technical than most others. If you are going to dig down to reveal whatever it is you have found, then you must also be familiar with excavation techniques as used by archeologists so that any evidence you do find cannot be argued with.

Odds and Ends

Sometimes, when dowsing, it is what is **not** there which is important. Instead of finding structures, old villages, or the like, you might be more interested in old mines. Instead of finding something in such places, you are more interested in finding empty spaces, the galleries or shafts the miners dug.

This might seem, at first, to be totally counter-intuitive. After all, dowsing finds **things**. It doesn't find **nothing**. At least, that's what our experience tells us. But, in fact, there is nothing different about finding empty spaces than there is in finding objects. It just depends on your focus and your dowsing ability.

An example of this type of dowsing took place in the opening years of the 20th Century in Paris, France. Over the preceding centuries the land underneath Paris had become riddled with excavations. This is where the actual Plaster of Paris came from. However, only a very few scientists actually knew of the extent of the workings and there were very few hand-drawn maps of them in existence, and they were under lock and key.

One scientist, interested in dowsing and having access to the plans, asked for any dowsers who might be interested in an exercise to meet on a plain field in the city. On the appointed morning, many dowsers showed up, not having a clue as to what they were going to be asked to do. In fact, the only instruction they received was to dowse and find out what was beneath the surface of the park they were in.

The results showed a remarkable similarity. Nearly all the dowsers reported empty spaces and virtually all agreed on the depth to the top of the empty space. Some found instead isolated areas which were marked out. These areas corresponded to the pillars left behind by the miners to support the roof. The depth and location of the spaces were also accurate, proving that you can find nothing, even if you don't know exactly that it was the object of the search!

Finally, there is always the unexpected historical aspect which can impinge on your work. When I was in the UK, I was called to a house to examine it for energetic problems having any influence on the ill-health of one of the people there. The man had had continual health issues with his left hip, his kidney and muscle problems with his thigh.

On examining the area I kept discovering very precise circles of negative energy dotted about the place. I had no idea what they were but one was directly under the area of his left hip, kidney and thigh as he would lie in bed. I had to do some research to find the answer. The area where the house was built had been used as a plague pit over 400 years ago, when the land would have been outside the city walls. But the same land had also been used earlier by the Romans as a burial site. And, the Romans had buried their people in circular pits, folding the body into them. This accounted for both the strange circular areas I discovered and also the noxious energy associated with it.

So, in this case, the archeological discovery helped me to understand a modern problem.

If history and mystery fascinate you, you will love delving into archaeological dowsing.

AURA DOWSING

Auras are the energy field each living thing has. The aura appears as shimmering energy surrounding the physical body.

A good clairvoyant can see colors and structure to the aura and is able to identify damage and dis-ease. Edgar Cayce, an American psychic of the first part of the twentieth century, could see auras. He related a story of one time he was waiting for an elevator in a building. When the elevator arrived at his floor and the doors opened, he noticed that none of the people in the elevator had auras. He decided to wait for another elevator. Shortly after the doors shut, that elevator plunged to the ground, killing all aboard.

The aura is a field of subtle energy surrounding a living creature, usually considered to be divided into several layers. The condition of the aura tells you a lot about your physical health. Every physical structure is represented in a part or layer of the aura.

Most people are not practiced enough at seeing the aura, and that is where dowsing comes into its own. If you can dowse, you can evaluate the aura of any living creature. You can also use dowsing to select healing methods that will repair and balance the aura.

The aura is often considered a template for a physical being. All parts of the being: physical, mental and emotional, are represented in the aura. Everything exists in the energy body before it is manifested in the physical body.

For that reason, treating the energy body is often much more effective long term than treating the physical body. It is also usual for problems to show up in the aura before they are physically experienced. By identifying problems in the aura, you can head off physical dis-ease.

You can picture the physical body as the end product of thoughts, feelings and beliefs that have manifested into physical form. Your thoughts, feelings and beliefs control your reality, and the aura is one way of accessing these energies to balance and harmonize them for good health.

Barbara Ann Brennan wrote a book called *Hands of Light* which has become a classic in working with auras and chakras. Often, a used copy can be obtained online or at secondhand bookstores for very little money. It is a good reference as you start using dowsing to work on the energy body.

The aura exists in layers which are interconnected and affect one another. The layers closer to the body are more 'dense,' while those farther away have a higher vibration.

Brennan states that there are seven layers to the aura, and she explains what each one is noted for. For the purposes of this lesson, it is enough to know that there are layers, and that the boundaries between the layers can be detected by dowsing.

The condition of your aura determines your health, so it is wise to keep your aura strong and balanced. The aura also functions as a protection for your physical body, and the stronger it is, the better.

The aura expands and shrinks due to its condition and the situation it is in. One person's aura can extend for many feet, while another person's may be only inches thick.

The following is an exercise in dowsing the border between layers of the aura, and how you can use dowsing to measure the overall size of the aura without having to know where exactly the outermost edge is.

Try It Yourself: Dowsing a Boundary Layer of the Aura

As mentioned at the beginning, every living thing has an aura. But the size of the aura can vary dramatically. In most cases, a large average size is regarded as a sign of health, power and enlightenment. A very small aura is usually indicative of dis-ease or the person being in a threatened state.

The size of your aura will vary not only from day to day, but from minute to minute. Each thought and feeling you have contributes to who you are and what you are experiencing.

Do not judge or compare aura size, as it is only a snapshot at the moment, and there are many complex factors that can affect it.

This exercise is best done with a human partner whom you can dowse on. Have your subject sit in a relaxed position, and ask them not to think about anything in particular. Stand about 8-10 feet away.

Take your dowsing tool. An L-rod is a good choice for this exercise, but any tool will work. Be sure you know what your 'yes' and 'no' responses look like.

Your dowsing question is to find a boundary layer of the aura by getting a 'yes' response as you walk towards the subject.

Be sure you are clear exactly when you want the response. Do you want it as your leading toe crosses the boundary or as the hand holding your L-rod crosses it? That will make some difference in your answer.

You might already be in the person's aura, but it doesn't matter. You are going to find the first layer of the aura which is in front of you.

You can mark the location in some fashion (a piece of tape or an object on the floor) and then go on to the second exercise, which follows shortly.

The size of the aura is affected by many things. When a person or animal is feeling scared, their aura may shrink. For a different reason, ninjas were taught to minimize their aural signature, as a person can sense another person when they contact the aura. Certain environments are quite toxic, and in such places it is likely the aura will shrink closer to the body.

We don't want to threaten or endanger anyone in an exercise, so we will use a harmless demonstration that allows you to see that the aura can change substantially in the space of a minute due purely to a thought or emotion.

The purpose of this exercise is to help you understand how you control the health and well-being of your aura by how you think.

Try It Yourself: Change the Size of the Aura

Have you marked the boundary layer of the aura from the previous exercise? If not, go back and do that exercise now. Put a mark of some kind on the floor to show where that boundary layer was when your subject is sitting in a relaxed and neutral position (thinking about nothing).

Now, having the subject stay in the same location, ask him or her to focus continually on something that he or she gets the most joy from.

Dowse where the layer you previously found is at this time. First, face towards the subject and ask if that particular layer is in front of you. Then turn around and face away from the subject and ask the same question. In normal circumstances, the layer will be farther away from the subject. Joy expands the aura.

Dowse exactly where the boundary of that layer is, and mark the floor again.

Now, ask your subject to think of something that frightens or saddens him or her while you dowse the same question. Check where the boundary layer now is, closer to the subject or farther away from where you stand. Dowse where the boundary of that layer is and mark the floor.

Note where your three marks are. In most cases, the neutral test will fall in between the joy and sadness test. The joy will have expanded the aura, and sadness will shrink it to less than its neutral position.

What if you don't get the expected results? Don't worry. Perhaps your subject's mind was wandering. Maybe he was thinking of someone he loves very much, but then he started thinking of his doubts about whether that person loves him, or perhaps thought of a betrayal.

Check with your subject and make sure the person is continually thinking of joy during the joy test, and sadness or fear during the other test. Plus, it is vital to stay neutral in the first exercise. It is hard to police our thoughts, and these exercises force you to be aware of what you are thinking and feeling. It also teaches you that those feelings and thoughts have an instant and direct effect on your aura.

If you cannot find a partner to work with, you can do this yourself. Instead of walking towards a person and finding a border between layers, face a wall and move slowly towards it from a particular spot with the intention of getting a 'yes' response when a boundary between layers of your aura meets the wall in front of you.

Once you have established that distance, you can continue with the previous exercises using the same principle.

Try This: A Fun Exercise with Plants

Now have some real fun. Find a houseplant (you may use an outdoor plant, but it might be less responsive.) Do the aura exercise with the plant that you did with the human subject.

First, find a boundary layer of the aura of the plant. Be very neutral in your search. Do not project any emotions or thoughts on the plant. Mark where that layer is.

Now send love to the plant. Tell it you want it to be very happy and healthy. If it is dry, give it a bit of water. Wipe the dust off the leaves in a loving way. Now test where that same boundary layer of the plant's aura is now. More than likely, the aura has grown.

Now tell the plant you are doing a test for educational purposes, and are going to ask how it would feel about certain things if they were to happen, but that you are not going to do those things.

Visualize the plant being consumed by fire. Or picture its leaves blotched and necrotic from a fungal disease. Or picture it being thrown away into the trash or ripped to shreds, eaten by a large plant-eating animal. Retest the boundary layer you found before. More than likely, it will have shrunk.

Now tell the plant you are sorry you scared it, and that you were doing an experiment for educational purposes, and that you only intend good things for it. Thank it for allowing you to use it as a subject. Promise it you won't harm it intentionally.

Doing this exercise with a plant will help you see that this is a true phenomenon. Do not repeat this exercise on the same plant. It can traumatize it and cause damage if done repeatedly.

Aura Problems

There are many manifestations of imbalance and dis-ease that the aura can have. The way you approach this subject will depend on the method you are using to evaluate the aura. If you are examining it clairvoyantly, you will be using your psychic sight to gather information. However, as a dowser, you will do it somewhat differently.

You can evaluate the health of your aura overall on a +10 to -10 scale. Negative numbers mean the aura is not doing well. Positive numbers are good.

Next, it can be helpful to dowse a list of common problems and find out which ones apply to your aura. The following list is a sample of some common aura problems:

- Tear

- Infection
- Hole
- Attachment of negative energies, entities or parasites
- Link to another person, place or time
- Burn
- Toxins

Just about any type of damage you can see in the body, you can see in the aura. Dowse the list and note which ones you have. You can also dowse to find out whereabouts the damage is. (Say you think you have been betrayed recently by someone, is the damage really in your back? After all, we say we have been 'stabbed in the back' by people. But is it really there, or is it elsewhere?)

Use the negative part of the scale -1 to -10 to find out how detrimental each damage is to your health at this time.

You can also dowse how long you have had the damage, what caused it, etc. It is not necessary to find this out, but it is good dowsing practice.

Healing Aura Damage

Dowsing is a great way to find the best and most effective method for healing the aura damage you find. If you have a healing method you are familiar with, test that first.

Use a scale of +10 to -10 to find out how effective that method would be at healing the damage quickly, easily, comfortably and safely.

There are many methods that work well. Here is a short list of some we have used:

- Visualization: once you know the type of damage, visualize yourself healing it in whatever way seems best.
- Crystals: dowse a crystal that will heal the damage and then dowse how to use it. For example, do you wear it for a while, point it at the damage, or do something else?
- Symbols: if you have symbols for healing or are good at drawing

your own, dowse one for healing the aura damage and apply it in whatever way tests best. You may look at the symbol, wear the symbol or draw the symbol on your body.

- Colors: Using a color wheel or something similar, dowse if there is a color frequency that will heal the damage per our original question, that is a 8 or better on a scale of 0 to 10. Then dowse how to apply the color. See it? Wear it? Both?

Sometimes the aura can be helped by treating the physical body in some fashion. A detox, parasite cleanse or supplementing with vitamins or minerals might also be useful for helping heal aura damage.

In general, we only use methods that dowse 8 or higher. Lower numbers mean the method will work, but the results won't be as fast or as good in some way.

When you are done treating the damage, go back and re-dowse and see if things have healed. If not, you may be dealing with a mechanism that is currently active and continuing to damage the aura on an ongoing basis. This is a more advanced problem, and we advise you to seek help if you feel you have a significant aura problem that won't heal. Such things frequently can lead to physical symptoms.

Strengthening Your Aura

Keeping your aura strong and healthy is going to help you stay physically healthy. You can strengthen your aura in a number of ways.

Visualization is a good way to strengthen your aura. You can see yourself surrounded by golden light in an egg shape. Or you can run through the colors of the rainbow, filling the egg shape with the bright, clear colors one at a time. Start with red and end with violet.

You will find that your best method of keeping your aura healthy is to think positively. That doesn't mean that you should be upset with yourself if you get angry or sad. It is natural to have such feelings. But teach yourself to let go of them in a nonjudgmental way. Reframe and focus on joy and how you intend to create it in your life. Remember the aura exercise and how the aura shrank noticeably when negative thoughts or feelings were dwelt upon.

Your aura is a part of you. Taking care of it will enhance your health and well-being. You can do the same for pets, plants and other family members. If you are interested in becoming a healer, then study all you can about the aura. And use dowsing to help you evaluate and heal the aura as needed.

Isn't it fun to see how 'big' you really are, how much more you are than this physical body? Dowsing will open doors for you into a world of wonder and awe.

CHAKRA DOWSING

If you have the good luck to have an amenable young child around who will sit still for you, you will probably be able to tickle them without touching them. All you need to do is think of your fingertip as being like a laser, and that you can shoot a beam of light out of the end of it.

Take your laser fingertip and, from a distance of about three or four inches, draw squiggly lines or circles over the thigh or the outstretched hand of your obedient little child. Inevitably, they will start giggling and twitching and saying that it tickles. Children are more sensitive than adults in this exercise, mainly because they haven't built up a set of beliefs about what they can and can't do. So they tend to be far more receptive to this game.

But what if you don't have a quiet and responsive child around that you can experiment with? Well, you can do much the same by pointing your finger at the palm of your other hand or your own thigh as you are sitting. Draw lines and circles on yourself from a distance of about three or more inches (you might have to get a bit closer when working on yourself before you start to feel anything). A lot of people will feel something. But what is it?

You are using the energy in your body and letting it out of one of your chakras. And that's what we're going to be looking at in this training: chakras and how dowsing can be used to explore them and help you to understand more about yourself and what's going on with you.

The word 'chakra' means 'wheel of light' in the ancient Sanskrit language. This is because, to people who are able to see them, they do resemble wheels and they seem to be made up of a very subtle light.

Chakras are part of the subtle energy body which weaves in and around all of us. The role which chakras play in our lives, according to general agreement, is to act as focal points for the transmission and reception of energies. As such, they are associated with specific areas of the body and are usually represented as having various levels of complexity and also have specific colors associated with each one.

Because they are assumed to be acting as links between the physical and the nonphysical aspects of existence, they are also associated with specific organs, emotions, and the spiritual aspect of individuals.

Because they act as ways of creating the physical body, they are often used as a way of assessing the general health of a person, or the probable future health. Nigel tells a story that illustrates this principle:

I was teaching dowsing and the use of dowsing to examine chakras back in the UK. One student in the class found that the chakra over her solar plexus was very, very weak indeed. Nothing seemed to be able to change it. She was very positive that there were no health issues in that area, but I urged her to see her doctor and arrange for a checkup.

Unfortunately, she did not and, within a year of that class she was fighting a very severe and sudden case of pancreatic cancer: the pancreas being one of the glands associated with the solar plexus chakra. The disease had shown up first in the chakra.

That was an extreme example, but it does illustrate that chakras can be used in helping you assess your own health.

And, just because you see pictures showing seven chakras, don't forget that there are a large number of chakras. It's just that the seven you normally see are the ones which are the most important.

How can dowsing help you explore and understand chakras better?

This is one of the few areas where a tool is really the best thing to use. In most cases, you don't need tools to dowse, but in working with chakras, it is much easier and the responses are far clearer if you use a pendulum.

Try It Yourself: The Palm Chakra

First, in order for you to see how pendulums and chakras interact, we will explore one of the minor chakras first, the one in the palm of your hand.

You might well have come across the following exercise if you have been to any classes to do with healing or energy. You rub the palms of your hands together vigorously and then, holding them close to each other, you feel the flow of energy between them. Sometimes it's like a magnet, other times it can feel like a warm breeze or a slight resistance. This shows that the chakras are there.

What you are going to do, however, is to use the pendulum to demonstrate **how** the chakra is working.

To do this, hold the pendulum in one hand and open up your other hand, palm up. Now, on your open hand, imagine there is a rosebud in the center of the palm. It represents the chakra. See it clearly as it is tightly wrapped but beautiful. Now, with this image clearly in your mind about the palm of your hand, hold the pendulum over that palm and allow it to start moving.

You want it to show you the chakra and how open it is, how much energy is flowing through it. So, let the pendulum move over the palm of your hand. Now, as it is moving, focus again on the palm and the rosebud you visualized there. Begin to see the rosebud unfurling and growing. Make it happen slowly. You should end up with the image of a full-grown, beautiful large rose in the palm.

As the rose is growing, your pendulum should be following its development by increasing the size of its motion. Normally, this is a circular movement.

Once you have that working well, begin to close the rose back down again and watch the pendulum as it, too, reduces in movement.

Practice with this until you are comfortable allowing the pendulum to move freely as it responds to the chakra.

Never leave the chakra shut down, as that can lead to a blockage of energy, followed by pain. Always leave your chakras open and functioning normally after an exercise.

Other Chakras

Although this exercise was done with the pendulum directly over the chakra, there is no need for it to be done that way. You can hold the pendulum as normal and simply ask for you to be shown the condition of any of your chakras.

It might help, to begin, to point with one hand at the chakra you are investigating. So, to begin with, point at your heart chakra and ask to see how it is energetically. Let the pendulum move as it wishes to.

Generally, the stronger the flow of energy in the chakra, the more vigorous the movement of the pendulum. Remember also that what you are doing is taking a snapshot of the chakra and a chakra is a constantly changing energetic aspect of your body, in the same way that your aura is constantly changing.

Your heart chakra might be very open and energetic, or it might be closed down and the pendulum movement small. It depends on you, what you have been experiencing and thinking recently. It is generally considered to be detrimental for the chakra to be totally shut down, and the pendulum will not move in such a case. This is rare, though.

Even normal physical activities affect your chakras' functioning. If you look at your third chakra, the one usually referred to as the solar plexus, over your stomach, it will change depending on when you look at it.

After a heavy meal, it will be acting differently than when you are hungry or very active.

Not every chakra will or should be fully open all day, every day. You'll find that your pendulum will show different movements according to how the chakra is working. Sometimes, it will show a smooth circular motion. Other times, the movement might be more lop-sided, more oval, perhaps even showing a movement like the petals of a flower. You will find it very interesting and revealing to make a note of the various ways in which the pendulum moves for different chakras at different times.

To do this, make a list of the chakras numbered 1 to 7, and next to them note your observations about each chakra.

If you prefer, instead of noting the type of pendulum movement, you could simply ask, on a scale of 1 to 10, how well each particular chakra is operating at that time, with a 10 being optimal.

So, let's assume that your crown chakra is not very open, but for you at that time, it is operating at its optimal level. In that case, even though it might not be fully open, it would still dowse as a 10 for you.

As you have seen, it is easy for you to focus on a particular chakra and alter it. You did it on your hand, but the same principal applies to every other chakra as well. Of course, if there is an underlying problem, then you will only be able to alter it for a short while before it goes back again. In which case, you will need to do further research. There is more detail about this aspect of chakras a little further on.

Maggie's mother had a bad pain in her right upper arm that had persisted for many days. She couldn't remember doing anything to it, and she wouldn't go to a doctor about it. She wasn't a believer in chakras and such, but she was frustrated enough to ask Maggie for help.

For persistent pain of unexplained origin, it's always helpful to dowse the function of the chakras in that area. Think of energy as flowing downstream and out the fingertips from the arm, for example. When the flow of energy is completely blocked, it can become painful. When Maggie checked her Mom's chakras in her right arm at each joint, she found the elbow chakra closed. She did the visualization to open it, and the pain immediately ebbed to nothing. It never came back. Her mother was both pleased and surprised.

What follows is just a very simple outline of the main chakras.

- The first chakra is also called the base chakra and is seen usually as red. It is located at the base of the spine.
- The second chakra, in the groin, is the sacral chakra. It is colored orange, and is associated with the sex organs.
- The third chakra, the solar plexus, is in the stomach area and is associated with the pancreas and adrenal cortex.
- The fourth chakra, the heart chakra, is related to the thymus and is often visualized as either pure green or green with pink.
- The fifth chakra, the throat chakra, is associated with the thyroid. This is usually seen as blue.
- The sixth chakra, the third eye, is usually seen as indigo and is associated with the pineal gland.
- The seventh chakra, or crown chakra, is usually seen as violet and associated with the pituitary gland.

The colors of the chakras in ascending order are the same as those found in the rainbow, making them easy to remember.

Chakras are to be found all over the body. The one you looked at in your palm is not as large as the seven major ones. Equally, there are smaller and smaller ones throughout your whole body.

Chakras, then, are the gateways between us and the subtle energies around us. For the chakras to work correctly, they need to allow the free flow of energy inwards and outwards. That free flow is helped greatly by us doing the right things such as healthy diets, reasonable exercise, reducing stress; all the typical things which we have been told time and again are important for us to achieve.

Dowsing can help you to investigate and explore your chakra system. The seven major ones are the only ones you need to examine on a regular basis, as it is these which control the flow of energy throughout the whole body.

For example, if you find that one chakra is consistently weak despite your best efforts and yet you are not aware of any particular physical symptoms, then you need to consult a book on this topic to explore more about that chakra, the organs it is related to, and find out what it might mean to you.

Try It Yourself: Finger Exercise

For the next exercise, you are going to be looking at the energies coming out from the tips of your fingers. These small chakras can be easily examined using a pendulum.

Begin by holding your pendulum over the tip of your thumb. Make sure you are not looking at the thumbnail or the ball of the thumb, but the end of the thumb. Allow the pendulum to show you the direction of the flow of energy coming out from there. Which direction is it moving in? How strongly is the pendulum reacting? Most people see either a clockwise or counterclockwise circular motion.

Now hold the pendulum over the tip of your forefinger. Is there a change in the movement of the pendulum there? If so, how is it different? In terms of direction or strength or both?

Continue examining the tip of each of the other fingers and note down what you discover. In most cases, the pendulum will change from one direction to another and back again as you go from finger to finger.

Now go through the exercise with the rosebud opening up in your palm again and, with the flower (chakra) fully open, test each fingertip again to see if there are any differences. The results for this will vary from person to person, so just be aware of any differences. See what happens when you close the chakra down again. Does that have an effect on the flow of energy through the fingertips? Remember to leave the chakra functioning optimally for you at the end of this exercise.

Polarity issues can also show up in the fingertips. If you are unsure of yourself, whether your polarity has flipped, dowse your fingertips and see which way the energy is coming out. You might well be surprised!

One of the most useful ways you can use the investigation of chakras is when you have an injury, particularly to a limb. As you will have recognized and demonstrated by now, chakras allow flows of energy to occur. To be healthy is to have freely flowing energy throughout the body. Places where the energy is blocked or inhibited in one way or another will be less healthy than others.

If you found that one finger chakra was weak, it may be that broken finger you had as a child, or that arthritis you have been feeling in it is blocking the flow of energy.

Incidentally, this is the basis of Feng Shui, the Chinese art of placement and energy flow. If energy flows too fast, in Feng Shui, it is considered to take beneficial aspects with it. If it flows too slowly or is blocked, then detrimental energy builds up.

So it is with the human body; too much energy flowing through you will leave you feeling weak, light-headed, uneasy, unwell, and so on. Blocked energy will leave you feeling stagnant, heavy, lazy, full of aches and pains and so on.

But with physical injuries, the flow of energy has been blocked by trauma.

Chakras and Injuries

Let's assume that you have pain in the calf muscle of your right leg. If you consider what we've been saying about chakras, then that would assume that the energy is flowing well at least through to the knee, but any chakras below the site of the pain or injury would not be as open.

You can begin to assess the flow of energy (or 'chi' as it is called in Chinese medicine), starting at the hip joint.

Either hold the pendulum over the hip, which can be tricky, or, more easily, hold the pendulum and simply ask to be shown how the chakra is operating in the hip above the knee at this time. Depending on how you have decided to do this, it will either be on a scale of 0 to 10 for optimum performance or it will be reacting to the openness of the chakra at that time.

For the purposes of getting a baseline, you can compare how the hip chakra on the healthy side is functioning. They will probably be quite similar if both are balanced and healthy.

Once you have a result, proceed to the next large chakra which is to be found at the knee on the sore leg. Again, either hold the pendulum over it (which will be easier this time), or do as before and discover how that chakra is operating.

Again, once you have a result, move to examine the chakra below the injury, at the ankle or in the sole of the foot. Remember, energy should flow freely through you. Chi is not gathered up and built up in large amounts. It should be allowed to move freely. Therefore, when you examine a chakra below your injury, you may find that it is less open, operating at a lower level than a chakra above the injury.

The study of energy flows through the body is very complex, but in basic terms, the body's energetic system takes in subtle energy through the root and crown chakras, and it is mingled together in the solar plexus area before being distributed through the body, exiting at the hands, feet and thousands of other minor chakra points (as well as the seven major ones).

Now, remember the rosebud exercise? You can do exactly the same for the chakra beneath the injury and open that up visually. In most cases, the pain will immediately lessen. It probably won't stay open for long, because there is a good reason for it being the way it is, but this simple technique can be used to help in many cases where there is pain.

Barbara Brennan's book *Hands Of Light* is indispensable for learning about dowsing the aura and chakras.

Most of us cannot see chakras, but anyone can learn to use dowsing to gather information that will heal, strengthen and balance these vital energy centers.

CHART DOWSING

The appeal of dowsing charts is the appeal of dowsing itself: charts give you answers, in many cases, answers you would never have imagined. We feel that dowsing charts can be a good tool in helping you sort out an accurate answer when there are many possibilities.

The key benefit of dowsing charts is that someone has put together a list of possible answers for you. That saves you a lot of time and effort, especially if you are not an expert in the field you are dowsing about.

Building confidence is so important in dowsing, and dowsing charts help build confidence. Dowsing charts often come in books. We have several books of dowsing charts ourselves, although we rarely use them anymore. Some books we have used in the past are:

- Walter Lubeck's *Pendulum Healing Handbook*
- Dale Olson's *The Pendulum Charts: The Doorway to Knowing*

If you use books of charts, you will discover that in any collection, there are charts you simply don't use much at all. For that reason, we've found that Nita Ott's individual charts, offered at her website Mirrorwaters, are appealing to dowsers who have specific subjects they want to dowse, but don't want to invest in an entire book of charts. See a link to her site in the Resources.

After using dowsing charts in various ways, Maggie began to experiment with making up her own charts. At first, she would make a fan-shaped chart and fill in the lobes with possible answers. Since she was doing a lot of health dowsing, and she was fond of certain remedies and products, she made charts of them as appropriate. For instance, she made a chart of a brand of certain human and animal supplements she liked.

Another type of chart that we don't use for ourselves anymore, but which some people enjoy, are number and alphabet charts. A number chart is a fan with numbers on it. The range of numbers represents the range appropriate to whatever type of question you are asking. Or, you can just have a chart with 0-9 on the lobes of the fan. You can then ask how many digits are in the answer; what is the first digit; the second, and so on.

With an alphabet chart, you can use your pendulum to spell out your answer letter by letter. Each letter of the alphabet is on one lobe of the chart. This is a laborious process, and it sort of reminds us of the Ouija boards we used as kids. But some people have fun using alphabet charts.

We knew our young cat Tuffy wanted a grown-up name, but when she tried to tell Maggie what it was, all Maggie could see was a massive golden light that seemed very powerful. Nigel dowsed the name by dowsing the individual letters, to be Sekh. It seemed to be a dead-end. We looked it up though, and it still didn't make sense, as that is an Egyptian word for the soil of the Nile. However, trusting in our dowsing, further research turned up the fact that Sekhmet is an Egyptian goddess with a lion head, and she is the daughter of Ra, the sun god. We determined that was the name she was trying to tell us. Since at the time neither of us were familiar with that goddess, the alphabet was a good way to determine the answer. Otherwise, we would have had no idea what she meant.

Try It Yourself: Making Dowsing Charts

What area of dowsing are you fond of? Whatever your specialty, dowsing charts can be used to get your answers. Let's spend a little time going through the process of making a dowsing chart.

First, choose the dowsing subject you are interested in. For example, if you like using supplements or certain healing modalities or crystals, you can make a chart of them using a list from a catalog or reference book.

What if you love using crystals, but you only have 15 different types? You can make a chart with all of your crystals on it, and have one lobe or possible answer be 'other.' Then if you land on that answer, you know it is a crystal you do not have. 'Other' should be an answer in all dowsing choices, as no one has all the answers.

What if your dowsing doesn't lend itself to lists of herbs, crystals or supplements? If you are an animal communicator, you can still use charts. You may find it useful to make more than one chart for your work.

For example, you can have a Master Chart that has general answers to a question concerning an animal problem. Choices might include:

- Health problem / dis-ease
- Emotional issues
- Nutritional deficiency
- Past Lives
- Fear or phobia
- Problem with a human
- Problem with another animal

Of course this is a short list, but you can see that it lends itself to further, more detailed lists. So for nutritional deficiency, you then would go to a chart you had made listing all your favorite supplements for animals. Or 'Fear or Phobia' would lead you to a chart listing all the common types of fears and phobias an animal experiences. 'Dis-ease' could go to a chart listing common causes of physical problems, like trauma, poor nutrition, parasites, etc.

So look at your dowsing specialty and decide if you need a Master List with subordinate lists or just a single list. Once you know the number of answers you will have on the chart, you can create a fan or a circle that has that many lobes or rays in it. Do whichever is your preference.

If you have a lot of choices, you can number the lobes or rays rather than writing a complete answer for each. If you do this, then make a master list of what the numbers stand for. This actually makes the dowsing more like blind dowsing, as you won't be influenced by the numbers (at least until you use it enough to memorize some of them).

If you made a Master Chart, each choice will then point to either a single answer or another chart that has many choices on it. You will find that putting the charts in page protectors in a binder is a nice way to keep them neat and organized. Label each chart as to its purpose or use.

Try It Yourself: Using Dowsing Charts

Let's practice using charts. The pendulum is the tool of choice when dowsing over a chart. We have found it useful to use a pendulum that is slim in profile and has a point on the end for this purpose. If you have a lot of detail or choices on your chart, your pendulum may not give you a clear reading if it lacks a pointed tip. Brass pendulums in various sizes often come with nicely pointed tips, and they are our first choice when dowsing charts.

Remember the four steps to dowsing you learned in Chapter 2. Why are you asking this question? What are your goals? Next, formulate a good dowsing question. Remember that a good question is often more detailed and longer than a poor question.

Put your pendulum into a neutral swing. If you are using a fan-shaped chart, the best neutral swing will be back and forth vertically across the middle of the chart. On charts that have zero in the middle, that means you swing it over the 0. If on the other hand, you are using a circular chart, your neutral swing might be a circle.

170

Whichever you use, you then get your question clearly in mind. Make sure you are relaxed and detached about the answer. Maintain a curious outlook so you can get into a dowsing state. Do not focus on the words on the chart. Clear your mind and focus on your question.

As the answer comes through, your pendulum will begin to shift in its swing. The momentum will carry it to the correct answer. It will swing over the correct answer and not move to another location. This may take a little time at first, but as you do this, the pendulum will move to the answer faster. Observe the answer. Write it down. If you need to follow up with other charts, dowse them the same way. Apply the answer.

The more advanced your dowsing becomes, the more charts you will find you need. Eventually, you may find as we did that charts are not the easiest way for you to get answers.

Going Beyond Charts

We ran into trouble when it came to charting essential oils, crystals and homeopathics. There is no way a single chart could list all the possible remedies. That is when we began to experiment with blind dowsing.

We had a deck of cards showing each of the Australian Bush Flower Essences. A chart of them would be too large to draw. Maggie tentatively started dowsing the cards for appropriate remedies, with much trepidation. It seemed too 'psychic' to have a large deck of cards, facing down, and be able to dowse through them to get the right remedy.

Her left brain said that she couldn't possibly get a correct answer without looking at the face of the card. But as it turned out, she did, and doing the blind dowsing became the way she sorted through large numbers of possible answers. She made remedies for several years using this method and got great results. This is an example of how blind dowsing can build confidence. But even the act of blind dowsing is a challenge in trusting yourself and your dowsing. Everyone doubts at first. Just give it a try.

We have a book that lists homeopathics, and one with an extensive list of essential oils. When you have a book that may have the answer you seek, you can follow the basic steps for dowsing and when it's time to ask your question, open the book at random and ask, *Is the answer to my dowsing question in the left group of pages? The right group of pages?* Whichever gives you a 'yes,' take that section and randomly split it in two and ask again. And again, until you get to a single page. Ask which part, front or back, has the answer, then if necessary, scan down the page to find the exact answer. This technique sounds like magic, but it's really just a modified version of list dowsing.

If you find that the simple types of charts found in books, and even your own personal charts, do not have the scope required to get you good answers, then you will want to branch out and find other ways of doing so. Otherwise, you will limit your dowsing.

Whole Brain Charts

The Whole Brain Charts are designed to use left and right halves of the brain, rather than just one or the other. They are designed in a decision-tree format with yes/no answers determining which branch you follow. Instead of having several charts, you have it all on one chart this way. And you don't have to think up either questions or answers.

We designed these as entry level charts for beginning dowsers, and also to simplify complex decision-making. We have included them in this chapter. They require no special tool or dowsing technique.

You could create your own charts in a similar format. The only caveat is that you need to be an expert in the subject, or capable of seeing all the possibilities, in order to create this style of chart and have it be accurate. It takes a lot of work, but they are very easy to use.

The Best Use of Charts

Charts are a powerful tool, but like all tools, they are best used as intended. To get the most out of using charts, consider these aspects:

- All charts should have a choice like 'other' that indicates an awareness that no chart is complete.

- Charts, like your world view, should be allowed to grow and change. If you make your own charts, update them as needed.
- Do not focus on the answer while dowsing. Be unattached to results. Allow other intuitive information to come through as you dowse. You may get information that isn't on the chart by doing this.
- Do not become dependent on any dowsing tool or technique, including charts.
- If you get to the point that you feel charts aren't enough, leave them and move on.
- Try a variety of charts to find the ones that suit you best.

There are no short cuts; always use the four simple dowsing steps we taught in Chapter 2.

For most people, charts are a doorway to a more advanced level of dowsing. So, get some charts and get dowsing!

CHARTS: WHOLE BRAIN DOWSING

How to Use These Charts

We created these charts specifically because complex decisions involve a number of dowsing questions and a variety of possible answers that can be overwhelming. We wanted our students to quickly be able to use dowsing for important topics, and to be able to get reliable answers without being experts at making a good question or knowing possible answers.

Anyone who can get a reliable yes/no response can get answers with these charts. By using them, you will begin to see the rational thought process that supports your dowsing.

Actual dowsing is intuitive, but creating a list of goals or forming a good question is a rational exercise. That's why we call these Whole Brain charts. These charts do all the rational work for you, but allow you to see the process clearly. All you have to do is dowse.

We suggest you keep a journal of your results and refer back to it as needed. See the notes that come with each chart before you dowse.

NOTES FOR ANIMAL BREEDING CHART

This animal breeding chart is not intended to replace the care of an appropriate professional. Please exercise good judgment and seek professional care as needed.

If you encounter difficulty getting answers that seem correct, we suggest you seek the help of a professional dowser.

The underlying premise of this chart is based on our experience working with animals who have had challenges with breeding: sterility, abortion, stillbirth, infant death, trying to kill offspring, harm, illness or injury to females during pregnancy, accidents during breeding/insemination, etc.

In many cases, the undesirable outcome can be avoided with proper diet/nutrition and attention to the energetic causes of problems. Of primary importance when breeding is to obtain the permission of the animal to breed it. If this is not obtained, and the animal is unwilling to participate in the process, problems will often occur.

A great deal of time, effort and money go into breeding programs. By using this chart and applying the results appropriately, you will in all likelihood save time, effort, money and heartache in your breeding program.

CHART: ANIMAL BREEDING

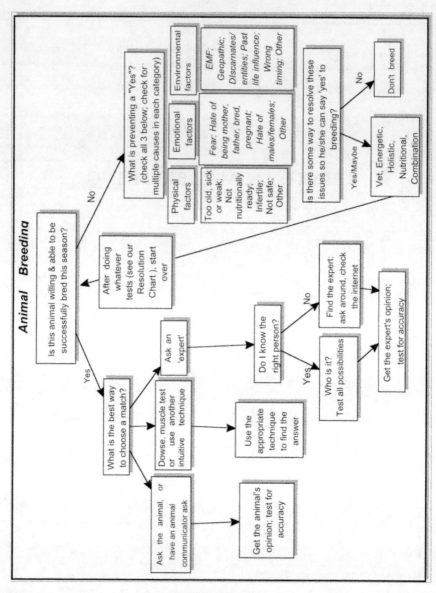

Animal Breeding Chart

NOTES FOR RELOCATION CHART

This chart is not intended to replace the advice or care of an appropriate professional. Please exercise good judgment and seek professional care/assistance as needed.

Moving to a new location is a big step that should be undertaken after considering as many factors as possible. Moves that are made for the wrong reasons often create problems.

Listening to your intuition is a valuable part of making a good decision about a move. If your dowsing indicates you shouldn't ask now, don't! Check back in a week or two, or even a month or two.

Bear in mind that there are appropriate times to ask, decide and act on something, and they aren't always at the same time. Once you get your answers, be sure to check when the best time to make the move is.

If you have family members or pets, or there are others who may be affected by the move, you can dowse the level in effects on them of the move. Be sure to check the effects for into the future, as well as now.

For example, your dog may be upset at first about the move, but in a year, he may be ecstatic. Sometimes there is a period of adjustment.

Blind dowsing can be useful when dowsing about a move. To blind dowse, you can write the options on separate pieces of paper and fold them up. Then dowse if the best place for you is in the pile of papers. If so, dowse which one is best.

Alternatively, you can do this and ask a dowsing buddy to dowse the pile of folded papers for you. Or, you can think of a question in your head and ask a dowsing buddy to dowse the answer for you. When doing the latter, it is important to focus clearly on the question.

CHART: RELOCATION

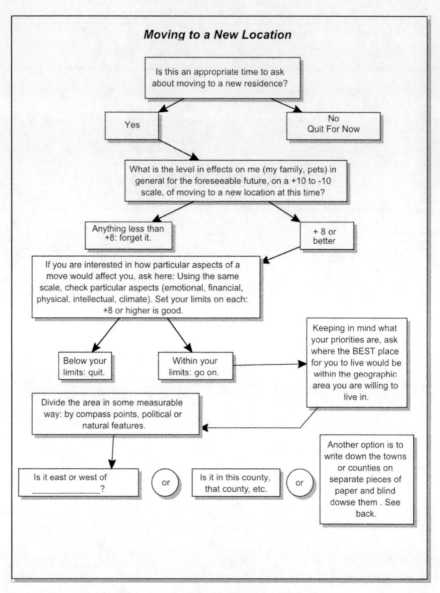

Relocation chart

NOTES FOR PROBLEMS CHART

This chart is not intended to replace the care of an appropriate professional. Please exercise good judgement and seek professional care as needed.

This chart is purposely quite general to allow its use in almost any problem or circumstances. Use this chart to define the cause(s) of the problem or symptom, remembering that multiple causes are possible.Then use our Resolution Chart or a book of dowsing charts to choose the best solution(s).

Level in Effects refers to the effect on you (on a scale of +10 to -10).

If you encounter difficulty in getting answers that seem correct, we suggest you seek the help of a professional dowser.

Types of Causes (Please note these lists are not complete):

Physical External:

- Diet

- Exercise (or lack of)
- Too much or inappropriate body movement
- Something ingested
- Something come into contact with skin
- Trauma
- Behavior-related
- Toxin
- Allergen
- Other

Physical internal:

- Genetic issues
- Malnutrition
- Parasites
- Allergy/sensitivity
- Old injury/trauma
- Inflammation
- Toxicity
- Other

Nonphysical External:

- Noxious earth energies
- Human energies
- Cosmic energies
- Alien energies
- Animal energies
- Discarnate entities (ghosts)
- Other

Nonphysical internal:

- Karmic issues

- Emotional issues
- Beliefs
- Energetic links to others
- Damage to energy body
- Other

CHART: CAUSES OF PROBLEMS/SYMPTOMS

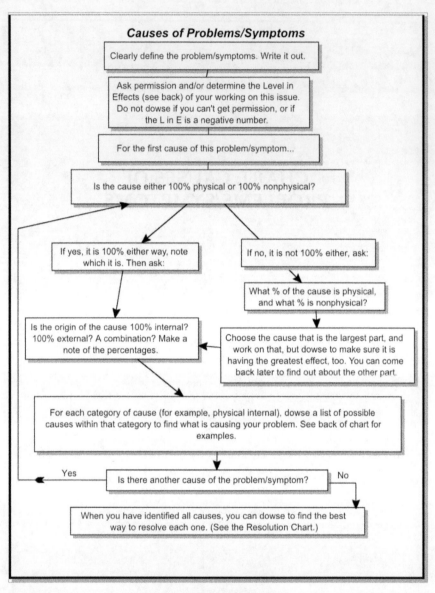

Causes of Problems/Symptoms

Clearly define the problem/symptoms. Write it out.

Ask permission and/or determine the Level in Effects (see back) of your working on this issue. Do not dowse if you can't get permission, or if the L in E is a negative number.

For the first cause of this problem/symptom...

Is the cause either 100% physical or 100% nonphysical?

If yes, it is 100% either way, note which it is. Then ask:

If no, it is not 100% either, ask:

What % of the cause is physical, and what % is nonphysical?

Is the origin of the cause 100% internal? 100% external? A combination? Make a note of the percentages.

Choose the cause that is the largest part, and work on that, but dowse to make sure it is having the greatest effect, too. You can come back later to find out about the other part.

For each category of cause (for example, physical internal), dowse a list of possible causes within that category to find what is causing your problem. See back of chart for examples.

Yes — Is there another cause of the problem/symptom? No

When you have identified all causes, you can dowse to find the best way to resolve each one. (See the Resolution Chart.)

Causes of Problems/Symptoms

NOTES FOR SOLUTIONS CHART

This chart is not intended to replace the care of an appropriate professional. Please exercise good judgement and seek professional care as needed.

If you encounter difficulty getting answers that seem correct, we suggest you seek the help of a professional dowser.

When dowsing 'methods,' be flexible. List any methods/therapies/treatments/actions that seem likely candidates. Then list others, such as symbols, color, sound, fragrance, affirmation, or other things you know how to do that can shift energy. It may take more than one method to resolve the particular cause.

Sometimes you will need to use one method for a while, then go on to another method. Determining the schedule of application will be very important. For example, is it best to apply the method once a day, more often, less often? For how long should you employ it for best results? Is it best to use all the methods concurrently, or one after the other? These answers can be determined by dowsing.

Concerning timing, sometimes doing nothing is the best thing to do. You can dowse if that is the the case, and/or if at some future time it will be appropriate to do something else.

This chart has purposely been made as general as possible, so as to apply to most types of problems. You may find a book of detailed dowsing charts comes in very handy after you have determined the basics using this chart.

CHART: SOLUTIONS FOR PROBLEMS/SYMPTOMS

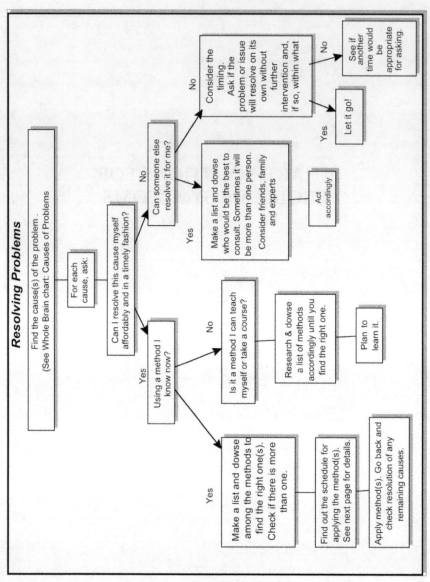

Resolving Problems

Find the cause(s) of the problem.
(See Whole Brain chart: Causes of Problems

For each cause, ask:

Can I resolve this cause myself affordably and in a timely fashion?

No

Can someone else resolve it for me?

No

Consider the timing. Ask if the problem or issue will resolve on its own without further intervention and, if so, within what

No

See if another time would be appropriate for asking.

Yes

Let it go!

Yes

Make a list and dowse who would be the best to consult. Sometimes it will be more than one person. Consider friends, family and experts

Act accordingly

Yes

Using a method I know now?

No

Is it a method I can teach myself or take a course?

Research & dowse a list of methods accordingly until you find the right one.

Plan to learn it.

Yes

Make a list and dowse among the methods to find the right one(s). Check if there is more than one.

Find out the schedule for applying the method(s). See next page for details.

Apply method(s). Go back and check resolution of any remaining causes.

Solutions Chart

194

NOTES FOR RELATIONSHIPS CHART

This chart is not intended to replace the advice or care of an appropriate professional. Please exercise good judgement and seek professional care as needed.

If you encounter difficulty getting answers that seem correct, we suggest you seek the help of a professional dowser.

If your dowsing indicates you shouldn't ask now, don't! Check back in a week or two, or even a month or two. Bear in mind that there are appropriate times to ask, decide and act upon something, and they aren't always at the same time.

Level in Effects describes the effect on you of any decision or action. A scale of +10 to -10 is customary. +8 or higher is considered good. You can determine how low a score you will accept, but don't accept negative numbers. We suggest going for +8 or better in all subject areas.

Factors that can be affected by a relationship: finances, career, emotional/physical/spiritual health, happiness, personal goals/dreams, relationships with significant others (family members/pets).

Blind dowsing allows you to dowse about a subject when you think you are emotionally attached to results. It reduces chances of incorrect answers in such cases. To blind dowse, you can write the options on separate pieces of paper and fold them up. When you dowse for the answer among the folded papers, you won't see what you have chosen until after the fact.

This chart can be used for current relationships with minor modifications. If you are trying to decide if a current relationship is toxic, worth the effort, or should be severed, this chart will help you formulate questions to help clarify your decision.

Whether you are asking about a mate, co-worker, friend or potential lover, this chart can help you avoid making decisions that will have unpleasant consequences.

CHART: RELATIONSHIPS

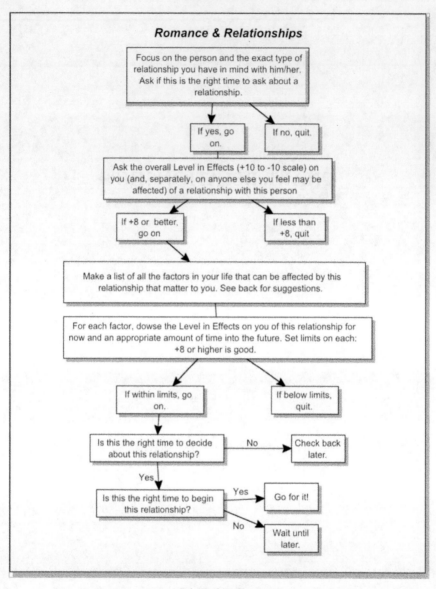

Relationships Chart

CLEARING THE ENERGY OF
ALLERGIES

Maggie tells how an allergy led her to a whole new way of seeing the world.

I had a dairy allergy from the time I was born that was quite serious. As a baby, I couldn't assimilate cow's milk, and my mother did not breast feed me. There weren't milk substitutes like there are today, and my survival was in question. I was put on solid foods quite early as a result, and that only led to more food sensitivities.

I learned dowsing from David Schultz, then President of the ASD (American Society of Dowsers) chapter in Phoenix, AZ. I liked his class so much, I took all the other classes he offered. One was about healing, as that was a specialty he had. He used a technique called SRT to heal all kinds of conditions. In the class, he asked for a volunteer who had allergies so that he could demonstrate how SRT (Spiritual Response Therapy) could be used to permanently clear a lifelong allergy.

I put my hand up fast, because my dairy allergy was really a nuisance. If I accidentally ate something with a tiny bit of butter in it, like veggies in a butter sauce, I would be awake for hours in the middle of the night with a sick stomach. I was ready to be rid of that allergy.

He did a 15 minute session using SRT to identify past lives, found several involving cattle and farming where things had gone horribly wrong, and cleared those energies. I went home and ate a bowl of ice cream that night and slept like a baby. I haven't had dairy problems since.

Those results led me to enroll in an SRT class and get my certification. But wouldn't it be nice if you didn't need to pay for an expensive class and learn a whole new healing system to clear allergies? Well, you don't. This article will teach you the easy way to clear the energies of allergies, and you will be off and running right away.

To your good health,

Maggie

Always seek the appropriate health care professional for help with physical issues. This article is not in any way intended to replace the effective care of your chosen doctor or health care professional, but rather to support your intention to be fully healthy, no matter what healing methods you choose to apply to your physical body.

Can Energy Clearing Resolve Allergies?

We believe that physical symptoms represent your body telling you about an energy that is present in your system and needs healing if you wish to be healthy. Each symptom represents a particular energy frequency that is about negative beliefs, fears and traumas.

Sometimes those energies have been passed down through generations or past lives, while many are a result of your current life experience. There are many books available for helping you decode the messages your body gives you, if this topic interests you and you want to pursue it for improving your health in general, as we have.

Since we believe dis-ease manifests first in the energy body and then in the physical, our focus is on healing energies rather than treating symptoms if we want to feel well.

Allergies tend to be an expression of certain energies, most of which revolve around not feeling safe in this life on earth.

Physically, those with allergies and sensitivities tend to have toxins built up in their liver and congested lymphatic systems. The liver detoxifies you of all kinds of toxins, including emotional ones, while the lymphatic system functions in part as the body's sewage system. If those systems get backed up, you get allergies.

A holistic doctor can help alleviate those physical problems, while an allopathic doctor only treats symptoms. In both cases, you can get some relief, but we feel the most permanent solution is to clear the energetic root cause of the allergy, then support the body in strengthening the liver and lymphatic system.

We have observed that success with healing lifelong, unexplained allergies is most often tied to healing past life issues. Do you have a lifelong allergy that has symptoms that annoy you or threaten you? This article can help you identify and clear the energies at the root of your issue.

As a dowser, this is where Step 1 of the dowsing process determines your success. What do you want, why do you want it, and why are you asking this question?

If you say you're suffering from an allergy-caused migraine and just want the pain to stop, what you dowse will be totally different from dowsing to find out **why** you tend to have migraines, so that you can stop having them altogether.

In this training, you will learn how to use dowsing to discover the energetic root cause of your allergic symptoms and clear that energy. The results can manifest in your physical body as the disappearance of the allergic reaction.

While we have seen this happen for ourselves and others many times, it is not 100% guaranteed, so please use good judgment. **Don't ever expose yourself to allergens purposely.** If you do this clearing, just live normally and don't test yourself. The goal of this clearing is to allow you to live more safely and comfortably on earth.

The Answer is 'Yes'

Most people have taken shots or gone through laborious and expensive desensitization techniques like NAET to get rid of allergies. And among the people we have worked with who have done one or more techniques like those, quite a few still had allergies.

The following technique is quite simple, but you need to approach it openly and with trust. If you don't believe something this simple will work, you aren't ready for this method. Not yet. As a colleague of ours used to say, put it in your back pocket if that is the case and take it out another day in the future to look at it again.

But if you are ready to be empowered to heal yourself by shifting your energy, this process has no down side at all. If it doesn't work, no harm done. You won't get worse. If it works, your life gets so much better.

Steps to Clearing the Energy of Allergies

The technique in this article is designed mainly for those who have had an allergy diagnosis that they believe is accurate, and they want to clear the energies of that allergy. If you have undiagnosed allergies, it's true that dowsing using lists and charts can help you track down the cause.

Step 1: Identify the Allergy

Let's say you know you are allergic to cheese, because every time you eat any, even a small amount, you vomit (this was true for Nigel's cheese allergy prior to SRT).

Using a +10 to -10 scale, with negative numbers indicating an allergy or sensitivity, dowse what the effect of that substance (in this case, cheese) is on you physically. Bigger negative numbers are more intense allergies and sensitivities.

Do not choose a life-threatening allergy for your first try using this method. Develop some success and confidence, and **always use common**

sense and avoid potentially dangerous substances, even if you think you have cleared your allergy.

Make a note of the number you got for your allergic substance. Maybe it was grass pollen, or smoke, or strawberries. It will be easier to see results if you clear an allergy that is a -8 or worse. Make a note of the symptom or symptoms you usually experience when exposed. This way, you can retest after clearing.

The basis of this technique, as in SRT, is that other lifetimes impinge on your experience in this one, and we want to eliminate those effects. We will use dowsing to identify and gather the necessary information about those lifetimes, and we will then clear them using intention. It's as simple as that.

Step 2: Dowse for Details

How many other lifetimes are affecting my allergy/sensitivity to _____*in this lifetime?* We dowse how many digits are in the answer: 0, 1, 2, 3. We have observed that in most cases, an allergy will have several tens of lifetimes contributing to it at most, but there are cases where the number is higher.

Ask: *Can I clear energetic root cause of the allergy/sensitivity without knowing the details of any of those lives?* In most cases, the answer will be 'no,' at least until you get really comfortable with the system. But if the answer is an unexpected 'yes,' proceed to the clearing methods directly.

If your answer was 'no,' then you need details of some lives, usually only a couple at most. Ask how many lives you need to know details of in order to clear the energies of the allergy/sensitivity completely. It is unlikely you will have a number over 3 in most cases.

Get details on each lifetime and write them down. You do not have to have all the same details in each life. You just need to know what you need to know to clear the allergy. And that can vary. Some questions to dowse are:

- Was the lifetime on earth?

- Time line: past, future, parallel or other? You can ask how long ago or how far into the future it was/is if you wish
- Were you human? If not, what were you? Animal, plant, mineral?
- Did the allergen cause you death or injury in that life? Did it have a direct result on harming you seriously in that life? For example, if smoke is the allergen, and you get 'yes' to the first question (did the smoke cause you death or injury), it is likely you may have died of smoke inhalation during a fire. Or perhaps smoke inhalation prostrated you, and you were burned badly and it ruined your life, and you always identified smoke with a ruined life. So it irritates you in this lifetime. When you get 'yes,' use your intuition and dowse to find out the connection.
- If you get 'no,' that the allergen did not have a direct effect on you in that lifetime, then you have a bit more of a job. It could be that the allergen indirectly killed you. For example, you are allergic to mold. Yeast is a mold. You owned a brewery, and your brother wanted it, so he killed you in the brewery near the vats, and somehow you associate death with yeast, which is mold. Thus, you are allergic to it (molds, not beer) in this lifetime. Other indirect traumas include something killed someone you dearly loved, leading to you committing suicide or lose financial support, leading to starvation and death.

It is also possible that you will occasionally not see any connection between the allergen and the past life. Here is where your intuition is vital. Maybe your subconscious has substituted a word that is similar. Or a concept that is similar. This does not happen often, and at first, you may choose to work on another allergy rather than face such a challenge. But be aware they do crop up from time to time.

At some point, you will have learned all you need to know about the past life. Just dowse if you need further info in order to clear the energies of the allergy. Then go on to the next life you have to research. When you have found details on all the ones you need to know about, then you can clear.

Step 3: Clear the Energy

Clearing the energies of the allergy is pretty simple. You use intention to power whatever method works best for you. The intention is the key thing. Your desire is to transform all the energies of that allergy, quickly, easily, comfortably and safely, as well as permanently. You may use a color, a symbol, fragrance or whatever you wish to anchor the intent. But use whatever works for you. Above all, you need to tell yourself that you are not in that lifetime now and that what was true then is no longer true now.

Bear in mind that energy can take up to 72 hours to clear fully. Do not intentionally expose yourself to an allergen just to test things. Just be aware of how you do the next time you encounter the allergen. Expect good results. Allow yourself to be surprised.

Avoiding Pitfalls in Allergy Clearing

Know Your Allergy

A potential pitfall is if you mis-identify an allergy. It is best to stick with clearing allergies you are certain you have, as they will allow you to see the confirmation and success of what you do.

However, once you are a good health dowser, you can dowse a list of common allergens and find which ones affect you, and then clear their energies. We used to do this with clients all the time, but we always liked to start with the more obvious ones so they can see the results immediately.

Some allergies are dangerous, as we pointed out in the story of our client's shrimp allergy at the beginning of this chapter. Anaphylactic shock can kill you. **Do not ever assume that you have successfully cleared a life-threatening allergy.** It's fine to do your best to clear it, but still avoid that substance. This technique is to improve your health, enhance your comfort and feeling of safety in living a normal life. Still carry your epi-pen.

Allergens Can Be Anything

You can be allergic to anything physical, but you can also be allergic to emotions, situations and energies. For example, perhaps you are allergic to 'being healthy', 'joy' or even 'happiness'. If you find that you have problems along those lines, you can usually go straight to clearing them using a statement of intention.

Summary

You have learned a powerful energy clearing technique for past lives that will permanently remove the energies that have led to an allergic reaction in this life. Remember that this method clears only the **energies** of the allergy. We do not claim this process will 'cure' the physical body. But we have observed that often, when you clear the energetic root cause of a condition, the physical body improves.

In Nigel's case he can eat cheese without problems but doesn't actively choose to have it consistently or as a snack, having had so many years of unpleasant reactions. But it is no longer a source of worry for him. For Maggie, eating dairy products no longer gives her the digestive distress it once did, but she eats those foods in moderation.

You can use this technique along with other physical healing modalities or alone and expect to have improvement. It is always beneficial to remove negative energies from your system, even if you don't see outward results. For us, the improvement has been nothing short of miraculous. We wish you the same results.

EARTH ENERGIES & DOWSING

You live in a complex web of energies that have a powerful effect on all aspects of your life. Your health is the most obvious reflection of the energies you live in.

One time we were dowsing the energies in a house in Sedona for the owners. They didn't tell us any of their history or concerns. After checking, we told them that the bed in the guest room had a couple of very noxious lines running through it at chest level before going out of the house. We informed them that anyone sleeping there would doubtless have health problems, probably quite severe, in the chest or the throat area, depending on how they slept.

That's when they told us that a sister who lived with them had slept there and had died of lung cancer. She was not a smoker. Earth energies have more to do with your health than you might imagine.

What is Energy?

The term 'energy' is thrown around a lot in New Age circles. But what is it? If you can remember back to your youth, in early science classes you learned that the Universe is composed of matter and energy. Matter is physical and it has mass and weight. Energy is nonphysical and often is invisible, though not always. The electromagnetic spectrum consists of a continuum of energies, and you can see the visible spectrum as light. But energy has no mass or weight and for the most part is invisible.

Even though energy is sometimes invisible, it is still quite powerful and has an effect on you. Quantum physics has proven that matter is just another form of energy. What this means is that your body is energy in physical form. Quantum physics also has demonstrated that everything is connected energetically. So it makes sense for you to learn about the energies that are out there, that are all around and even passing through you, and how to deal with them.

Energy is always neutral. It isn't 'good' or 'bad' in itself. Judgment is a facet of duality, and it can lead you into trouble when dealing with energies. Energy simply *is*.

Energies are usually **not** conscious. They don't have agendas. Their effect on you can be detrimental or beneficial. And sometimes their effect changes as you change.

Even more confusing, their effect won't necessarily be the same on another human, and often it is quite different for another species of animal, or a plant. That is why it is not appropriate to categorize energies as universally 'good' or 'bad.'

There are many types of energies. You can categorize them in many ways. We like to use categories that relate to the origin of the energy. We use three basic categories: earth, human and cosmic energies. Although humans live on earth, they have created quite a few unique non-natural energies, and we like to separate them from the natural earth energies.

In this training we will focus on earth energies, as they have been studied by humans for thousands of years.

Types of Noxious Earth Energies

When we talk about negative earth energies, what are we referring to? There are many types of geopathic energies. Geopathic stress is a term used to describe noxious earth energies (energies that are harmful to humans).

Noxious earth energies include, but are not limited to, the effects of:

- Underground water
- Underground faulting
- Radon gas
- Negative lines of energy running on the surface, above or below it
- Negative vortices
- Negative spots of energy

Try It Yourself: Earth Energy Detection

Go to a busy location near you: a hospital, a shopping mall, a subway station. Do not have any particular preconceived notions or judgments. You can take your pendulum if you wish, but you don't have to.

Pick a spot that is on the edge of the activity and sit down or stand quietly. Choose to be aware of (but not participate or process) the earth energies present. Allow yourself to perceive the energies in whatever way is best.

If you are visual, you might scan the area visually using very soft focus. Note that some areas might appear dark or dirty out of the corner of your eye, or even when you look directly at them.

If you feel things in your body, then close your eyes and choose to be aware of the energy present. You may feel it in a particular location of your body, or as a particular feeling or emotion, such as sadness or heaviness. Sometimes, you might feel it physically like a pressure in your head and sinuses.

If you don't feel anything there, move to another location. Try a few areas until you get a sense of the energy present. Make notes about your perceptions.

Dowse the list of earth energies above and see which of them were present, and how intensely negative they are on a scale of -10 to +10, with -10 being worst.

Now do the same thing when visiting a location like a cathedral, holy spot or healing spring. Compare your perceptions and dowse the list again. You will note that the energies in such a place are much less noxious, and in some cases, even register positive numbers on the -10 to +10 scale.

Quite often you will find that you have been unconsciously reacting to the energies of a place already, but hadn't realized it until this exercise. An example we've frequently seen is people constantly finding reasons to leave their house if the energy is quite noxious there. It's always good to be aware of your physical and mental reactions to places; they can give you much information.

Bear in mind that you have to be aware that you are just searching for earth energies. Anywhere where there are large numbers of people, you can often be confused by the energies given off by the people or by manmade energies. This can be confusing at first, so this is also a good exercise in discrimination; for only finding what it is you are searching for, and filtering out everything else.

How Earth Energies Affect You

Why bother detecting earth energies? Because some of them are quite detrimental to your health. You can die if you spend a lot of time in very noxious earth energies. It happens all the time.

Almost any physical and some mental/emotional symptoms can be caused by earth energies. For example, cancer is often called a 'disease of location' due to its tendency to be associated with noxious earth energies.

Here is a brief and partial list of symptoms that are common with geopathic stress:

- Serious diseases like cancer, MS and SIDS (Sudden Infant Death Syndrome)
- Ongoing, low level health issues that seem to relate to a compromised or weak immune system
- Behavioral problems with children and animals

- Tension and irritation
- Sleep disorders
- Difficulty concentrating; fuzzy thinking
- Seeing apparitions or ghosts
- Smelling strange smells, but not finding a cause
- Hearing knocking or tapping sounds, but not finding a cause
- Nightmares in children
- Plants dying or not growing well in spite of proper care; strange growths on plants
- Headache, sinus issues or pain or trouble in one part of body (can relate to energies in your bed)

Noxious earth energies have been shown to have an immediate effect on a number of physiological factors. The immune system seems to be most at risk, but whatever is your weak 'link' in the health chain, that is where things will start happening if you have noxious earth energies.

As you can see from the above list, it isn't easy to pinpoint something as caused by environmental energies. However, if you clear your space and the symptom goes away, that pretty much proves what the cause is. And research has proven that even terminal cancer can be reversed once noxious energies causing the cancer are removed.

The challenge is that any symptom on the above list can also be caused by other factors, so you can't be sure what the cause is. Even if you are an excellent dowser, it can be hard to pinpoint the causal factors, as sometimes there is more than one. Dowsing does give you a measure of confidence that is way beyond anything else you can use, though.

The main thing to remember is that each species and each individual responds uniquely to energies, and that what is harmful to you may be beneficial to your cat. One type of plant may be killed by an energy, while another will thrive in it.

That is why it is wise to avoid judging or naming energies as if they are 'good' or 'bad,' because that judgment is purely selfish and does not apply uniformly to all life forms. The energies are there, because they all are part of the whole, and each has its role to play.

The Solution: Space Clearing

Space clearing is the most common phrase associated with removing, neutralizing, or harmonizing the energies of a particular location. We like to use the term Environmental Harmonization, as we feel that 'clearing' sounds a bit judgmental, but either term works.

While we don't like to judge energies as good or bad, we believe it is smart to choose to live in energies that are healthful. Thus, it makes sense for you to learn to detect energies and keep your space beneficial for you and all the life forms on it. Check out the space clearing article in this chapter if you want more details on this subject.

You are a part of Earth's ecosystem energetically as well as physically. Earth energies are here to support you in your goals. Use dowsing to guide your way to find and create happy, healthy space to live.

ETHICS IN DOWSING

Dowsing is an incredibly powerful tool for change of all kinds. As with any kind of power, corruption and ego can follow. Just because you **can** do something does not mean you **should**. Just because **you** feel something is good does not give you the right to impose it on others.

We have seen and heard of professional dowsers telling people to use dowsing to change other peoples' space, attitudes and behavior without permission, just because they feel it would be 'good.' This is just plain unethical.

In this article, we will share with you our perspective on how you can use the power of dowsing wisely and well for positive change without creating negative karma for yourself.

Humans seem to be unable to restrain themselves from using a power once they discover it. Much of the time, boundaries and guidelines for the use of a power only come about after the power has been in use for some time, often after it has had disastrous consequences. Even when guidelines are set, there are always some individuals who refuse to be bound by them.

Dowsing is powerful. We encourage people to learn to dowse. We love to empower people. But at the same time, we are passionate about people learning to use their power ethically. This can only be done when you consider the consequences of your choices and how they affect yourself and others.

Living ethically requires a certain degree of self-reflection. You need to be willing to think about what matters to you and what goes into making healthy choices. It requires you to think about how your actions have consequences not only for you, but for others as well. Unfortunately, most people don't take time to do this for themselves. They prefer to have an authority figure tell them right from wrong.

As you learn to dowse, one of the most amazing discoveries you make is that you can do virtually anything with it. But trying to use dowsing to change the external world in some fashion to suit your world view is a sign of fear. People want to feel safe and secure, and when they have noisy neighbors, Republicans in office or a sick relative; they feel threatened. So they use dowsing to change what scares them. This is not an enlightened approach, and it is not ethical. More to the point, it isn't effective. When you use dowsing to force others to change, the change will not last for long. Maggie learned this lesson as a new dowser. Her story took place in the late 90s.

I was very new to dowsing when a dear friend asked if I could help her. Her daughter was going through a horrible divorce. The ex-husband was a lawyer, and he was totally uncooperative and making the process an ordeal for her and the children. He never signed any papers on time. He lied. He used the system to cost her time and money and keep her from doing what she wanted to do.

I knew my friend's daughter was a nice person, and I had no doubt that my friend was being honest. I wanted to help her. She explained that her daughter needed the ex to sign a paper by a certain date, or it would cost her a lot of time, money and effort. I used what I had learned in class. Believing that fairness to all was a good goal, I dowsed to see if his High Self would give me permission to facilitate a fair and timely response, because I knew it was pointless to ask him directly. I got 'yes'. So I set my intention and went to work on it. I learned that he signed the paperwork uncharacteristically quickly (on time for the first time) right after that. But then he went back to being his normal self again.

In the years following that event, I came to feel that I had overstepped the bounds of ethics when I did that. If someone does not consciously agree to change, it is inappropriate to ask their High Self to permit it. What I did overrode his free will temporarily to get the outcome my friend's daughter desired. In a sense, it was a judgment not only against the ex, but against her, saying she was a victim and unable to choose to be a victor. I saw myself as riding to her rescue with my power. I was acting out of ego. I would not use dowsing in that way again.

It's easy to take a step on a slippery slope such as this. Don't do it. Don't assume you always know what is best for others.

Unethical behavior is often about ego or fear, and both cause one to rob others' of the right to choose what to experience for themselves.

If you use dowsing unethically, it is our opinion that you create negative karma. You will be given opportunities to change your ways. If you don't, the lessons could become increasingly harsh. At first, the lesson is that when you change something without permission, it soon relapses to its original state. That is a cue for you to rethink things.

It is appropriate for you to use dowsing on yourself, your property and to help others with their express permission to do so on them and their property. Always ask permission of a child or animal before dowsing for or about it. The responsible adult and owner need to give permission, but so does the subject. In this case you can ethically use dowsing to see if the subject gives permission if they cannot speak for themselves, as with a person in a coma.

It is also permissible for you to use dowsing to alter space in which you work or visit, even if you are not the owner of that space. Your office cubicle is in your care. Do not clear the entire workplace for others or the company without appropriate permission, though.

When clearing space for a client, only clear the space on their property. Don't change anything that is affecting adjacent properties without the owners' permissions, which you don't have in most cases.

Don't decide that a place is 'bad,' and that you have the right to change it because of your judgment. Changing the crime rate in a location can be an egotistical exercise. It won't last without the agreement of those in the location, even though it can be done.

Try It Yourself: Making Ethical Choices

Here are a few scenarios that give you an opportunity to practice ethical dowsing. See what you would do and compare it to what we recommend is ethical and effective (unethical is also, ultimately, ineffective).

Situation 1: Using dowsing to create peace and quiet

You have noisy and disrespectful neighbors. They keep you awake at all hours, harming your health and concentration at work. You are either afraid to ask them to quiet down, or you have asked, and it didn't help. How can you use dowsing to change this situation?

1: Would you decide to clear their space and clear them of negative energies, hoping that would calm them down and make them more open to being good neighbors?

2: Or would you work on yourself and find out why you are attracting this experience? What is it precisely about their behavior which you find so distressing, and why is that? Then use dowsing to change whatever energies are within you that are not in harmony with having respectful, peaceful neighbors?

We have heard of both choices being used, and both getting results. However, we feel choice #2 is more ethical and will more likely have lasting results. Plus there is less fear, judgment and ego in it.

Situation 2: Getting what you want out of negative people

Your spouse doesn't believe in all this metaphysical mumbo-jumbo. He is negative and won't listen to what you say. You know he has a serious addiction to nicotine, and his health is at risk from his smoking, but he either can't or won't quit. You are truly concerned for him, but his health and well-being also impact you. If he dies, it will seriously change your life, perhaps for the worse. What can you do?

1: Do you use dowsing to clear his addiction energy without telling him, so that he will want to quit smoking?

2: Or do you work on why you can't get respect from your own spouse? Do you clear yourself of the energy of not being valued/not being heard/being ignored? Do you look for the judgment you have on smoking and clear the reasons behind that so you can release your fear and judgment? Do you try to discover why you are afraid of losing your spouse to lung cancer/being alone/being on your own?

Either choice may give results. But choice #2 is more ethical, as your spouse does not want you to change him. It allows the other person to have free will. It also is not done out of fear or judgment.

Dowsing makes you very powerful. We know you want to use that power for good. We believe the best way to accomplish that is to work mostly on changing yourself, your outlook and beliefs, and your energy. Be the change you want to see.

FOOD DOWSING

Dowsing and food might seem strange bedfellows, but in reality, you can use dowsing to a great advantage in all aspects of your relationship with food. Here are just a few ways:

- Selecting produce, meats and brands of food at the supermarket
- Choosing what to plant in your vegetable or herb garden
- Preparing a menu for guests or a special occasion
- Finding out if you or a member of your family has allergies or sensitivities to foods
- Choosing the right cooking time and temperature
- Selecting appropriate cookware for a given task
- Selecting the perfect gift of candy, wine or other food item
- Checking digestibility of a given food for yourself or a family member
- Choosing the best item on a restaurant menu
- Helping with a dietary regimen

Our relationship with food is complex and often filled with problems. Nourishment is vital for health, and yet most people spend very little time consciously choosing what to eat or drink. It's no wonder that people are waking up to the fact that the most significant factor in your health, after what you think, is what you eat and how well you digest it. Borderline malnutrition is rapidly being recognized as a major underlying factor in many health problems.

As a dowser, you can heal your relationship with food by asking good dowsing questions that give you accurate information that leads to happy choices regarding what you eat and drink.

Many questions related to food will not have clear yes/no answers. You will find it more useful to employ a scale instead. We use a +10 to -10 scale, with negative numbers being detrimental and positive ones being beneficial. The larger the number, the stronger the answer. Zero is of course neutral.

You can see the value of a scale if you are trying to determine how allergic you are to shrimp or how much Aunt Joan will like that Cabernet Sauvignon wine, as a scale gives more than a yes/no answer. Likewise, if you are in a wonderful restaurant and spoiled for choice on the menu, it would be ideal to find what item is a +10 for you.

We find that numbers greater than 8 tend to be significant enough to act on. Don't spend money on a bottle of wine that dowses +3, even though the number is positive. Aim higher. For more on how to use scales, see that topic in Chapter 4.

Try It Yourself: Practice Making a Good Question

Pick one of the subjects below and record your dowsing responses to the questions. If possible, think up questions that will give you further details on the subject. Choose something you can get confirmation on, so that you gain confidence in your dowsing ability. Included in this exercise is using a sliding scale to dowse about a subject.

How do you create dowsing questions that use a scale of +10 to -10? Start with this phrase and add one of the ones below to complete the dowsing question:

On a scale of +10 to -10, with positive numbers being beneficial and negative ones being detrimental,:

- *Are any of these avocados a +8 or better for use in a green salad this Tuesday, if I want the avocado firm but ripe, beautiful and tasty as well as nutritious?*
- *How much will Dad like this brand of scotch if I buy it for his birthday next week? (This presumes you have dowsed Dad likes scotch and will drink it if presented with some.)*
- *Is there anything on this restaurant menu that is a +8 or better for me today in terms of nutrition, tastiness, digestibility and overall enjoyment?*
- *Will planting tomatoes in my garden this year be a +8 overall in terms of enjoyment, success, productivity and nutrition?*
- *Is serving lamb to the Joneses next week a +8 or better in terms of their overall enjoyment of the meal?*
- *How is this tap water for me at this time in terms of my overall health and enjoyment?*
- *How will my system react to shrimp if I eat a serving of shrimp scampi tonight?*
- *How digestible is spinach lasagna for my Mom at this time?*
- *How 'done' (be sure you know how you define this) is the steak on the grill at this time, with +10 being perfect? (Remember it cooks after you remove it, so factor that into the question.)*

As with many dowsing questions, your answers will probably prompt even more questions. Don't stop at one answer. Maybe you would like to find out why a particular answer was negative or only a low positive.

Break the question down into specific aspects and dowse some more. Take the avocado example above. If you got a negative number, you could ask the following questions:

*Are there **any** avocados here that are +8 or better for my needs? (Sometimes we forget that maybe there aren't any good choices.)*

Are there any that would be +8 in terms of appearance and taste in a green salad this Tuesday? (Maybe they all lack nutrition based on poor farming practices, so you won't find a nutritious one, so eliminate that aspect and re-dowse. You can do that for each attribute.)

Perhaps they are all need more ripening. So ask, *Are any +8 or better for a salad on Wednesday, Thursday, etc.?*

What if you are getting a negative number because you have an allergy to avocados that you didn't know about? This shows how important flexible thinking is during a dowsing session. You weren't thinking about allergies or digestibility when you asked the question, but that will impact your answer.

Or what if you are planning on making this salad for guests, and one of them hates avocados, but you don't know it? You may very well get a negative number for all the avocados in that case.

As you can see, dowsing about food will cause you to think in broader terms about it, which is quite useful. We have found that dowsing actually does have the effect of helping one see the many and complex relationships between things, regardless of the type of dowsing you are doing.

Try It Yourself: Dowse for Food Gifts

Selecting food gifts and preparing meals for guests can be a nightmare filled with anxiety. No one likes to spend money on meals and wine and candy that are not appreciated or enjoyed. Dowsing is an indispensable tool for making sure your dinner parties and gifts are always loved and enjoyed.

The first thing to dowse in such circumstances is:

On a scale of +10 to -10, how much does _____(fill in the person's name) like _____(fill in the type of wine, food, candy, etc.)

If you get a +8 or better, that's great. But don't stop there.

Next, dowse if that person eats/drinks/uses that item at this time or would use it/eat it/drink it if given to them as a gift. You would be amazed how often people swear off something, go on a restrictive diet or otherwise give up on something they like. So asking this question is vital.

Then, once you are assured they will enjoy and use what you want to buy, you can use dowsing to pick the best brand for their tastes. Remember to go for a +8 or better. You can use the term 'overall' in the question, but if there are more specific aspects of like and dislike that you know of, add them in for better accuracy. Then pick the best individual item of that brand. You don't want to get a bad bottle of merlot.

For example, Dad might like scotch and still drinks it, but you can't get a good number on any brand you are testing because you forgot Dad likes single malt, not blends. Or Mom likes dark chocolate, not milk chocolate. Being specific will give you even better answers. So be as clear and specific as you can when making up your questions.

Try It Yourself: Dowsing a Restaurant Menu

Most people go out to eat occasionally, even if it is just fast food. Picking a meal that you will enjoy is very important. But have you ever thought of all the factors that go into your enjoyment of a meal? Maybe not.

When looking at a menu in a restaurant, consider what factors matter to you from the list below. Everyone has their own priorities. If you can think of something to add to the list that matters to you, do so. Some possible aspects include:

- Tastiness
- Digestibility
- Lack of allergens
- Nutritional value
- Compatibility with your diet, if you are on one
- Freshness of the food, lack of toxicity
- Enjoyment of the seasonings and presentation

So as you scan the menu, you might ask,

Considering my goals, on a scale of +10 to -10, are there any items on this menu that are +8 or better for me overall today for lunch? But you can also program into the term 'overall' any of the above items you wish. Or you can dowse them each separately by plugging them into the question in place of 'overall.'

Program yourself to get a negative number if food will give you unpleasant symptoms of any kind. (By 'program,' basically we mean intend that outcome. This technique is discussed in detail in Chapter 4.) And do whatever your dowsing says. You never have to experience food poisoning or an allergic reaction to MSG again if you dowse.

As with all dowsing, you can't always imagine the causes of low numbers. But you will sometimes get confirmation later. For example, you may wonder why you dowse -1 for your favorite food, but then the waitress tells you they are out of that item today.

Try It Yourself: Dowsing about Allergies

Dowsing is a great way to determine whether or not you have an allergy or sensitivity to a particular food or drink.

Caution: You should not dowse about this subject if you have any emotions about allergies, attachment to a certain answer, or strong opinions about whether or not you are allergic to something. Do not substitute dowsing for appropriate health care. Always seek an opinion from a trusted health care professional.

As with all types of dowsing, you will be better at dowsing for allergies if you take what we term a Whole Brain approach. Read up on food allergies. Find out the most common allergens. Learn the difference between an allergy and a sensitivity. Find out what allopathic medicine does for allergies, and what natural medicine does for them. Do not absorb this information as gospel, but use it as a basis for when you dowse.

Allergies and sensitivities can happen for a number of reasons. You may have an allergic personality and many allergies. You may have a clogged lymphatic system or a toxic liver. In all cases, allergies are merely a snapshot of the condition of your system at the time you are tested. Allergies do not have to be forever.

Allergies can be life-threatening, as is the case in anaphylactic shock. This is relatively rare.

Do not use your dowsing as the sole basis for any action regarding an allergy. Be sure to consult a professional.

Once you have good definitions of allergies and sensitivities, you can find a list of common allergens. You want to formulate a good dowsing question to ask. An example is:

Using a +10 to -10 scale, with minus numbers indicating a degree of relative allergy or sensitivity to a substance, what is the level in effects on me of ingesting/breathing/ exposing myself at this time to _____. Fill in the blank with each item in the list. Make a note of what number you got. Any that give you a negative number are giving you a negative physical reaction at some level.

We generally use 8 or higher as a significant number. If you have a -8 or worse on any substance, then you may have a strong allergy or sensitivity. Eliminating that substance from your diet for at least two weeks will allow you to confirm your dowsing. (This may be harder with allergens you breathe.)

When a food is removed totally from the diet for two weeks, the body heals significantly. Then if it is reintroduced, you will see a reaction to it if you are allergic or sensitive. Common reactions include many things, such as hives, increased mucus/ drainage, poor digestion, gas, diarrhea or constipation, headache, nausea or even neurological symptoms.

You may eliminate the substance for two weeks on several occasions to test how accurate your results are, and to determine the symptom is truly related to that food. Once you have determined you are sensitive or allergic, you may do whatever you feel is best in terms of dealing with the allergy.

We have an article in this chapter on clearing the energy of allergies if you wish to pursue that further.

Deviceless Dowsing about Food

You don't have to take your pendulum shopping with you and make a scene when dowsing about food. You can learn any one of many types of deviceless dowsing, and no one will know you are dowsing in the store or restaurant. We use deviceless dowsing (see Chapter 2 and the Appendix) most of the time ourselves, and we recommend you become confident using one of those methods. It will help you feel comfortable using dowsing in public places like shops and restaurants. Plus, stealth dowsing is fun!

Everyday dowsing sometimes seems boring, but in reality, the little things you do everyday are what build your skill for dowsing big life choices.

FINDING LOST OBJECTS

If you have a beloved pet or a favorite heirloom ring, you know how it would feel to lose them. In either case, you often associate your identity with precious objects and pets, and losing them feels like losing a part of yourself. So misplacing or losing something can be a stressful situation.

Dowsing can help you find anything you have lost. But you will discover that finding lost things using dowsing is not a slam dunk. There are many pitfalls, and if you are unsuspecting, you can be led in frustrating circles instead of finding what you seek. This training will help you have the most success possible whenever you search for something you have lost.

As you know, dowsing can be used for anything. But there are certain subjects that people associate with dowsing more than others. Most people think of water dowsing when dowsing is mentioned. But perhaps the second most common association with dowsing is the finding of lost things. We have had more requests from strangers to help find lost pets than any other type of dowsing request.

We have been asked to find lost jewelry, money, pets and people, but finding lost objects has never been a forte of ours. All the professional dowsers we know have special areas of interest at which they are quite good. Most of them use dowsing for healing and personal growth, or to clear space, as did we.

There is a huge market for successfully finding lost stuff with dowsing, but we don't know of anyone doing that professionally. Should you wish to start a dowsing business, after finding water, finding lost objects is in our opinion the top application for creating income.

But it is not as simple as you might think. Here is a short list of some of the major factors affecting results:

- Energy of karma exists for the lost object and person who lost it.
- The level of consciousness of what has been lost will affect the outcome.
- The energies of the various searchers can leave false trails.
- The difference between what the seeker wants and what the lost pet or person wants may be a problem.
- Things you seek don't always stay in this dimension.

A loss is a complex, dynamic situation that merges the energies of the person, object and any seekers into a karmic drama with no guaranteed outcome.

Lost Object vs. Lost Creature

There is a fundamental difference between a lost 'thing' and a lost person or pet. Living beings have a level of consciousness that potentially (though not always) complicates the process of finding them. Your lost sock doesn't have an agenda or feelings that amount to much, but your dog or cat is capable of independent thinking, mobility and resistance to your plans.

Your sock didn't get lost on purpose or run away out of fear of your new baby. Pets that get 'lost' often have left of their own volition due to fear, a desire for freedom or a need to escape something they didn't like. Even the best owner can be unaware of these motivations and expects his or her pet to be eager to be found.

Obviously, this can complicate the procedure. If a pet doesn't want to be found, it won't be found. So one of the first things you want to check is whether the animal wants to go home. You can use dowsing to find this out.

How to Avoid Pitfalls

There are many pitfalls to finding lost objects. If you avoid them, your success rate will improve.

- Don't be attached to outcome. Being emotional about a lost object will make it harder to find it.
- If it's a lost animal, find out if it wants to be found. If not, you are not likely to succeed.
- If it's a lost animal, dowse to find out if it is alive at this time. Sadly, if the animal has died, you probably aren't going to find it. (But be aware that even asking this seemingly innocent question can have complications. For example, if you believe in reincarnation or the continuance of the soul, you might have to be very precise indeed in your wording of your question concerning whether the animal is 'alive'.)
- Ask if it is currently in this dimension, especially if it is an object. If it isn't in this dimension, you won't find it until/unless it comes back.
- Ask if any thought forms have been created by searchers. Thought forms will mislead and give you false positive responses.

Create a series of questions that give you important data that may help you resolve the situation. Subjects to ask about include current health; whether it's inside or outside; stolen or not; on the move or stationary; distance from home, defining home carefully; what compass direction the current location is from home; etc.

Useful Techniques

When looking for lost objects, a sketch or map can come in quite handy. It helps you narrow the locations or directions to search in. It can be used at a distance for giving accurate information to the searchers. Therefore, learning to map dowse is useful for finding lost objects. We have an article that subject later in this chapter.

Long distance work with dowsing is just as effective as in person. Using a map to dowse lets you help find an object that is far away from you. Long distance work can be a hard concept to get your head around, but we worked with a global clientele for many years, and we promise you, distance is not a problem. Finding lost objects for friends and family can give you the opportunity to experiment with dowsing long distance.

Communicating with the object or pet using dowsing can also provide useful information about location. In a communication class we taught, we had students communicate with Nigel's bicycle and with a large stuffed dog I used as a surrogate for distance Reiki healing. The results were amazing, considering the students knew nothing about these objects.

A student said that Nigel's bike was unhappy because it wasn't being used much, which was true. About the stuffed dog, a student said the dog was in the dark and didn't know why. (I had packed it in a large garbage bag in storage to keep it clean.) If these were lost or stolen objects, a dowsing session communicating with them would be quite helpful. However, be aware that sometimes what you are seeking will not be willing to communicate with you! An animal might even lie to you, as the Bernese Mountain Dog in the story we told about the lost dog in an earlier article.

If you get involved in a search, it is possible you will be asked to dowse more than once. Keep a record of the times, questions and answers you got when dowsing, so that you can be aware of the progress of the case.

Usually you will either succeed quickly or not at all. Our experience is that if our answers don't turn out right the first time, dowsing again later won't change anything. Partly, this is due to the energy of the owner and how it affects the process.

Unless you get great results, you will feel better if you offer your services for free for dowsing for lost things. Otherwise, you get attached to the results. If you are a rare person who can always find lost things, charge well for your service. It is valuable and needed.

A Common Problem: Thought Forms

Thought forms are a major pitfall in finding lost objects. If you think of something with strong emotion or intention, you can create a thought form that dowses the same as the 'real' object.

This technique is used by some dowsing teachers in class to create underground water streams for students to dowse.

You can't easily tell the difference between a lost animal and a thought form of that animal. If you come late to the scene, and there have been other dowsers or searchers, you may find the search confusing, as you can't get a single clear trail or hit for the object. You may dowse it is somewhere simply because another dowser believed it was there and created a thought form.

Thought forms are a reason that finding hidden treasure is difficult. So many people have looked for the treasure, each sure he or she knew where it was, that many thought forms were created. The same happens with lost objects. Being the first on the scene is helpful for avoiding thought forms.

If you are an accurate dowser, you may be able to dowse if there are thought forms, or if the location you come up with is merely a thought form. However, your own emotional attachment will come into play in such a case. We all like to be 'right.'

Karma: The Curve Ball

Things don't happen by coincidence. Everything is interconnected. The cat didn't slip out of the house by accident. Yes, it may have wished to have freedom. Or it might have been scared. But the event happened due to the karma or personal energy of the cat and the owner. It is easier to find lost things if you can resolve karmic/personal energy issues that are blocking finding it.

Doing this involves clearing energies for the animal, object and owner. Most owners are not interested in seeing that they had a part in the loss. They don't want to change. They just want to find what was lost. If they have issues around loss, drama and blame, those issues may prevent them from ever finding what was lost. If they see themselves as victims and are focusing on negative outcomes, it is unlikely they will be successful. Victims can't be victors.

Sometimes a loss repeats something that happened in a past life, and this time there is an opportunity for different results. However, if there is not an awareness of that information, it is hard to overcome the karma from the past life, as the 'players' tend to repeat past performances.

The lost object or animal likewise has karma or personal energy. Maybe the cat wants freedom so badly it runs away. Even if you find it, it will probably escape again unless that issue is cleared.

Someone once called us about finding a lost ring. The person had major issues about the ring, not feeling she deserved it, and in a sense, not liking it. It reminded her of things she wanted to forget. So the ring got 'lost.' Without clearing the cause, it was impossible to locate the ring. Deep down, she didn't want to find it. We weren't able to help her.

Try telling the owner of a lost dog or heirloom ring that the reason it's lost is due to them and their energy. They will act like you are crazy. In a small percentage of cases, you can find things in spite of this, but it really makes it harder.

As a dowser, you can ask some questions to see how much the situation is being driven by the personal energies or karma of the participants. It will always have some effect. The larger the effect, the harder it may be to find the lost object or pet.

Going on Vacation: Visiting Other Dimensions

An unusual but not that uncommon occurrence that makes finding lost objects hard is that sometimes they go into other realities or dimensions. We have found this happen a number of times, but only once were we given positive proof. Maggie tells the story:

A client bought one of our personal harmonizers, a small custom-made device we used to make for enhancing the energy field and protection. She liked to sleep with it in her pillowcase at night. One morning, she went to retrieve it, and it was gone. She searched everywhere, but couldn't find it. She began to look in all kinds of places, but no luck. Finally she called me and told me about the loss. She truly had looked everywhere. She was ready to order a replacement. I told her that it was going to come back, and she should wait.

She called me back a couple weeks later. She had washed her bed linens a couple times and had kept looking for the harmonizer, but still couldn't find it. She called and said she was tired of looking and wanted to buy another one. I suggested that she speak to the harmonizer, wherever it was, and tell it she loved it and wanted it back, but if it wasn't back by tomorrow, she'd buy a new one. Then act accordingly.

The next morning she got up and checked her pillow case. The harmonizer was there. Bear in mind that the sheets and pillow cases had been searched, washed and replaced a number of times. There was no way the harmonizer was there all the time. She called me, delighted that it had returned.

Don't expect this to happen often, but don't forget to ask, because you aren't going to find something that has gone to another dimension.

A Weirdly Effective Method: Calling It Back

So if you can't find an object or animal, is there anything else you can do? Yes. Call it back to you like our client did. This may sound silly, but it often works. Here is another story from Maggie that is just as amazing:

I had a pair of earrings I really liked. My mother had made them for me. I lost one of them, and that was so frustrating, because I couldn't wear just one. I looked and looked and tried to dowse, but couldn't find it.

So I decided to call it back to me. I told it I loved it and wanted it to return right now in good condition somewhere that I could easily find it. Not 15 minutes later, I went into the bathroom. There, stuck by the French earwire into the top of my bath towel hanging on the rack, was my earring, as if someone had put it there.

The strange part is that I had showered and used that towel to dry not one hour before, and the earring could not have been there at that time. I was overjoyed to have my favorite earring back, but totally mystified.

This 'calling back' technique was developed by a dowser in the UK. He used it successfully on many occasions. Your confidence will have an effect on the outcome, as will your heartfelt desire, and at the same time, a detachment from the outcome. This can be a tricky combination to achieve, but it is worth practicing it, as it gives spectacular results. Give it a try next time you lose something you care about.

Finding lost objects and animals can be frustrating or fulfilling. You may be gifted with a talent for this dowsing application, or you may not. But regardless of your skill level, you can learn to find things better by applying the suggestions in this training.

FUTURE DOWSING

The Main Objection to Dowsing the Future

We discourage students from dowsing the future. Why would we tell you not to use a divination technique for divining the future? Because it's really hard to dowse the future accurately when you are dowsing out of fear of what may happen.

We gave you four simple steps to the dowsing process in Chapter 2. Step 1 was knowing your goal, your 'why' for dowsing a certain subject. We emphasized that fear blocks intuition, and that it behooves you to reduce fear in your life, which will improve your dowsing.

Future dowsing, more than any other dowsing application, even health dowsing, makes you face fear before you ever get beyond Step 1. That is because almost every time you dowse the future, you are dowsing because you are fearful about it.

If you are dowsing because you are afraid of making a mistake, afraid of poverty, afraid of rejection, afraid of failing or afraid of dying, it is unlikely you will get an accurate answer. Strong fear blocks a good dowsing response. Fear prevents detachment.

What we have learned over the years is that it helps to really be honest with yourself before you dowse. Admit if you are fearful about a certain outcome, if you are using dowsing to create a sense of control or security. It's normal and OK to feel that way, but whenever you find yourself wanting to dowse mainly out of fear of what might happen in the future, we advise you **not to dowse**. Instead, do something to release fear.

By using one of the techniques we suggested in Chapter 1 to release fear, you can then decide to focus on what you want instead of what you fear. You can empower yourself to find solutions to whatever problem you have by using dowsing. That is when you can expect to get a useful response.

The most important nugget in this article is that teaching yourself to focus on what you want to create and using dowsing to chart a path to your goals is an approach that will change your whole life for the better. Dowsing this way is empowering.

There are some situations where dowsing the future fulfills this goal, where dowsing gives you the ability to create better outcomes by focusing on what you want. In this article, we will examine them.

Predicting the Effects of Decisions and Choices

This is our favorite way of using dowsing to create positive future outcomes. We all have major decisions we have to make that will affect the rest of our lives. Some examples are:

- Marriage proposals
- Job offers
- Where to live
- Where to go to college and what to major in
- What career to choose
- Business decisions
- Investment strategies
- Major purchases like a home or car

Then there are more minor decisions, but they can also have quite an impact, like where to vacation, what time would be best for a specific appointment, or when to plan a family event.

The first problem you run into is that you are too attached to the outcome to dowse for yourself. It is unwise to dowse when you have a vested interest in the outcome. By practicing dowsing all the time, you can learn to achieve the detachment needed to dowse the future accurately.

Be honest with yourself and don't dowse on things you are emotionally involved in. You can get a dowsing buddy to dowse your question for you, or you can blind dowse the question to eliminate your attachment.

Be clear in your mind why you want to dowse. What outcome do you desire? That's the first step. Step 2 is forming a good dowsing question. For important decisions that will affect your future, this is vital.

Here is a question that can form the basis for your own, more specific dowsing questions about a choice you have to make:

On a +10 to -10 scale, what is the overall long term effect on my goals of attending the University of Virginia if I intend to become a successful criminal lawyer within the next ten years?

You have who, what, where, when, how and why in this question. The 'how' is underlined. Your goals are simply referred to as 'goals,' and the assumption is you have clearly defined them. This is a good basic template for any life choice you have to make, whether a major or minor one. Remember, there are only four simple steps to dowsing.

The Time Element

Your future can depend on how you resolve a problem in the present. Health issues are perhaps the most common situation.

We frequently are able to get accurate dowsing answers to asking a question about when a health problem or symptom will resolve. Likewise, you can ask the effect of a particular medicine, therapy or treatment on you at some specified time in the future.

The +10 to -10 scale comes in handy here. Also, take the time to formulate your question well by thinking of all the things that matter to you in terms of success.

If necessary, you can create a set of dowsing questions to evaluate different aspects of the problem.

Here are some examples of the applications of this type of future dowsing:

- Asking when a rash or headache will be completely gone. (Example question: *If I continue to take Tylenol as directed, when will my headache be totally gone? Less than an hour? Less than a day?* Then refine questions based on what answers you get, until you pinpoint the time.)
- Asking the overall effect on your symptoms or situation of taking a particular medication as directed for 10 days
- Asking the overall effect on you of taking a particular medicine for 10 days (notice the difference: this question will pinpoint side effects, while the previous one only measures how effective the medication is on the symptoms.)

Diet, fitness and weight loss programs can be evaluated in the same way. You want to lose X pounds by your birthday? Find out what diet will do the trick. Always dowse for side effects. (Example question: *If my goal is to reach my target weight of 115 pounds by my birthday, will the South Beach diet be a +8 or better for achieving this goal and maintaining that weight into the future?*)

As always, we expect you to consult a health care professional about any health-related issue you have. Do not rely solely on your dowsing. Your dowsing is just one tool in your tool kit. Don't throw out the other tools.

We have trainings on health in this chapter if you wish to pursue health dowsing further.

Divine Timing: It's Not Always When You Wish

Planning the best time for a future event can be challenging. Dowsing can help you pick the best time to achieve the results you want.

Some examples of applications include:

- When to move
- When to change jobs
- When to get married
- When to start the new project for your business

Of course, the above assume that you have already determined that doing those things are a +8 or better, and you have made a detailed list of factors involved that matter to you.

Here is an example:

You want to move to Santa Barbara. You have done the research on the job market and real estate. You have even gone and visited various neighborhoods to get a feel for the area. You still feel good about moving, but you aren't sure when is best. You may have an idea, but you aren't sure.

You can make a list of your priorities for the move. Some might include:

- Being able to get a good job at a good salary
- Finding the perfect place to live
- Being able to live close to where you work
- Having a property that has good resale value

Of course, there could be many other priorities. And it is very individual. You formulate a dowsing question based on your needs and wants. Your question might be something like:

On a scale of +10 to -10, if I want to move to Santa Barbara and start a job I love at 50K annual salary or more, when is the best time for me to move? This year? Next year? Then narrow it down until you get a month. (Of course, you've already dowsed that this move will give you these things; you're only checking for the best timing.)

Do the same for each priority. You may be able to move at a time that gets you all the things you want, or you may have to sacrifice a little. But if you can dowse, you can make a good choice and be more likely to get your priorities taken care of.

We have a Whole Brain Chart in this chapter on relocation if you want to dowse more about this subject.

Try It Yourself: Simple Future Dowsing

There are also very simple applications for dowsing the future that can make your life a joy or at least more fun.

Here are some examples:

- When will the last guest arrive at your dinner party?
- When will the steaks be done perfectly?
- When will your spouse be home from work today?
- If I leave the house at 3:30pm, will I get to the movie before it starts? (sometimes there are long lines or traffic)
- If I wait to get gas at the next exit, will I run out of gas before I get to the gas station?

Your subconscious believes you can't predict the future. Every time you successfully do so, you challenge that belief. Then when you really need to dowse the future, you will have eradicated some resistance to success. So have fun predicting these everyday occurrences. At first, your success may be no better than guessing, but don't give up. You will improve if you persist.

Gambling: We Advise Against It

One of the most common subjects non-dowsers will ask about dowsing is for winning the lottery or some other form of gambling. We don't suggest you use dowsing to gamble. Your ability to win at gambling will be determined by your beliefs and karma and energies around money. Dowsing won't change that.

Most people lose, as they expect to lose, in a gambling situation. They are not gambling to win. They are gambling to find hope. To feel good. Or for entertainment. They don't really feel they are winners, and they don't feel they deserve to win. They just want hope. For that, they are willing to pay.

If you want to win at gambling, put your dowsing to work at changing your relationship with wealth and sudden riches. Check out the article in this chapter on Money Dowsing if you'd like to learn more about this application.

Summary

We have found that dowsing the future works best when dowsing practical applications that are related to present choices. The formula for that is, "If I do this now, what will happen in the future at some specified date?" By anchoring your dowsing to your current choice, you make it more likely you will get an accurate answer. You have a stronger desire for a positive outcome, and your intention is focused.

Dowsing the future is fun and can be quite useful for creating positive outcomes. Don't model your future dowsing on the picture of the psychic predicting the winning lottery number. Some day you may be able to do that, but don't try now. Build confidence by dowsing practical future outcomes that you can measure.

GO BEYOND DOWSING WITH A PENDULUM

In this article, Nigel explores interesting non-dowsing uses of the pendulum. (Incidentally, this is the subject he first discussed with me via email when we met online in a dowsing group.)

Strange but Fascinating: Dowsing Shapes

Your normal, average pendulum, whether made of stone, crystal, metal or wood, can be surprisingly helpful in giving you information which you didn't even know was there! And, to prove it, let's begin by using a pendulum over some simple shapes.

Take a blank sheet of paper and draw a square on it. It doesn't matter if you use a pen or a pencil. Keep it to a size that's going to be easy to dowse over. I'd suggest anything around two to four inches on a side would do, but, as I said, it is only a suggestion.

Now, you have a two dimensional shape on a piece of paper. You didn't do anything special to it, I hope, just drew it.

Yet there is something more than the simple square there and you can prove it. You are going to use your pendulum to examine what is going on. However, to give you some sort of baseline to compare, take a blank sheet of paper and, with your pendulum in the ready position, just ask to be shown what energy, if any, is there.

Depending on where the paper has been stored, what it has been used for, you could get a range of movements. And let the movements just be that; movements. Let the pendulum move any which way it wants. After all, it's doing what you want it do, showing you how your body is responding, so let it be.

Now, swap sheets of paper and dowse over the square you just drew. Again, all you are doing is asking to be shown what energies are there.

You can dowse along each line, in the middle of the square, at each of the corners, just outside, just inside. Take the time to investigate all the square and all the parts of the square.

Again, what you get as a response will depend on many factors including type of paper, size of square, drawing implement, and so on. But what you will find is that there is a difference between what happened to the pendulum over the blank sheet of paper and what happened over the square.

Remember, you aren't asking for specifics here. The only thing you are interested in is to discover the way the energy flows in, around and about the simple shape you have just drawn. So, take the time to see what your pendulum is doing.

Is it moving in circles or spirals? Does it show direction or distance? How does it feel in your hands?

This is where the experience of your own dowsing comes into its own. This is not just yes/no. It is more subtle than that. What impressions do you get as you dangle the pendulum over the shape? What questions come to mind as you watch and feel the pendulum moving? Write them down. Follow up on them as you let them come to mind.

This technique is more advanced than simple dowsing. It requires you to think and to let impressions come through, ideas to form. You can begin to perhaps see that square in a new light. Perhaps you can relax and feel in tune enough to put the pendulum down and sense with your bare hands, and maybe that will give you more information.

Do not rush this exercise. Let it unfold. If you want, stop and think. What is happening to make me move this pendulum in this way? What is it moving to? What am I sensing? Go back and repeat anything you want.

Then, when you want, take a fresh piece of paper, or separately on the same piece, draw a triangle and repeat the procedure. Go from one shape to the other and see how they differ, where they are the same.

Draw a circle and see what happens. Draw just a straight line. Do the same movements happen for you only over a line you've drawn yourself? Or can you repeat it with a line printed in a book or on paper from somewhere else?

And all this, remember, is with two dimensional objects. Lines on paper. Nothing else.

If you have a three-dimensional shape to hand, you can compare that with the two dimensional one. A cube, for example, compared with a square. A sphere with a circle. What is happening to the energy: which is the same and what is different? Is the energy stronger in three dimensions than it is in two?

The Long Pendulum: Way Beyond 'Yes' or 'No'

The previous set of exercises were really just allowing you to explore whatever you could find. There was no right or wrong answer or even a right or wrong way of going about it. All that mattered was that you used your pendulum and your sensing abilities in a new way. In other words, the pendulum really showed you something new and it was up to you to understand what was going on.

There is another method using a pendulum which can also reveal some very interesting aspects of the world around you. However, instead of your normal pendulum, you will require one which has a much longer string. Around five feet should do. Seriously!

I found that a plumb bob purchased from a hardware store was just about perfect for this. Just be careful that the thread or rope or whatever you attach to the weight does not stretch, as you will be needing to mark it accurately, and you don't want the length to change.

Once you have your pendulum, you need to make sure that the string is stretched taut as you mark inches along it. I found that making one color for every fifth inch and a different color for all the inches in between allowed me to see what length I was working with much more easily.

The end result should be a pendulum with a lot of string (preferably wound round something) on which you have clearly marked each inch. I found a colored Sharpie worked well for this.

You may be wondering how on earth you can possibly use a five-foot-long pendulum. In fact, it is possible, you just have to be patient. I have used a six-foot-long pendulum on a pair of steps to get sufficient height. Normally, however, the longest range you would use is between three and three-and-a-half feet. It might seem crazy, but bear with me and I'll explain.

This idea of a long pendulum was proposed by a very inventive and inquisitive dowser named Tom Lethbridge. Years ago, he took up dowsing after he retired from education, where he had been a don at Cambridge University in England. His inventive mind was intrigued by dowsing and he devoted a good deal of his time to discovering what he could do with it, along with several other subjects of interest which were not in the mainstream of scientific thinking.

What follows is a brief outline of what the long pendulum can do for you, courtesy of Mr Lethbridge.

First, though, you have to get used to using such a lengthy pendulum. You will need to be able to slowly unravel or lower the pendulum, but giving it time to react to whatever is the object of your inquiry. Depending on the type of pendulum you have, your arm will tire after a certain period of time.

This use of the pendulum is nothing like the usual use of the tool. The usual use of the pendulum is of movement which is an interpretation of your intuition, to a degree. The long pendulum, on the other hand, is a far more physical approach where the action of the pendulum is not determined by any question but by what is being examined.

What Lethbridge discovered was that a pendulum of a certain length dangled over a piece of iron and set to swinging back and forth or side to side, would change to a circular motion when the length of the string above it was exactly 32 inches long. If this same length was held over silver, it would not react, but continue on its back and forth or side to side motion. Only when the string was set to 22 inches in length would it react to silver.

It was invariable. Specific lengths of pendulum would react to specific materials.

In order to prove this works for you, take up your pendulum and have a very short length of string and then set it moving in a to and fro motion (side to side or back and forth, or even on a diagonal, it doesn't matter). Beneath the pendulum, have something made of glass. Keep the pendulum moving as you slowly unravel the line, letting it slip through your fingers of one hand as you unwind with the other. If the pendulum stops, you go too quickly, or you let too much line through at a time, stop, rewind a little way, start the pendulum moving to and fro again and continue until the pendulum begins to move in a circle above the glass. Make a note of where that point is on the thread and then measure the distance from the mark to the top of the pendulum.

For most people, that distance will be 14 inches. Your measurement might be off a little by an inch or two because you are not yet at ease with allowing the thread through your fingers at a slow enough rate, so you missed the point where the circular motion really became strongest. Make sure that you are keeping in your mind that it is glass you are seeking a response to, not just the object beneath the pendulum. I have no idea what maybe beneath your pendulum as you do this, but it could contain any number of chemicals, minerals or even emotions, each of which will have their own specific lengths of pendulum.

However, this technique is just a matter of familiarity and nothing else. Repeat the process until you are satisfied that you can let the thread out at a slow rate at the same time as keeping the pendulum moving. I normally hold a pendulum in my right hand and I find that if I do the same here and let the thread out slowly between my fingers, holding the ball of thread in my left hand a little to the side, I am more in control of the process and can be far more accurate.

There is a table of 'rates' at the end of this article. Scan it through first before moving on, as I will be referring to it in a moment.

Note, the term 'rate' is simply a way of referring to the length of thread or string necessary for a circular reaction for each object. So a 'rate' of 30 means a pendulum length of 30 inches, measured from the fingers to the top of the pendulum.

If you look at the rates, you will notice that some appear to be quite strange. For example, you can, according to this chart, dowse to find love or evolution or youth or age, amongst other things. These things are characteristics, each of which have their own frequency or rate. So, if you received a letter from someone, which they had written, you could adjust your pendulum to 20 inches and see if it circled over the letter. If so (and assuming your rate for love is 20), then you could say that whoever wrote it, wrote it with love. Or you could dowse over the same letter at 10 inches and see if it was a youth who wrote it. And so on.

By the way, evolution, in this sense, merely means change, or a step forward. Not a change for the worse, decay or anything like that, but an improvement.

If you look at the chart, you will see that at the 22 rate silver, lead, sodium and calcium all exist. How can that be? It would seem to make this method useless.

In fact, this apparent problem highlights another wonderful aspect of this technique. If you take silver, for example, and let the pendulum begin to rotate over it, you will find that, after a while, the rotations cease. The pendulum reverts back to its to and fro motion. If you count the number of rotations it makes, you will find that, over silver, it is always the same number. If you try it over calcium at the same rate of 22, you will find that the number of rotations is different. (For Lethbridge, the numbers of rotations were Lead, 18; silver, 22; sodium, 30; calcium, 35.) So silver you could write down as 22:22, meaning a 22 inch pendulum rotates 22 times over silver.

This method of counting rotations allows you to distinguish between apparently similar objects with ease. The only difficulty you will have at first in doing this is counting when the rotations start and when they end. So, to begin with, you might be one or two out, but you will soon learn how to distinguish the feel of the pendulum and when to start counting.

As I said, this method is entirely different to the usual use of a pendulum. It isn't dowsing as such. It isn't about intuition. It uses a regular methodical approach which has nothing to do with formulating good questions. It relies more on keeping focus on what it is you are holding the pendulum over or keeping count.

Lethbridge, for example, wanted to find the age of a coin in his collection. He took one at random and kept it in its paper wrapping so he didn't know what it was and then set his pendulum to 30 inches, the length for age and began counting. He counted 642 revolutions! Subtracting that from the year, 1968, gave him 1326, the date of manufacture of the silver farthing in the paper. But, as he admitted, it was a long and tiring business. Nevertheless, this is a fascinating approach to investigating the world around you and can be verified by another person using the same technique.

But it is more than that, as Lethbridge himself realized. Look, for example, at what is dowsed at 10, 20, 30 and 40 inches. You can begin to see a certain connection there.

North, South, East and West. Fire, Earth, Water, Air. Life and Death. Youth and Age. There seems to be some sort of reflection of life, of how we perceive ourselves here.

It is very easy to add your own information. And, as you build it up, you can begin, perhaps, to see relationships developing. Certain sorts of trees, for example, in folklore, had specific legends or properties attached to them. How they react with, interfere or not, with other trees or plants, or finding out which plants get on with each other and which should be kept apart can all be discovered using the long pendulum and examining rates.

You can investigate one object for different attributes. For example, if you take a nickel coin, a nickel itself if you are in the US, then you can check for the nickel in it at 32.5 inches, and also the copper in it, at 30.5 inches. Or, if you have heirlooms, you can find the age of manufacture (if they were not mass-produced), what it was made of, made by a man or woman, old or young and so on.

Or, if you are interested in crystals and the like, see if you can distinguish between the various varieties of quartz, or find the difference between emeralds and garnets. You'll need pure samples of these because they can contain many tiny quantities of other minerals, but, then again, that can also be a fun thing to find out!

You can use a normal pendulum to examine aspects of shapes and the way energy interacts with you. And you can also use a long pendulum to delve into far more detail about objects, ideas and emotions than otherwise possible.

The Long Pendulum Rates in Inches

What follows is a list of various rates for various objects/ideas/minerals, etc. which were discovered by Tom Lethbridge over a period of years. The precise rates might vary for you a little, but, once you have discovered them, they will not change.

- 3: Rosemary
- 3.5: Lavender
- 4: Currant
- 4.5: Bramble, Rose
- 5.5: Ash (tree), Phosphorus
- 7: Brown, Sulfur, Mercury, Scent
- 9: Purple, Elder, Chlorine, Safety
- 10: Red, Graphite, Light, Sun, Fire, East, Truth, Youth
- 10.5: Ivy

- 11: Oak, walnut
- 11.5: Hair
- 12: Orange (color), Cherry, Carbon, Disease
- 13: Rowan, Slate, Concrete
- 14: Silica, Glass, Flint
- 15: Glaze on pottery
- 16: Grass, Dung, Scarabs
- 17: Beech, Truffles
- 17.5: Mahogany
- 18: Apple (tree)
- 19.5: Blood
- 20: White, Life, Heat, Earth, South, Electricity, Magnetism, Love
- 20.5: Hazel
- 21: Fungus
- 21.5: Grey, Potassium
- 22: Silver, Lead, Sodium, Calcium
- 22.5: Magnesium
- 23: Elm
- 23.5: Amber, Vegetable and Mineral Oils
- 24: Diamond, Male Principle
- 25: Aluminum
- 25.5: Alcohol
- 26.5: Oxygen
- 27: Garlic, Thought, Memory, Stink
- 28: Yew, Tin
- 29: Yellow, Gold, Female Principle, Danger
- 30: Green, Hydrogen, Water, Moon, Sound, West, Age
- 30.5: Bue, Copper, Cobalt
- 31: Pine
- 32: Violet, Iron, Health
- 32.5: Nickel
- 34: Cypress
- 36: Evolution
- 38: Tomato
- 39: Potato
- 40: Black, Air, Death, Anger, Sleep, North, Falsehood

HEALTH DOWSING: MAKING
EVALUATIONS

Maggie has always been passionate about health and healing. Her earliest application of dowsing for health was in making simple evaluations of different physical systems for her animal companions. Here's a story of success from that time:

Shortly after I began to dowse, I combined my love of animals with dowsing to evaluate the health of my dog. My 9-year-old Akita Tammi had been shy and even potentially dangerous around children since she became an adult. We assumed she was just being an Akita. My dowsing indicated she had serious dental issues.

I consulted with a veterinary dentist. He found she had an abscess on her canine tooth that was the biggest he had ever seen (and he was a specialist who treated the big cats at the Phoenix Zoo). He said she had probably had it for many years. I knew how long. She had broken that tooth on her crate during training as a puppy, and her vet at the time had said it would be ok. The specialist said it was a very painful condition that would cause her to protect herself from being touched or pressed on the face.

As soon as he did her dental work ($1300 in the late 90s, including a gold crown on her canine tooth), Tammi became a new dog. She played joyfully with my young niece, who had always caused her to act aloof or even defensive.

I felt bad she had suffered for over eight years, but I was grateful to dowsing for helping me to give her back her health and a good reputation as a dog who could be trusted around kids.

Health dowsing is one of the most exciting and rewarding applications of dowsing you can learn. Don't get scared away because you don't have a degree in Biology. If you can master good basic technique and proper detachment, you can do wonders with health dowsing.

Dowsing is not intended to replace professional health care in any way. Please consult your health care practitioner if you are having any health problems. Note that Maggie consulted a dentist for confirmation and help with her dog.

Dowsing about your health is a good step towards showing your commitment to live a healthy life. It engages your powerful intuition and shows your intention to be an active participant in this process. And it's easier to do than you think.

There are many areas that you may apply dowsing that will enhance your health and well-being. In this lesson, we will address the interesting topic of 'diagnosis' as relates to dowsing.

It's perfectly legitimate to diagnose for yourself in this way. However, it is always important to know your limitations and get professional help when that is appropriate. Never use dowsing instead of getting professional help, if that is what is needed.

A Good Place to Start: Health Evaluation

The physical body is made up of many organ systems. If you are new to health dowsing, this is an easy place to start. You can get a list of systems from online and read a little, if you want, about what they do.

Start simple. For Maggie, when her dog seemed leery of being touched on the face, she dowsed about the function of the teeth and gums and went from there. She didn't have to do any more than realize her dog needed dental help. The dentist then tested and fixed the problem.

In that case, her goal was to find out how well her dog's teeth and gums were functioning for overall health and well-being, including comfort. She asked the question:

On a scale of 0-10, with 8 or higher meaning good to excellent function overall and 3 or less meaning not functioning properly to the point of dis-ease, what is Tammi's dental health at this time?

She got 3 or less. She then dowsed about seeing a vet to resolve the problems and got a high number. So she did it.

You can substitute any organ or organ system in this question. You can create further questions if you get a poor number, or you can choose to see a professional if that dowses as helpful for your goals.

The cool thing is that if you check yourself or your pets monthly when things appear fine, you will gain confidence. And then, if help is needed, you will see the change from a high number to a much lower number and understand something is going on.

Doing this type of evaluation of major organ systems before you have symptoms is a great way to improve detachment and your skill.

When You Have a Symptom

One of the biggest mistakes most people make in terms of health is that they judge any symptom that is painful or unpleasant as 'bad.' They then go to a doctor and ask for medicine to erase the symptom, because the symptom makes them uncomfortable or insecure and fearful about their health. Suppressing the symptom is like killing the messenger. We prefer to take a less judgmental approach.

A symptom is just to get your attention. Sometimes a symptom is a sign of a dis-ease process, an imbalance in your health. At other times, a symptom is a sign of change, shifting energy, healing or detoxification, and those are all positive processes.

We use a +10 to -10 scale to determine the overall "Level in Effects" of a given symptom on our health. Obviously, if you have pain, that would seem to be negative. But if you are asking how the cause of that pain is affecting your health overall, you might find that it is a sign of positive change. An example is, if you start an exercise program, you may be sore the next few days, but overall, that is normal and a good sign.

Your dowsing answer will determine if you have an imbalance that requires correction or a healing process that requires your support. In either case, further dowsing will allow you to respond appropriately. As told by Maggie, this anecdote illustrates the value of this approach:

One day while showering, Nigel noticed that one of his moles had changed. He showed it to me. Having lived in AZ for some years, I know the classic signs of a 'bad' mole. This one had them all. Instead of rushing to the dermatologist's, we dowsed the overall level in effects on his physical health of what was going on with the mole. We both independently got a very high positive number.

This indicated that a positive process was ongoing. We double checked our answers by asking the overall effect on his health of going to a doctor and doing what was advised. We both got a very big negative number. So we dowsed what he could do to support the process and help a positive outcome be quick, easy, comfortable and safe.

We each repeated dowsing the same questions every single day. The only answers that changed were what he could do to support the process. Topical applications and other remedies were used as dowsed.

After a few weeks of doing this, Nigel observed the mole fall off in the shower one day. Underneath was perfect, clear skin.

We are not advising you do this if you are not a veteran and experienced health dowser. You can see a situation like this tends to be more charged with emotion than the evaluation example we started with.

Don't use this protocol until you have mastered basic dowsing and have enough detachment to be able to receive whatever answer is correct.

One thing that helps you do this is to realize that knowing a situation needs outside help is good, not bad. Being ignorant of a problem is detrimental to your health goals. So, learning to be open to finding out something needs to change is beneficial. Dowsing is always beneficial, even when it exposes a problem like Tammi's dental issues.

Never make major health choices based solely on dowsing. Note that Nigel had backup in the form of me, and that we asked multiple questions to assure ourselves that our choice was correct. And we checked each day.

Always consult a professional for any health issue you have.

The purpose of this anecdote is to show you how to react and dowse about a symptom. Don't have judgment just because the symptom elicits fear, discomfort or negativity. Ask a variety of questions in different ways. Get backup help to assure yourself you are correct. Then act with confidence.

If the overall Level in Effects of your symptom is negative, unlike the above instance, then your dowsing would be aimed at finding out the proper course of action for restoring balance and health. If you have enough education in health, you can learn to ask questions about trauma, parasites, infection, nutrition, degenerative disease, toxicity, etc. that will lead you to actions that will help.

Alternatively, you can use dowsing to find a health care practitioner if you are not confident of your own abilities. Use the same scale and choose one that is +8 or better for resolving your problem quickly, easily, comfortably, safely and permanently. Note, this was the procedure Maggie used for Tammi. At the very least, you can become good at doing this, so that you know when to seek professional help and who can help you best.

Summary

Set goals for your health and take appropriate actions with the help of dowsing. Use dowsing to select good health care practitioners to support you in your health goals.

Start with simple topics and work up to more challenging ones, always seeking outside help as needed and getting a second and third opinion before taking action.

The road to good health is a journey, and dowsing can make it a successful and interesting trip.

HEALTH DOWSING: NUTRITION, DIET, FITNESS

Maggie tells the story of the incidents that kick-started her self-empowerment about health.

In 1990, my health collapsed after I had knee surgery for the second time. All the doctors (except the anesthesiologist) said it was due to a reaction to the general anesthetic. It doesn't really matter what's to blame when you lose your health. You just want it back. Unfortunately, no doctor I went to had the answer for turning things around.

When the liver goes south, it is accompanied by annoying and scary symptoms. For weeks I could barely walk or eat anything. I broke out in hives when I did eat. I had diarrhea frequently. I finally got fed up with how long it was taking me to return to 'normal.' When I went to my doctor, he said he couldn't help me, and it would be best if I just let him write me a prescription for Seldane for the hives, because allergies were too hard to resolve (notice he homed in on one symptom and had no interest in causes).

I wasn't satisfied with taking pills to cover symptoms. I wanted to feel good again. Finally, I decided that since I had two degrees in Biology, I could do research and fix myself. I had no idea where that decision would ultimately lead me.

It was my health collapse that led me to energy work and holistic health methods and from there to dowsing. It took me several years to restore my health using natural methods. I had a lot of help from natural health care practitioners. I also learned energy healing methods and dowsing as a result of my search for good health.

*Now my health is better than before. But more than that, I consider my health **my** responsibility. I use dowsing to help me make good choices for achieving my health goals. I get professional help when I need it, but I am in charge of my health.*

In this training, we give you some useful tools for taking charge of your health. Using dowsing to help you choose what to eat and how to exercise for your goals is truly empowering.

Dowsing is not meant to replace professional help. If you have a health problem, see an appropriate health care practitioner. Dowsing can help you do that. Dowsing is not meant to take the place of your doctor.

Setting Health Goals

Most people would agree that their health is their most valuable asset. Without health, money does you no good. Yet who has real goals about their health and a program for reaching them? After this, you will!

Try It Yourself: Goal-setting

Let's do a brief exercise in goal-setting. Think for a few minutes about how you want your health and level of fitness to be. Jot some phrases down that describe it. Be as specific as you possibly can.

Each person is unique, but here are some goals that might apply:

- I want to be able to hike 10 miles easily and comfortably.
- I want to bike the 15 miles to the beach every weekend easily and comfortably.
- I want to feel energetic all day.

- I want to sleep well at night and wake rested each morning and ready to meet the day.
- I want to be slim, trim and strong.
- I want to feel comfortable in my body.
- I want glowing and healthy skin.
- I want to have good digestion.
- I want to react well to all kinds of foods.
- I want to be mentally alert and have good memory skills at all times.
- I want to feel calm and centered all the time.

Make sure the things on your list are things you really want to achieve. You must also believe that it is possible to achieve the goals.

Nutrition, Diet, and Fitness

Modern life is unnatural. The proliferation of fake foods, environmental toxins and stress have created real health challenges in humans. Modern living hasn't given humans longer, healthier lives. Quite the opposite.

So, the first place to look if you want better health (beyond how you think and what you believe) is what you eat and how you move your body. You probably are aware that a healthy diet consists of whole, unprocessed, organic fruits, veggies and meats. And you instinctively know that it's healthy to get outside and walk. So, do those things for a first step.

If those things don't allow you to reach your goals, then dowsing is the next step. You can dowse your diet, your exercise regimen, your supplements or anything else you are contemplating for improving your health.

The same four simple steps of dowsing apply here as in all dowsing applications. You have your goals, which are the first step.

Next, you create a good dowsing question. Using scales is very helpful in health dowsing. Any question is going to have who, what, where, when, how, and why as needed. Here are some sample questions:

- *On a scale of +10 to -10, with +8 or above being very good to excellent, how does the keto diet rank for my overall health goals if I follow it for 90 days?*
- *For my overall health goals, how does a step aerobics class rank on a +10 to -10 scale, with +8 being good to excellent, if I take the class at the gym starting this month?*
- *On a scale of 0 to 10, with 8 or higher being very good to excellent for my health goals overall, how does the Brand X probiotic supplement test when taken for 90 days as directed?*

You can see the pattern repeating in how you make good dowsing questions about any topic. It's really pretty easy!

Once you have the questions, you can dowse. Make sure to maintain a detached and curious attitude. Won't it be great to know what to invest in, instead of throwing money at health problems? Think of all the times you've bought pills or potions that did nothing at all for you. That will now be a thing of the past. (Within reason. Remember, nothing is 100% accurate.)

What about Thoughts?

While what you eat and how you exercise is fundamental to your health, what you think has even more of an impact on your success. Changing your diet and joining a gym often aren't enough to reach your goals.

Most people have limiting beliefs that make it hard to do things like be beautiful, be healthy or be happy. A perfect example of this is the difficulty of losing weight. Getting rid of excess weight is not simply about burning more calories than you ingest. That's claptrap from the media and health system putting guilt on you and getting you to spend money on weight loss. If you have ever had a weight problem, you know this is true.

We could make a joke and say your health problems are all in your head, but in a sense, that isn't a joke. The subconscious beliefs you have, the way you hold past trauma, how you think of yourself: these things are the major factors in how you experience life.

Subconscious beliefs can only be known in two ways: through dowsing or by keenly observing your environment and analyzing it carefully. Most people aren't good at the latter, but anyone can dowse.

If simply working with your body doesn't give you the results you want, we suggest you consult the training in this chapter on subconscious beliefs and clear as needed on the following subjects:

- How hard it is to make changes
- How safe it is to make changes
- Deserving what you want
- Letting life be easy and comfortable
- Being powerful
- Feeling safe in physical form
- Being a victor/winner
- Accepting love and abundance

You deserve to have a healthy, beautiful and strong body. It is actually your natural birthright. Your body has an intelligence and knows how to create good health if you give it what it needs and if you don't block success with negative thinking. Dowsing is a powerful tool you can use to reach your health goals.

INVISIBLE BEINGS & DOWSING

Dowsing is an ideal way to get information on things you can't see. Some invisible things are dangerous to your health, while others may be beneficial. This is as true of invisible beings as it is with energy in general. While it is beyond the scope of this training to go into detail about all types of invisible beings, we will mention the main categories that might be of interest to you as a dowser.

Beneficial Invisible Beings

This category refers to beings that are not visible, but which demonstrate a willingness to work in harmony with humans, and even aid them in achieving their goals. Included in this group are:

- Angels
- Fairies
- Devas
- Guides
- Guardians of the land
- Other non-terrestrial advanced beings who are benevolent towards humans

Detrimental Invisible Beings

Some invisible beings have a detrimental effect on humans and/or animals. Included in this group are:

- Discarnate humans or animals (ghosts)
- Non-terrestrial entities
- Some 'aliens'

It is useful to bear in mind that our categories are based purely on selfish judgment. Too often, people feel that if something is harmful, it must be bad, and thus evil. In the vast majority of cases, detrimental beings have no agenda against you. However, if you choose to 'demonize' them, they will sometimes turn their rather formidable energy of anger and frustration on you, which can make things much worse.

We adopt a different attitude. We don't feel there are 'good guys' and 'bad guys.' We are not doing battle against evil demons or aliens. We regard detrimental beings in most cases as misplaced and lost. It is possible as a dowser to help them move on to their right and perfect place. This is a win/win attitude, and much safer than taking an adversarial approach to their removal.

We have seen people become inconvenienced and even ill when they chose to have a judgmental attitude towards entities. If you see yourself as a warrior or a victim, you are choosing a path that might lead to negative consequences for you, as it will attract more and more entities. We urge you to have a less judgmental approach and use your dowsing ability to create balance and harmony without judging the beings you encounter.

Another possible complication is that people who are sensitive to such beings tend to have poor boundaries, particularly energetic ones, and can easily become swamped by them. Do not 'dabble' in working with invisible beings without using proper protection, avoiding empathy and having appropriate boundaries. Your health can be compromised if you don't take precautions.

A third situation we have seen often repeated with those who are new to energy work and dowsing is that they seem to have put out a 'free lunch' sign for entities to be cleared, and they end up being overrun by them. While it is empowering to learn clearing techniques and it makes you feel good to help beings find their right and perfect place, for most people, it is not your life purpose.

If you find yourself overwhelmed with entities wanting clearing, put out a clear intention that you do clearings on your own schedule, not on demand. In other words, 'just say no' appears to actually work!

Invisible beings are everywhere. They have always been around. They are the rule rather than the exception, especially these days. You can use dowsing to determine what exactly is in your environment. Then you can take appropriate action.

How to Deal with Beneficial Beings

Angels, guides, devas, fairies: they can all help you in many ways. To get help from spiritual beings, it is best to address a particular being or guide you know rather than just send out a plea for help. Otherwise, help may come from a questionable source with strings attached.

Learn a bit about these different types of beings and what they do. Then you will be prepared to include them in your goals.

For example, when you create a garden, you may ask the help of the guardian of that land, the deva of the plant species you are planting, or fairies that live there. You can send your intention out as a prayer or statement based on your goals and ask that they contribute to the attainment of those goals in whatever way they choose. Thank them for their assistance.

When you ask for spiritual assistance, you get it in a variety of ways. One way might be that your dowsing becomes more accurate. Or your intuition may speak to you in other ways to guide you toward you goal.

You can dowse about what recommendations a spiritual helper has, but that can be a tedious and lengthy process. If you do it, you will be asking yes/no questions about your goals and trying to elicit information about what advice your helpers have: a very slow process.

How to Deal with Detrimental Beings

It is much more common for dowsers to find themselves dealing with detrimental invisible beings. Perhaps that is because of their noxious effect on humans and animals. Ghosts and entities can attach to people and animals with disastrous results. Even if they are just free-floating in the environment, entities can have a strong negative effect on the humans and animals nearby.

Any type of symptom can be caused by entities. If a discarnate human attaches to you, and that human had a condition at the time of death such as a broken leg, you might find your leg hurting for no good reason. Nightmares are common when entities are in the environment. Sometimes you hear unexplained sounds, especially at night. Apparitions, of course, are a sign of beings. Seeing red eyes or feeling watched is another symptom that has been reported.

A change in behavior in pets and children can mean entity attachment. Among the most extreme symptoms, mental imbalance, suicide and psychotic behavior are all possible with entity attachment.

Caution: Nonhuman entities can be dangerous to deal with. This is not a subject to delve into if you are a novice dowser or have fear about entities. Be sure you have adequate protection before dowsing about entities, and do not hesitate to ask for professional help if you have trouble.

Detrimental Beings: the Importance of Protection

Your intention to stay safe while dowsing about or dealing with entities is an important part of your routine. Develop some method of protecting yourself that dowses as a 10 on a scale of 10 for keeping you safe, healthy and balanced throughout the process. If you don't get a 10, or the protection collapses, you need to stop dowsing, as those things are often a sign from your intuition that you are in over your head.

It is beyond the scope of this article to talk about protection in great detail. There are many books written on the subject, and we encourage you to read about it. The method we outlined in Chapter 4 is a good starting point, but if you regularly come into contact with entities, we advise you do more research on this important subject.

Here are some useful facts we have learned during our many years of working with clients:

- Unlike other forms of noxious energy, beings have consciousness. When they 'see you coming', they often leave the area so that you dowse there is nothing there. Then they come back later on.
- Some entities are quite good at 'hiding', and your dowsing may be influenced by them to show that there is nothing much there, or that there is less there than is true.
- Do not dowse about entities if you are fearful of them.
- Do not dowse about entities if you are adversarial towards them, and see them as 'bad guys' or 'demons.'
- Do not send entities to the light with the mistaken idea that is where they all belong.
- Do not dowse about entities if you are feeling very angry, frustrated, confused or lost. This energy might resonate with theirs and cause them to attach to you.
- On rare occasions, entities may actually be embedded in a person or animal. Regular clearing will not remove embedded entities. If you dowse there are embedded entities (and remember it is not that common), consult a professional about removing them. (when we see embedded entities, they are usually causing physical symptoms that immediately clear up after removing the entity.)

Steps for Clearing Entities

Keeping the above in mind, you will want to dowse about the situation to determine what's present. The following is a series of useful dowsing questions and actions, but it is not complete, nor is it applicable in all cases. Experience will teach you what to ask.

- *How many entities are usually present at this property/attached to this person?* Check 0, 1 digit, 2 digits and so on until you get a 'yes,' then if it is 2 digits, test 10, 20, 30, etc until you get a 'yes,' and so on.
- Your goal in clearing them is to send them to their 'right and perfect' place, wherever that may be. There are many types of entities, and we don't pretend to know exactly where they belong. Sometimes a simple statement of intention does the job. On other occasions, you might need to employ a symbol or some other method to effect the clearing. A good statement of intention is "Please send all of these entities to their right and perfect place in the right and perfect way."
- After you have done the clearing, dowse to make sure they are all gone.
- It is common when there are groups of entities that it might take a few tries to get them all moved on. Just repeat the process until you dowse there are 0 entities. If you find there are one or two who won't leave, the next step is to find out why.
- Dowse if they are staying out of fear. This is the most common reason. If 'yes,' just tell them that their right and perfect place is not somewhere to fear, that it will be good for them. Then try to clear them again. In most cases, that will do the trick. In extreme cases, we have found it effective to open a portal to their right and perfect place, tell them it will stay open for ten seconds, and they can have a look and come back if they don't like it. We've never seen one return when doing this. Then close the portal.
- On rare occasions, a spirit or nonhuman entity may linger for other reasons. The most common we have seen is when a human discarnate, or ghost, has a message for someone living there. In most cases, this will be a relative who has recently died wishing to communicate something before they will leave the area. You may use dowsing and other forms of intuition to find out what

the message is. Then they usually are willing to move on if you will pass the message on.
- Consult a professional if you have entities who won't leave when instructed.
- On rare occasions, entities can become 'embedded' in people and animals, leading to unwanted physical and mental/emotional symptoms. Removing this type of entity is work for a professional.

As a final note, keeping your personal energy and your home space balanced and harmonious will reduce the number of entities you attract. Anger, stress, fear, frustration, confusion and loss are common energies found in entities. If you are resonating with those energies, you will attract them. Being balanced and joyful will be your best protection. And it must be through and through. A veneer won't work.

Some locations naturally attract and pile up entities. Cemeteries, bars, morgues, hospitals, prisons, crime scenes, busy shopping malls and doctor's offices are just a few of the more 'dangerous' places to go if you want to avoid picking up entities. Use your protection whenever you leave your property. Don't use it out of fear, but out of the choice to be strong and healthy and safe.

If you are in a 'high risk' job, such as mental or physical health care, counseling, military, police or have a high level of contact with the public, we suggest you do daily clearing of yourself to remove entities, as well as using proper protection at work.

Aliens: Real or Not?

It might seem strange to assume that you believe in human ghosts and entities from other dimensions, but not aliens. Aliens are a group of beings that have a long history of contact with the human race. There are many theories about aliens; many sources of information about their agendas; a lot of speculation about their effect on us.

Our point of view is that there are other intelligent beings, physical and nonphysical, in the Universe, and that some of these beings are beneficial (listed in that topic above) and some are not. Those beings who originate from off-world can be called 'alien.'

We have spent many years as professional dowsers and space clearing experts, and we find plenty of evidence of alien energies at many locations on this planet. While the physical presence of aliens is probably quite limited, the energy of aliens, past and present, is quite common. In some cases, it is highly detrimental to humans and animals.

You may dowse about this energy as you do about entities. Because this is also a conscious type of energy, it has the same pitfalls as those listed above for entities in general.

Some areas have more alien energies than others.

Alien energies can also be acting at a distance, and sometimes aliens have an agenda involving the humans they are affecting. This is not usually the case with entities. If you dowse that alien energy is present and affecting you at the level of -8 or worse, we suggest you consult a professional to have it dealt with.

As a dowser, you have the ability to identify and appropriately handle detrimental beings in your environment. Your life will be richer and safer as a result.

MAP DOWSING

What is Map Dowsing?

A map is a sketch that represents an area or location. You can use map dowsing to find your way around an area that is far away or to mount a methodical and successful search.

Some of the many applications of map dowsing include:

- Prospecting for minerals and gemstones
- Space clearing and identifying noxious environmental energies
- Finding lost objects, pets or people
- Siting a water well
- Treasure hunting
- Evaluating a person or animal using the drawing as a surrogate

Map dowsing is thus about finding things. Once you find them on the map or sketch, you can locate them in the real world or decide how you intend to deal with them. The technique is the same regardless of what you are seeking.

Does It Work Long Distance?

One of the most common applications of map dowsing is in long distance searches. We used map dowsing for years to do space clearing for our global clientele. You can help a friend search for his lost cat in another state. Distance is no problem; maps shine as a tool in long distance dowsing.

Three Effective Map Dowsing Methods

You can dowse using a map or sketch in whatever way works best for you. The basis of any map dowsing method is to find a way to survey the entire map area and locate whatever is the object of your search without too much repetition or leaving any areas out. Three good methods (in order of difficulty) are:

- **#1: Break the sketch or map into natural areas** and dowse each area, one after the other, until you find what you are seeking.
- **#2: Quarter the map** (divide the map or sketch into four roughly equal sections by drawing a vertical and a horizontal line across it at the middle) and dowse each section. When you find the section that gives you a 'yes,' divide that section into four quarters and dowse each one, repeating the process until you have narrowed the search down enough to locate the item you seek
- **#3: Use a ruler as a guide.** In this method, envision the location of what you seek as being marked by a cross consisting of a vertical and a horizontal line whose intersection marks that exact spot. Using a ruler, you locate the vertical and horizontal lines and find the point of intersection.

Method 1: How to Dowse a Map Section-by-Section

The simplest type of map dowsing is to use the natural sections on the sketch or map and dowse each one in turn until you find what you seek.

A floor plan is easily done this way. Simply dowse one room after another.

Even a sketch of the body can be dowsed using this method. You could dowse each arm, each leg, the head and the torso. If there are not obvious boundaries, just draw them on the sketch.

For a search of a map of land, sometimes there are natural or manmade sections and boundaries that you can use. An example would be city limits, property lines or rivers.

When your map does not lend itself to this simple method, you can try quartering, which allows you to make your own boundaries.

Method 2: How to Map Dowse Using Quartering

Say you have lost something; your keys, for example. You know you lost them in the back yard during Sunday's barbecue, but you don't know where. Sketch the yard (make a map) with as many landmarks as possible, like the well head or the swingset or grill, plus the fences, if present.

In this variation of map dowsing, you will be dividing the area into four approximately equal sections, or quadrants. You simply draw a line across the middle of the sketch horizontally and another one down the center vertically. Then, you can quickly ask your question, *Are my keys in this quadrant?* over each area.

When you get a 'yes' in one area, divide that section into four and repeat the process, narrowing down the search area each time until you have a space you can easily search visually. The landmarks will be helpful when you do this.

Using this method, you can quickly search large areas very successfully. The only skill it requires is good basic dowsing technique. You do not have to have a sketch or map that is drawn to scale, but of course, especially for large areas, that would make your dowsing even more accurate and easy.

Method 3: How to Use a Ruler to Dowse a Map

The only additional skill needed for this technique is a little manual dexterity. Don't be put off if it takes a little while to master. It gets easier every time you do it. When you really need a specific location, this method excels. It's tremendously helpful when dowsing a large area using a map, as you would if you were seeking a lost pet or siting a water well.

Have your map flat on a table where you can sit and do your dowsing comfortably. Using a ruler (a metal 18-inch one works well), lay the ruler on your map at the top (you can start at the bottom if you prefer).

The object or location you seek is envisioned as being marked by the intersection of a vertical and horizontal line that form a cross on the map. Your goal is to find the vertical line and travel down it until you locate the intersection with the horizontal line, which marks what you are seeking. (Alternatively, you can lay your ruler vertically on the left or right edge of the map and use it as a guide to find the horizontal line, then follow that to the point of intersection with the vertical line.)

Hold your pendulum in whatever hand feels best and put it in a neutral swing. With the other hand, point along the ruler from left to right with a pencil or your index finger, asking your dowsing question while in a dowsing state. A possible question, once you have clearly defined the phrase 'what I seek,' is:

Give me a 'yes' when I point at the spot where the vertical line that passes through what I seek intersects this ruler.

When you get a 'yes,' turn the ruler 90 degrees, passing through that mark perpendicularly. Dowse along the length of the ruler using a question like:

Give me a 'yes' when I point at the location of what I am seeking.

What you are doing is locating the vertical line that passes through the spot and then traveling down it to its intersection with the horizontal line, which is the exact location of what you are seeking, whether it is a treasure, the best well site or a lost object. This is by far the best method to use when dowsing large outdoor areas.

Note: You don't need to use a pendulum with this method. If you prefer, you can use blink dowsing.

Extrapolating Map Dowsing to Other Applications

In many cases, you are looking for one particular thing (a lost object or pet) or one type of thing (gold or water) when you map dowse.

If looking for one specific object, then you only expect at best to find one location. If looking for water or gold, you may get multiple hits.

Maps and sketches don't have to only be about geographic locations. A sketch of the human body including the aura can be map dowsed. In that case, you would be searching for the root cause of a physical symptom, damage to the aura or where a person is holding energy of a particular trauma, for example.

Summary

You can use your dowsing skill to find something which is hidden from you and which requires a plan, sketch or map for you to accurately locate it. For this to work well, you can draw simple plans or elaborate maps, or use existing maps and plans, according to the task in hand. Use whichever of the three methods adapts best to your situation and goals.

Learning to dowse a sketch or map will expand your dowsing to new applications. Some of those are rewarding in terms of money, some in terms of the joy you give other people and some, both. Map dowsing also gives you new confidence of using dowsing at a distance.

MONEY DOWSING

If you look online about dowsing and money you'll inevitably come across a phrase like, "dowsing should be for need, not greed," or "dowsing for money is a misuse of your spiritual gift."

To be honest, we think that they are nice sounding phrases, but we also think they don't mean very much. Behind them lies an unspoken fear that something bad will happen to you if you indulge your perverted desire to make money from using a skill which anyone can use. Additionally, we consider dowsing to be a natural ability everyone has, not something exclusive.

We believe that it is ethical and moral to use dowsing to improve your life, and that pertains to finance as well as other areas. The hard part is going to be dealing with your own issues about money and wealth, because they will block you from getting accurate answers. If you doubt us, just try to dowse the winning lottery number for Saturday's draw.

Before you dowse anything financial, we suggest you check out the article on dowsing subconscious beliefs and work on as many aspects of abundance, money and wealth as you can think of. Clearing out false beliefs will go a long way towards helping you dowse about money. It will also make it easier to attract whatever abundance you desire.

Your Subconscious Money Issues

Let's give you some background on why you might have money issues you don't know about that are affecting you and can block a good dowsing response. You can use these ideas as a springboard for dowsing subconscious beliefs using the techniques in the training on that topic in this chapter.

Since the subconscious is all about keeping you alive, the problems you have often stem from fear. Fear of death, fear of rejection, fear of bodily harm, fear of losing what you love most, etc. You may have had several past lives where being rich caused you to be killed, judged, rejected, jailed or tortured.

So, when you consciously decide you want to dowse to win the lottery, find a great paying job or invest and make a lot of money, your subconscious turns to its rule book and asks, "How safe is this?". The past lives where wealth killed you or harmed you terribly activate and become energetic blocks to wealth in this life, thereby 'saving' your life. But it's all a mistake. Being wealthy in this life doesn't mean you will die. Those energies need to be cleared.

Read the article on dowsing the subconscious and find out how aligned you are with your wealth goals and clear what you can to remove blocks.

Something Else to Consider

Another interesting exercise you can do is to find out what exactly you mean when you think of being wealthy. Remember, we're talking of your subconscious mind here.

Some people will discover that being wealthy only means having enough money to pay the bills and nothing else. Others will discover that being wealthy means having one billion dollars. Still others will discover that they can never have much money because being wealthy means having to give away or spend any extra money as soon as it comes into your hands.

What you need to do, if any of those apply to you, is to decide what exactly you would like the word 'wealthy' to mean to you whenever you think or see it. Consciously decide what precisely it will take for you to consider yourself to be wealthy. And then you can see if that looks even remotely possible.

If it doesn't, then you need to re-think your definition or discover ways (apart from the lottery) which can get you to that goal. This, in turn, might lead you to more hidden beliefs about wealth and wealthy people which you need to work on.

These hidden problems are often the reason behind apparent difficulties which dowsers come across when using dowsing in some form to make money.

One example of this would be dowsing and horse-racing. For most dowsers this is the usual course of events when using dowsing in the following fashion.

First, you begin by thinking to yourself, 'Why can't I use dowsing to predict the winners and make a tidy little fortune?'. Then you decide to practice first. So you find lists of runners and riders and begin to dowse, but without putting any money on your results. After all, you're new to this and you want to make sure it works before you put any money down.

You find that your results are way better than average! This excites you, so you keep track of your results to make sure it's not a fluke, just a run of luck. And you keep picking more winners than losers and some of those are at good odds.

Heartened by your success at picking them, you then decide to place money on the rides you dowse. Impossible! It can't be! Hardly any winners at all! And you're now out of pocket and can't explain it. You did so well. You had the winners in your trial period.

So you decide it must be that you have missed something out. You decide to read more about the horses, learn about their previous races. You discover a world of information about handicaps and distances and jockeys and different weather conditions.

MAGGIE PERCY & NIGEL PERCY

You become more serious and more devoted because you know your dowsing doesn't let you down. But, no matter what you do, your dowsing results give no better odds than mere chance would.

Dejected, saddened and a little poorer, you decide that dowsing is a complete waste of time and effort and throw away your pendulum, never to believe in dowsing again.

OK, so maybe the ending is dramatic, but the main part is often true and has been reported by many different people; what starts out looking promising ends up as a failure as soon as you start committing money.

And the reason for that failure usually is because, when you actually use money and place a bet, that is, when you actually could become wealthy from using dowsing, your hidden beliefs kick in and stop you by picking out the wrong horses.

It is not a failure of dowsing because you can pick the winners using it. It is, if you like, a weakness of your own subconscious personality which is preventing you from accessing your full dowsing ability. But, as you now know, you can clear those hidden blocks and beliefs; dowsing can help you find them.

Dowsing for Profit

There are many ways you can use dowsing for profit. The principles are roughly the same no matter which area you dowse in, with the exception of mining or drilling based on your dowsing.

Let's assume that you will be dowsing for money from your armchair, rather than in the field. In which case, the most usual areas are:

- Stocks and shares
- Racing or sports of various kinds
- Gambling via the lottery, online or in a casino

Stocks and Shares

In this area, the key factor which overrides everything else is what profit can be gained from either buying something right now or selling something in the future. The process of selling something is not really part of the dowsing approach, as the price at which you sell will be dictated by the price you bought for.

However, you can always use dowsing here as well to make sure that you will be selling at the best price and that it won't go up today or next week. However, your profit margin and your overall goals will be what determine your initial interest in selling. So dowsing won't be the way to start your interest in selling, just as a method of determining when to sell.

The most important aspect of this type of dowsing for money is to determine for yourself what exactly your goals are. In other words, as always, it comes down to the precision of the question.

The exact question will depend on your own goals, the amount you are willing to invest and the timescale you have in mind for a profit. The size of profit, both from individual shares and from your portfolio, is, of course, yours to decide for yourself. But, without that, your question will be lacking important details and your results will, accordingly, be less precise and accurate.

So, your question will be something like the following:

Given my intention to make x amount of profit in y timescale with an outlay of z per month (or whatever time period you have in mind), will buying shares in (company name) today be a +8 or better on a scale of -10 to +10 in achieving my goals?

Or, you could ask it slightly differently, as follows:

If I buy shares today (or whenever) in (company name), will this significantly help me to achieve my stated goal of profit (or return) in x amount of time as quickly as possible, given all my other current investments?

You can probably think up your own variations of questions tailored to your specific requirements. But, you must make sure that you take into account all aspects of the question, especially the 'when' part of it.

There is another, less intense way, of working with dowsing in this field. Instead of dowsing each company and the share prices and so on, you can stand back a little from the process and dowse a much broader but simpler question each day.

For example, again assuming you have specific goals, you could dowse something like the following:

Given my stated goals of x return (or profit) in y amount of time with z amount of investment, and given my current investments, is it a +8 or better (on a -10 to +10 scale) for me today to buy (or sell) shares? This would, in fact, be two questions; one for buying, one for selling.

After that, you use your own knowledge or intuition or however else you work, and follow the guidance accordingly. But, it is important to remember that, if you dowsed it was a better day to buy than to sell, then that's exactly what you must do and not be seduced by what might seem like tantalizingly good offers.

Racing and Sports

With these areas, the approach is much simpler and clear-cut. In races, you are dowsing to find the winner or one of the first three. In sports games with betting, you are also after a definite goal; the winning team or player, or the number of points (or goals, runs etc) or the spread of points.

That makes the question process much easier and, after having dealt with any of your subconscious issues, it should allow you to see success more quickly.

Casinos and the Lottery

Almost every dowser is tempted to dowse about winning the lottery, and if you go to a casino, you may be tempted to dowse which one-armed bandit to play. There is absolutely nothing immoral or unethical about this type of dowsing, but perhaps more than investment dowsing, this application has many potential blocks you must overcome in order to succeed.

If you've ever bought a lottery ticket or gambled in a casino, adding dowsing to the process simple focuses your intuition on your goal. You will probably suddenly realize that in the past, you didn't really have a goal when doing these things, which is why you didn't win. We're not saying having a goal makes success inevitable, but that not having one makes it pretty unlikely.

So if you decide to use dowsing this way, have clear goals. They will be unique to you. Maybe you just want to pay for your vacation. Or you want to buy a new car. You get to decide. Then you focus your intuition via dowsing and ask an appropriate, detailed question.

It would be best to work on subconscious money issues before doing this sort of dowsing. See if you have any beliefs about gambling that would block an accurate dowsing response. Maybe subconsciously you feel gambling will send you to hell. That is a spiritual death your subconscious will protect you from.

The reason most dowsers don't successfully use dowsing to gamble is not because it is wrong, but because at some level, they believe it is wrong, or they don't deserve success.

Getting Paid to Dowse

There is one final area where dowsing and money meet, and that is charging money for dowsing. If you have a desire to become a professional health dowser or water dowser, your goal is to make a profit by dowsing.

In this case, the problem of self-confidence can compound blocks you may have about money itself. Hopefully, you will have realized that you are able to offer a service which some people will find very useful and will be willing to pay money to access it.

Whether it is to help them find something lost, discover more about their health or to answer questions which are difficult using traditional methods. In whatever form you offer your dowsing, you have a right, should you wish to, to ask for money when using your skill.

If fear of making a 'mistake' is your main concern, and for many people, that is the big one, then be upfront about it and say that you cannot guarantee 100% accuracy but that you will do your best for the client. If they accept that from you, then you have no problem with going ahead and being paid for it.

Remember, no professionals guarantee results: doctors and lawyers would be in trouble if they had to guarantee certain results for their patients and clients.

This article has been about how dowsing for money, in various ways, can be difficult for one or more reasons. However, it is important to remember that it is not the dowsing which is a problem, but the blocks, hindrances, beliefs or whatever else you want to call it which are there inside you and which only show up when challenged by the prospect of making money.

ON-SITE DOWSING

What is On-Site Dowsing?

Using dowsing at your current location to find specific targets is one of the earliest uses of dowsing. Historically, humans have used on-site dowsing for at least hundreds of years to find water and minerals.

Regarding tools, a good, multi-purpose tool for this purpose is a sturdy L-rod. It is less likely to be influenced by wind and can indicate direction easily.

A pendulum which is heavy enough not to be affected by wind will also be tiring to use for a long while, and sometimes, on-site working can involve plodding around while dowsing, and you will have to allow for your other body movements when interpreting the pendulum's movements.

In most places, you buy L-rods as a pair and all the teaching manuals assume you use two at a time. While it is certainly true that you can use two rods at a time, we have found that it is just as easy to use one. In fact, it's probably better, in most cases, to use just a single L-rod at a time, as there are advantages to that.

Using just one frees up your other hand. You can use this to hold marking materials, a witness, if that is the way you choose to work, or indeed anything else at all. You can find direction, location and depth using just one rod as well as you can using two.

You, of course, need to make the choice which suits you and the circumstances best. What works well in one situation might not be as effective in another. Not every on-site job will require a 'witness' or sample of what you seek, but certainly in gas, oil, diamond, mineral and water location, there are some dowsers who would not dream of working without one.

The witness is usually placed inside a chamber or in a container small enough to hold in your hand easily as you dowse. The idea is that it allows you to focus on your target more effectively and reduces the number of false reports you might encounter.

It is a matter of personal choice as well as experience whether you prefer to work with a witness or not.

Simple Applications of On-Site Dowsing

The thought of oil wells, diamond mines and buried treasure may seem a little exotic, but there are other ways you can dowse on-site around the home. It is relatively easy to practice your skill in there. All that is required, at first, anyway, is your imagination!

For instance, you can try any of the following exercises;

- Locate pipes, studs and wiring in or behind walls
- Locate a leak in a pipe
- Locate a lost or hidden object

You probably get the picture. You are attempting to find out information about something which you can't see.

No matter what you do, or how you do it, with which tools and so on, you absolutely must check up on your answers. Were you accurate? If not, why? Was the question poorly worded? Were you right, completely?

Almost right? Try and find out **how** you were wrong because the more knowledge you have about that, the more it will help you next time.

Try It Yourself: Finding Things On-Site

For this to work, you need the help of a friend. This friend will bury several items in your yard or other convenient location for you to find. A variety of objects will work; pottery, metal (if you can use silver and gold as well, all the better), oil in a can, or whatever type of target you are interested in going after.

The important thing is to have variety, for you might find you can locate silver very easily, but ordinary pottery just isn't something you can find at all.

Once you have established what there is to be found (you might just want to know the number of items, or you might want to ask how many metallic objects there are to be found), then you can proceed to dowse for them.

If you can, use different tools and also dowse with and without witnesses to see what you feel most comfortable with.

This is a relatively simple experiment to set up, but it does allow for a variety of dowsing practices and can be used prior to actually setting out on a real exercise.

If you decide to use a witness, then see if you can find a way of making it easy to hold and dowse at the same time. Some pendulums have witness chambers in them, and some L-rods have the same capability. Normally, however, very small glass containers are used, but go with what works for you and your circumstances.

One word of warning, though. As you are dowsing, you could pick up other objects neither you nor your friend knew were there. That's OK. In fact, it's really good practice, finding anything at all and then thinking back about the strength of reaction, or the type of reaction. It all helps you in your learning.

But what about if you don't have a handy friend around? You can always do this yourself. If you have a grassed yard area, let the grass grow long and then, with your back to it, throw the objects of your search over your shoulder where the length of the grass will hide their location. Obviously, you're going to be using small objects for this, so don't throw those diamond cuff links into the grass just yet, because, just possibly, you might not find them until a long time later!

How do you actually go about locating small objects in a large area?

You will find it very useful to have something like a peg or two to put into the ground as markers when you begin.

Start by walking along the edge of the area with your tool, asking to be shown the shortest direction to what you are seeking. So, you will be walking along and the rod will begin to turn, say, to the left. At that point, start walking in the direction that the rod has pointed in until it signifies that you are near or over the object you have in mind (you do have the object in mind, don't you?). Place a marker at that point and then go back to the edge again and carry on walking, repeating the process again and again as necessary.

You will end up with several markers all quite near to each other (hopefully!). Inside those markers is the area where you now concentrate your search. You can do this by walking carefully to and fro marking each place you have a dowsing reaction. (Remember, there might be similar objects unknown to you already buried in the area, so you might get several 'hits'.)

Once you have swept the area as carefully as you can, you then begin to do a visual search of the markers and see what you have located.

This is the great thing about on-site dowsing. Either what you are searching for is where you dowsed it is, or it isn't! It is wonderful because you get to see results, both positive and negative, and you get to see them right away. There really is nothing else to compare with the excitement of on-site work in this regard.

The chief problem areas you will come across at first are the use of tools outside and the ability to narrow in on a small area quickly. Once you have dealt with these issues, you will be able to develop and expand this most useful aspect of dowsing in any number of ways.

Finding Buried Objects

Sometimes what you seek outdoors is underground, like a water pipe or septic tank. One of the things you are going to need to know before you start digging is how far beneath the surface the object is.

'Depthing,' as it is often known, is relatively easy to do. The simplest method is to stand over the object and ask a series of questions. If you are relatively sure it is close to the surface, you can begin by asking, *Is it less than 10 feet below the surface?* If you get a 'yes,' then you can ask, *Is it less than 5 feet?* If 'yes,' then ask for each foot until you get an answer.

This method can be used for much larger numbers. Let's say that you are standing over something quite deep. You can begin with, *Is it less than 100 feet below the surface?*. Continue going up (or down) until you get a response.

Suppose you know it is between 300 and 400 feet deep. You can then begin asking about units of ten feet at a time. So, *Is it less than 350 feet?-* '*yes'-340?'-'yes'-330?* You get a 'no,' meaning it is between 330 and 340 feet. Then ask again, but this time in units until you have the depth.

Ways to Use On-Site Dowsing

If you have access to a yard area, then you can dowse a variety of targets. For example, depending on where you live, you can dowse the direction of sewage or water lines or even electrical cables.

You can stake the location as you go along, or make a mark in some fashion so that you can look back at the end and see if the course you have plotted looks reasonable. Sometimes, utilities will take unusual directions or they could split and you end up following two lines.

There is no reason why you cannot use this technique in many other areas. For example, it would be possible to track an animal. You can follow the path it took with your tool, even though there may be nothing visible to the eye.

Some dowsers use this process to locate the best place to cast their lines when fishing, having dowsed where the fish are to be found.

You can, of course, use this skill to dowse for oil or for diamonds. Diamond firms will sometimes use a dowser to research a possible site before doing more expensive exploratory work. Many oil wells have been dowsed prior to being drilled.

Then again, there is the whole field of treasure dowsing. Do be aware, however, of the problem of thought forms in treasure dowsing. They are more likely there than in any other form of dowsing you will do, for obvious reasons!

A quick word on legality. Different countries and different states will have different laws which will govern access to land and what you can and can't do on it.

If there is any doubt, then don't do it until you have done the necessary research or received the necessary permission to go ahead. And, if you do find anything valuable, the law dictating what will happen to it or who it belongs to varies considerably.

The message is clear, if you are interested in dowsing for treasure, be very aware of the legal restrictions surrounding this subject.

Avoiding Pitfalls

There you are in the middle of a field and you've just realized that great-grandfather's gold hunter watch is not where you dowsed it was. Instead of feeling despondent and giving up, let's look instead at some possible causes for this apparent failure.

Insufficient focus: It could be that you were distracted as you were walking and dowsing. It can be difficult at first to do both at once, especially if other people are watching you. Maintain a crystal clear mental image of exactly what it is you are looking for. Don't be vague and just be searching for iron, because you might react to iron filings, a certain percentage of iron in the soil, old nails buried years before or even iron salts suspended in water flowing underground.

Tools not showing clear indications: Because you are walking and there might be a wind, you might have misinterpreted the reactions of your tool. There might have been a stronger gust of wind, or you might have lurched a little on a patch of uneven ground, either of which caused the tool to move as if it was indicating a positive response. It can take practice walking and holding a tool to begin with until you are confident that you can distinguish between the occasional movements of it due to you or the environmental conditions and a real dowsing reaction.

Dehydration: Dehydration or lack of mineral salts or electrolytes in your system will cause your dowsing to be 'off' no matter what type of dowsing you are engaged in. It is essential to make sure you are well-hydrated to begin with and to refresh yourself as necessary as you work.

Thought forms: If you are particularly sensitive, you could even be reacting to where onlookers think there should be a target, so you end up with these false positives which are not really your reactions at all, but the reactions of other people to certain areas. This type of interference can be quite difficult to deal with, particularly in areas where many people have tried to find gold or treasure, for example. They've all brought along, and then left behind for you, their ideas of where they think such things should be. Again, it takes practice to overcome such things, but it can be done.

Summary

On-site dowsing can, in many ways, be the most rewarding type of dowsing to do because it invariably allows you to confirm or deny your accuracy. That is why it is such a useful type of dowsing, even on a small and limited scale.

It may be that, one day, you end up bringing in oil wells, or finding that lost Inca treasure, but, in the meantime, you can keep honing your skills outside and inside.

PAST LIFE DOWSING

Past Lives: Real or Not?

Christianity and Islam are the two major religions which generally deny reincarnation. However, Eastern religions by and large accept it as a concept, and there is a growing number of Westerners, including Christians, who believe in reincarnation as a fact.

The space-time continuum is not fully understood. Many theorists believe that time is not linear. That means the past doesn't come before the future, and the future doesn't come after the present. The truth is that our perception of time may not be accurate.

Quantum physics allows for the possibility of other times and places. These other times and places may energetically connect with what we perceive as the present. They may be running in parallel dimensions. It is difficult to conceive of how it all works, because we don't think beyond our own 3-dimensional version of reality, or 4-dimensional, if you include time. But there are scientific theories that suggest and support the existence of other realities.

You don't need to fully understand quantum physics or the space-time continuum to dowse about other lifetimes. You can get useful information by using some basic concepts. With respect to lives, keep the terminology 'past,' 'present,' and 'future,' and add 'parallel' and 'other' just to cover all the bases.

Be open to expanding your understanding of how things work, and try not to reject any idea, no matter how crazy it sounds. Do as a friend of ours says and put it in your back pocket to be examined at a later date if you can't accept it right now. Avoid judgment of any kind concerning this area of exploration. If something seems strange or ridiculous now, it just might change into something really useful later on.

So don't dismiss the new and the strange just yet. Personal growth is about change, and you may be surprised how much your perceptions change over time.

Why Bother About Other Lives?

For many reasons, we have found it useful and sensible to accept the belief that we have lived other lifetimes. This is not a totally outlandish idea, as most of the world's people believe in reincarnation. It's just that in Western culture, it is not a common belief.

If you are willing to be open to the possibility that past lives may exist, then your next question is going to be, "So what?".

If it isn't this life, what's the point of knowing about it? Or maybe you feel just the opposite. Any other life intrigues you and seems more interesting than your present one. Whichever way you are feeling, there is more to it than you ever imagined.

Other lifetimes can affect you now. You create karma by your actions in other lives, and that karma exists in you today as a mute testimony to other times and places. (Karma is basically the energetic result of every decision you make and action you take. It is neutral. Karma is somewhat like the physics law that states every action has a reaction. Karma is a natural fact of life.)

People tend to classify karma as good or bad based on their subjective feelings, but it is best not to emphasize judgment. Just know that your actions have consequences, and those consequences can follow you from one life to another in many forms energetically.

Phobias that can't be explained by present life experience usually stem from a bad experience in another lifetime that left a strong negative impression. Past life regressions have shown this to be true, and that the phobia can be cured by dealing with that other life.

The significant people in your present life were also significant in other lives. A person you have an unexplained jealousy of in this lifetime may have stolen your beloved in another lifetime. An adversary you face in this lifetime may have been an enemy in a past life. Problem relationships usually have a karmic element, and finding out about the experiences in other lifetimes can often lead to resolution of the problems.

Your health is often a reflection of other lifetimes. Maggie's dairy allergy, which began the day she was born, stemmed from several past life experiences around dairy farming that were very negative and caused her to react negatively to dairy products in this lifetime. When those lives were cleared (it took about 15 minutes), her lifelong allergy to dairy products cleared immediately.

It has been found that one way curses can be used more effectively is by causing you to connect to other lifetimes, making you more susceptible to the curse for a variety of reasons, such as you had a negative outcome with the person in that lifetime who is cursing you in this, so that intensifies the results. It's kind of like programming an outcome.

These are just a few examples of how other lifetimes can affect you now. As a dowser, you can discover other lifetime influences and resolve them.

Pitfalls to Avoid

Dowsing about other lifetimes can be fun. There's no doubt about that. It can be entertaining to find out some of the experiences you had in other lives. It's unlikely you were anyone famous, but you may have been close to someone famous, or you may have had an important part in some historical event you read about in school. Most lives, though, are pretty ordinary. But even ordinary other lives can hold the key to resolving present life problems.

The biggest pitfall to dowsing other lives is the ego. Your ego may reject the facts. It may fear the truth. It may want to be massaged. If the ego gets involved in your dowsing, you won't get accurate answers.

The bad news is you won't know your answers are garbage. You may want to think you were always a great person in every other lifetime. Or that you never did anything you would consider 'bad.' You can't accept that you poisoned your mother in another life. Or you may feel so disempowered in this lifetime that you wish for a past life when you were powerful, a life you can tap into. That wish will influence your dowsing.

The best advice for dowsing other lives is to develop that detachment we speak of so often. The more detached you are, the better your dowsing becomes. Detachment is what comes from releasing judgment. The more you judge things as right or wrong, good or bad, the less detached you are. And it follows that your dowsing won't be accurate.

Try It Yourself: Other Life Dowsing

This exercise will give you a chance to find out information on another lifetime that is affecting you in this one.

First, think about someone you have difficulties with. It can be a person you are currently struggling with, or someone from your past whom you no longer see. It doesn't matter. But it should be someone you have had strong issues with.

Remember to detach yourself from the process. You are going to dowse some questions. You are merely curious about the answers. You have no judgment.

This may be harder than you expect. If this person has betrayed you or done something you think is horrible, you won't find it easy to detach. But that is very important. Be open to whatever the dowsing says is true.

Dowse the following questions and record your answers, filling the person's name in the blanks:

- *Have I ever known the person who is presently called _____ in other lifetimes?*
- *How many other lives have I had in which _____played a significant role?* (Bear in mind how you define 'significant' will affect the numbers.)

To dowse how many lifetimes, just say 0, 1 digit, 2 digits, 3 digits...and so on until you get a 'yes' response. Then take that response, say, 2 digits, and test 10, 20, 30, 40...until you get a 'yes.' Then ask *less than 20?* or *more than 20?*. Go from there to pinpoint the exact number by saying the numbers in sequence until you get a 'yes.' Then double check by asking if that is the number of lives in which this person played a significant role. It sounds clumsy, but it very soon becomes very quick.

The number may be small or large. You may assume that if the number is large, this person is someone you share a lot of karma with. But that can be true even if the number is small.

Now make a statement of intention that you want to find out the details on the most significant life that is affecting your present life negatively. This assumes you will just be dowsing about the details of one lifetime. Ask the following questions about that one life:

- *What is the time frame: past, future, parallel or other?*
- You can then dowse how many years before or after this life it was, if it is past or future. If parallel, that doesn't matter. If other, you need to choose a lifetime that will give an easier answer. Go back and ask for a significant life that is past, future or parallel.
- For example, if it dowses as a past life 1000 years ago, that gives you a time frame for reference.
- Now you can ask for more details. Ask if you were human, on Earth and what gender you were (male/female). Do not assume it will be a human life, or even a life on Earth. Those are easier, but it's not guaranteed that is what you will come up with. Ask

the same questions about this person. Was he/she human, what gender, on Earth? Now you know what you were and when.

- Next, you can ask questions about what relationship there was between you. You can dowse if you were related by blood, by marriage, by business or were strangers to one another.
- If you were blood relations, find out if you were mother and son, sister and brother, etc. If you were related by marriage, find out if you were married to one another or were in-laws of some type. If you were related by business, see if you were competitors or partners, etc. It is highly unlikely you were strangers, but if so, that's fine. The relationship will suggest things that may occur to you intuitively before you even dowse. Don't reject those thoughts, but be open to testing them out.
- Once you know the relationship, you can begin to see how things were between you. Don't assume they were bad in that life. Maybe they were, but maybe there weren't. See what emotions were on each side. Love? Hate? Jealousy? Envy? Did you love each other? Was it reciprocal? Was there animosity between you? Was there a misunderstanding? Ask questions that paint a picture. Don't assume you were nice and he was bad. Often, it is the reverse. Just be open to whatever the answers are.

Here is an example of an exercise. You may decide you want to ask about your sister Joan. In this life, you and she are not close. She seems to be very jealous of anything good that happens to you, and you don't recall ever doing anything to deserve that.

When you dowse, you find you had 43 other lifetimes with Joan. The most significant one for the jealousy in this life is a past life on earth, where you were both human females. You were sisters, just like now (that is not always the case). You both fell in love with the same man, and he chose you. She went on to commit suicide out of despair.

So in this lifetime, she has carried the jealousy over and it activates strongly due to cellular memory. (Remember you are just as likely to be the villain as the hero in other lifetimes.)

Dowsing Other Lives Can Change This Life

There are many useful things that you can do with information about other lives. Using a similar set of questions to the above exercise, you can find out how other lives impact you in this life. Some examples:

- Curses from other lives can affect this one. They can activate at any time, or can be active and then dormant and activate again later. You can disempower the curses once you discover them. Use whatever clearing method tests as most effective.
- Allergies can sometimes be cleared by dowsing the energetic cause from the lifetimes affecting you. See the article on this technique in this chapter.
- Relationship issues often stem from other lifetimes. You may think you know why you don't get along with someone, but it's likely to be about other lifetimes as much or more than this one. Dowsing about other lifetimes as in the above exercise will help you to see how karma carries over. You will also have compassion, because in many cases, you were the victimizer, not the victim. You will start seeing that judgment is counterproductive, and that it is best to release it. You can heal relationships by having an understanding of what drives them.
- Phobias often stem from other lifetimes. If you can't explain your phobia, or sometimes, even if you can, it will help heal it to find out about other lifetimes that it started in and clear the energies of them.
- Issues with your life's purpose often will relate to bad experiences in other lives. If you can discover why you are afraid of being a leader, or why you do not want to be well-known, you can clear those energies and be more successful in this life. See the article on dowsing subconscious beliefs in this chapter for more details on this topic.
- It is not advantageous to be energetically connected to other lives. Dowse how many other lives you are currently connected to. If the number is greater than 0, use whatever clearing method you wish to disconnect from other lives, to clear issues that

perpetuated those connections, and to clear whatever came over as a result of those connections. This is very useful and healthy to do.

The goal of dowsing about other lives is to allow yourself to enjoy this lifetime more and to have greater success in it. Your dowsing about other lifetimes can bring greater success, understanding and balance to this one.

PET HEALTH DOWSING

One of the biggest challenges a vet has is figuring out what's wrong with his patient. Animals can't tell you where they hurt or how they feel. The vet has to be highly intuitive and experienced to diagnose unusual conditions. Too bad they don't teach dowsing in vet school. It would be one of the most valuable courses they could offer. But you can dowse for your pet, and use the information to help your vet get the best possible results.

The application of dowsing in pet health care could easily be a two- or three-day workshop. In this article, we will condense some applications into a form that will allow you to immediately begin to see the value of dowsing for your animal's health.

Dowsing is not meant to take the place of appropriate health care for your animal companion. However, you can successfully use dowsing to complement whatever professional care you get. Use your judgment and always get confirmation of your dowsing if you are not a confident health dowser.

Try It Yourself: Dowsing Food and Supplements

What you feed your animal is vital to his/her health. Evaluate:

- Food
- Treats
- Water
- Supplements

Using a +10 to -10 scale is the best bet here. It gives you a nice spread on answers that will help separate the excellent from the moderately good.

Here is a sample dowsing question for the above subjects:

On a +10 to -10 scale, with positive numbers being healthy, and larger positive numbers being more healthy, what is the rating of _____(brand of food; water source used, brand of supplement, treats) on the overall health and well-being of _____(name of pet) at this time?

We use +8 or higher as the cutoff for making a purchase. Just because something is 'good' does not make it worth buying. So disregard products that test less than +8.

Note that we have a time mentioned. Why? Even the best food or supplement is likely to be incomplete or a potential allergen if fed exclusively or for a long time. What tests well this month, because your animal is changing constantly, may not test well next month. We have found that changing brands of food is helpful in avoiding allergies and deficiencies.

Set in your mind that you want a negative number to come up if there is an allergy problem, negative side effects or toxins or something that would indicate you are better off not buying that brand. Each animal is unique, and even a good product can be harmful to a particular animal. So be open to getting whatever is correct for your pet.

Do not dowse after you have invested in a product. You won't be detached enough to get an accurate answer. Also, make sure you approach all of these questions with an open mind, as things change, and you need to be open to hearing what is true.

The key issues that cause negative numbers are usually toxins, allergic reactions, negative side effects, etc. Also a given brand may not test the same each time, not only for the animal, but due to changes in quality.

Try It Yourself: Dowsing a Practitioner

It is fun and rewarding to use dowsing to select a professional to work with. It is important that you have a clear and specific question to dowse. Don't just ask, *Who is the best vet?*. That is too vague. For example, vets have specialties. You may do well taking your dog to Dr. Smith, but you might get better results with Dr. Jones for your cat. And again, time is a factor. Sometimes professional people are subject to burnout or are having temporary personal issues affecting their approach.

Make a list of the priorities you have. Some might include:

- Convenience of location and hours
- Good communication style
- Prices
- Caring nature
- Good with animals of your pet's type
- Experienced
- Open to working with you to find solutions to problems
- Willing to listen to you
- Good followup routine
- Open to new ways of doing things
- In alignment with your belief system

The +10 to -10 scale works well here, too. Put your priorities together and form a question that assigns a number on the +10 to -10 scale to each professional you are testing.

Make sure you set your intention to get a negative number for anyone who is dangerous, incompetent, etc. Look for +8 or higher in order to select someone.

If no one comes out at +8 or higher, widen your search. If too many come out above +7, then add more priorities to your list and retest. Remember that things change, and over time, you may decide it is wise to re-dowse and make sure you are still using the best professional.

Try It Yourself: Dowsing the Recommendations of a Professional

Your health care professional will most likely have recommendations. He or she may suggest a therapy, a supplement, or a procedure (surgery or euthanasia). Or your vet may render a diagnosis of a problem.

You are not a trained professional, but you have to choose whether to proceed with the recommendation. You have to decide whether it will be worth the cost for your goals and whether you believe it will work . Dowsing is an unbiased and wonderful way to make a good choice.

If you have been practicing your dowsing, you are becoming less fearful and more open to hearing the truth. When a vet or other professional says your horse has a terminal condition, and you should put it down, your reaction hopefully will not be purely emotional, but will be a balanced response that gives you a clear feeling of whether the suggestion is appropriate or not.

Health care professionals do a hard job. They see your animal rarely, and they spend most of their time giving vaccinations and neutering pets. Many of them have limited experience in other areas.

You know your pet better than they do. Your opinion matters, and your impression is important.

If the professional is suggesting a therapy or procedure, you can dowse how much help, or how effective that particular therapy/procedure/drug will be in resolving the issue/symptom permanently with no negative side effects. Use the +10 to -10 scale for this.

You have to keep the overall health of your pet as the key goal. If you damage the liver with the drug to cure the problem, then you have just created another issue to deal with. It becomes expensive to do this, yet both humans and animals are subject to this sad pattern.

Another thing you can dowse is possible side effects. Use a 0-10 scale with under 3 being negligible and 8 or higher being dangerous. This is a very valuable technique for testing prescription drugs or recommended surgery or the timing of either.

Try It Yourself: Dowsing Symptoms

This is the one of the trickier dowsing exercises you can do. When you see a symptom, you are going to automatically feel it is bad. You are also going to fall into the mindset of wanting to be a 'good' caretaker for your pet, and that will color your perceptions. Ego and attachment do not mix well with dowsing.

What we have found is that sometimes a symptom is not a sign of a disease process. So your first question will be to find out the overall long term effect of this symptom and the process it represents for your pet. Negative numbers mean disease or imbalance, while positive numbers mean healing crisis, detox or other positive transformation.

Depending on the number, you can then ask questions about the best course of action. Remember your overall goal is for your pet to have optimal health and wellness. Do not just focus on getting rid of a symptom. Learn to read the symptoms as a sign of your pet's condition.

The number may be positive if you have been doing healing work on your pet, have changed her diet or started a new supplement. These actions can lead to symptoms which are a sign of positive change, because they are aimed at creating change.

If the number is negative, especially if it is a large negative, the main question to ask is whether it is appropriate to seek professional help for resolving the problem. Each person is an individual, and your priorities will have to be taken into account when asking this question.

We have presented this application in the Health Dowsing: Making Evaluations training, and the process is the same for your pet as it is for you.

Some factors that you might want to consider are:

- Cost
- Side effects
- Is the professional better able than you to resolve the problem
- Is the professional the only person who can resolve it
- Is there an excellent professional nearby for resolving this issue
- How serious is the condition
- How fast do you need to act to resolve it
- How many trips to a professional will it take to resolve it
- Is the professional open to your input
- Is the professional in alignment with your beliefs and viewpoint

You can program a short question as we taught in Chapter 4 to make dowsing this subject quicker and easier, especially in emergency situations.

Having a dowsing buddy or using blind dowsing is also helpful in such situations. Do not dowse for this type of thing unless you are an expert and have practiced a lot. At first, you can dowse what is best, and then do whatever you feel is best and see how the outcome goes. But always be cautious. Never risk the life of your pet.

What if you dowse that you can deal with this issue better than a professional? Then, once you have confirmed that you are dowsing accurately, you dowse a list of the remedies and therapies you have at hand and create a program to restore your pet to health.

Homeopathics, clay, flower essences, hands-on healing techniques, color therapy and sound therapy are a few possible things for your list. It makes sense for you to use techniques and products you are familiar with, so your list may be different from mine. We even use symbols at times.

If in dowsing the effect of the symptoms, the number is positive, then you need to find out if there is some way you can support the process to make your pet more comfortable. Often, a herb, supplement, flower essence or the like will assist the process and make it faster.

Try It Yourself: Dowsing the Results

It helps if you are good at dowsing outcomes. In cases where you are getting treatment or giving therapy to a pet, you can dowse when you will see improvement; when your pet will be back to normal; when your pet will no longer have pain/fever/whatever. By dowsing about when you will see a change, you can then measure progress. It gives confirmation on your dowsing, too. This is an important part of the process.

Be very clear about what you are asking. And always remember that you probably are not thinking about all the possible outcomes. You may not want to think about your pet dying, but that is possible, and if you dowse that your pet is in transition, then you can do things to make the transition easier for him/her. Dowsing is also useful for making a decision about euthanasia.

Broaden Your Horizons

Everything we've taught you in this article can be applied to human health. If you feel detached enough, go ahead and use these protocols to improve your health program. It is very empowering.

What If I Make a Mistake?

The biggest challenge people face when health dowsing is fear of making a mistake. Dowsing is not 100% accurate. But nothing else is, either. Your vet's recommendations are never guaranteed to create positive outcomes. You basically invest money in a situation that has no guarantees. When it comes down to it, that is true about most life choices.

Dowsing is not about guaranteeing anything. It's about improving your odds of success. That is all. Simply doing whatever the doctor says or flipping a coin may work. But dowsing brings another source of information online to help you make an even better choice.

Always follow what feels best to you, but never make choices based on fear. Use intuition and rational knowledge. Health choices are often a gamble. We recommend using everything you can to improve your odds of success, and dowsing is a valuable tool.

In this article you have learned some important dowsing applications for pet health. As you become more expert, you will get confirmation about your dowsing that will make you more comfortable using this tool. It will empower you and help your pet. It will save you money and time. It might even save your pet's life.

PLANT DOWSING

One of the great things about dowsing is how practical it is. Using the results of your dowsing, following up on what you have dowsed, can really make huge changes in the quality of your life in all sorts of ways. In this article we'll be looking at how dowsing can help the plants in your life, whether it's just one potted plant or a whole orchard!

Remember that, if a plant of any kind is to reach its true potential, it has to have all the elements necessary in place and working effectively for it to do so. Or, to put it another way, you need to check the following aspects to ensure success:

- The physical location
- The soil composition and nutrients
- The amount of moisture required
- The energetic environment
- Other plants nearby

Having checked those, you can then begin to address any issues which arise using a wide variety of possible solutions which, again, you can filter through quickly using dowsing. After all that, you then apply the fixes and wait for the wonderful results!

Let's begin to look in detail at each of those elements and see what they mean.

The Physical Location

Where you live will determine, to a great extent, what you can grow easily. So it's unlikely that you will grow good pineapples in Alaska, for example. But there are always micro-climates where it is possible to grow plants not native to the area. There's a lovely sub-tropical area on an island off the coast of England, where all sorts of exotic species (exotic for that part of the world, anyway) grow quite happily.

By and large, though, you are limited by the climate in your area. Within that, of course, there are other physical considerations. The amount of shade and moisture, if the ground collects water or allows it to run off very easily, whether there are issues of toxicity from neighboring sites such as factories or from careless use of chemicals, as well as the numbers and hunger of local animal life likely to eat what you grow. All of these are important issues to at least understand before starting your garden.

If you are only growing indoors, then similar ideas, but scaled down, need to be understood; light, moisture, chemicals and so on still have effects indoors as well.

You can easily work out a scale of probability of success of growing various plants in your chosen location through dowsing, prior to doing anything with the soil or any other aspects. This will give you a baseline from which to work.

For example, you could ask a question like, *On a scale of 0 to 100%, indicate the likely success of my growing (name of plant or vegetable) in this plot successfully so that it (here state your goal, such as yield, height, color, shoots, healthy fruit, etc.) without doing anything more to the soil other than digging it over.*

The Soil

The most immediate physical aspect which has the greatest effect on plants is the composition of the soil. Modern farming techniques have introduced the use of huge amounts of various chemicals to encourage increased growth rates in many species.

Unfortunately, this undisciplined dosing of the soil has poisoned it, and overuse has reduced the amount of minerals which plants can pull from it. We eat plant materials in order to obtain vitamins and minerals. But the present state of affairs means that we have to supplement what we eat with vitamins from health shops, because plants just don't have minerals like they used to.

Because plants require certain minerals to be available, for color, for strength, for yield and so on, there is a tendency to assume that increasing amounts of a certain few minerals will be sufficient to ensure success. In fact, the chemical balance of the soil is not only delicate, but it is also complex. It is not always just a matter of dowsing what chemical to buy and then adding it by the spoonful or bucketful and then sitting back.

First, you should dowse what, if anything your soil is missing for the plants you have in it. No soil is perfect for everything, so you need to be specific in your question. Then you need to dowse to find out what you can do to improve things.

Just adding minerals and inorganic bits isn't nearly as sound a practice as making sure that the soil organisms are healthy and productive. They are responsible for many of the vital aspects of soil that feed your plants. There are companies now that sell products designed to support and create a balanced living soil environment, from earthworms to mycorrhizae.

Of course, if you are not yet ready to plant, then you can take advantage of this to add in bulk whatever you dowse is needed. Digging it in, adding sand, or clay, or compost, or whatever, and making sure the soil is well aerated are all tasks which can be dowsed over and carried out and re-checked with dowsing.

Water

All plants need water. The trick is knowing how much and when.

If you are growing potted plants indoors, then the need for water is crucial. However, the situation is not necessarily straightforward.

For example, let's say that you dowse that your pot plant needs watering. That's not much help, because, as I just said, all plants need water. What you need to determine is when it needs water and how much does it need?

Now, water is a remarkable liquid. From Dr Emoto's work photographing water crystals after being exposed to various influences, we can be pretty sure that it can carry energies in it. Therefore, you need to be able to dowse the water you are using to see if it is the best possible water for your plants. Spending a few moments holding the water container while thinking happy thoughts or loving thoughts will change the energy and help your plants grow.

But it is not only the energy of the water. Some water is heavy in minerals or has traces of chemicals in it which can influence your plants one way or another. You can certainly purchase kits to test your water for various chemicals, or you can dowse to find out how beneficial the water is that you are using. The results may help you to understand more clearly the results of your dowsed soil analysis, for example.

A sample question might be phrased, *On a scale of -10 to +10 with positive numbers indicating better quality, how does the water I use on my plants rate for helping their growth?*

Outside, it might be that you have to dowse how to improve the water quality permanently. Your well might be the source of the problem, as might your storage method, if that is what you use.

For example, if the answer to the previous question was a negative or low positive, then you might ask something like, *Can I improve the quality of the water?, Does it require that I use more than one fix?, Which is the first fix to apply?*, and so on.

In any case, whatever it is that you dowse needs to be done about the water, it can be treated in exactly the same way as you would treat a space which needs balancing and harmonizing. Work out what you need to do: symbol, color, sound, crystal, etc, and then apply it and re-test the quality again.

The Energetic Environment

Having an understanding of the physical environment is important, just as is getting a feel for the energetic aspect of your chosen site.

Quite often, simply taking the time to look around and see what is growing where will give you a good first impression. Bare patches, bent and twisted shrubs, huge numbers of weeds, many signs of rabbits, moles, gophers, ants and the like will all indicate an area which is energetically not helpful to your proposed plans.

Of course, there are always those plants which thrive in areas which are noxious for us humans (many medicinal plants fall into this category), so it is important that, when you dowse the site with your plantings in mind, you do so without prejudice even though, to your eye, it looks poor.

If it dowses that the energy is not helpful to what is already growing there or what you propose to plant there, you will need to use what you learned in the space clearing training in this chapter to balance the energies according to your needs.

It is important that you take the time to check this aspect out at regular intervals. About four times a year should be enough, although if anything strange happens to your plants at any time, then you should always check this first. By keeping an eye on things energetically, you will always know that whatever else is going on, you can discount that aspect.

Energies can be affected by construction nearby, by pollutants in water which flows under your property, and by such things as curses and EMFs, amongst other things. So, if there are new things happening in your neighborhood, check to see what is going on energetically which might affect your plants.

Other Plants

Gardeners have long known that certain plants tend to grow well in the company of other species. It's called companion planting and has been practiced since, probably, Roman times. In this, for example, tomatoes grow well with asparagus, but you should avoid planting cabbages with them.

This technique is useful because each plant species requires different chemical balances, attracts different insects and produces different amounts of shade and has differing water requirements.

While the list of companion plantings is relatively easy to look up and learn, you can use your dowsing to find out other, more subtle relationships.

Plants of all kinds have, for the want of a better term, personalities. While this might sound strange to a non-gardener, if you put this concept to someone who has a wonderful garden, they would probably immediately agree with you and launch into various descriptions of their favorite plants and what they were like, giving them human terms and labels.

What dowsing can do for you is find out which plants actually like each other. For example, let's suppose that you have several pots of houseplants in various areas of your home. Some are on the windowsill, others on low tables, still others on shelves in various rooms.

By dowsing, you can discover which potted plant wants company and which one want to be left alone. Some want a greater share of the sunlight, even if only for a few times a week, or for short periods in a day. Others want to be with only one plant and no one else.

The complexity of the relationships is something which is quite fascinating the first time you do this. You will discover plants that are only happy in groups and others who will only allow others within a certain distance, and yet others who are happy to be wherever they are, but have their own preferences nevertheless.

In order to find this out, you dowse each plant with a list of possible questions, such as;

- *On a scale of 0 to 10 with 10 being best, is your happiness in this present position an 8 or better?* (I'm assuming that anything below an 8 means the present setup is only so-so and can be significantly improved.)
- *Would having a companion next to you increase your happiness and well-being?*
- *Would more/less sunlight/a different room/etc increase your happiness?*

And so on. You can refine the questions to your specific requirements, but do make sure that you cover the various possible parameters of their environment and of their inter-relationships.

Once the plants are in their new positions, you can check out the results by straightforward dowsing, or, and perhaps more interestingly, by looking at how the aura or energy field of each plant has changed. The ones who like being in groups will have auras which intermingle, whilst those who prefer being alone will have wider and stronger auras with distinct boundaries.

If, on the other hand, you are thinking of companion planting outside, then the easiest method of doing this is to have the seed packets or seedlings together and ask the same sort of questions as above of each type of plant.

Once you have a good idea of who is growing with whom, then you need to check when each needs to be planted and the density of the final garden. But, in essence, the approach is exactly the same as for indoor houseplants.

Growing plants is one of the easiest way anyone can interact with Nature, no matter where they live. Whether you grow plants in pots or outdoors in a garden, dowsing is a valuable tool for helping you to grow the most beautiful, nutritious and happy plants.

SPACE CLEARING

Your Environment Can Heal You or Kill You

One of our specialties in dowsing was for the purpose of space clearing. Early in our dowsing careers, we learned about the dangers of noxious earth energies, called geopathic stress. As we studied more, we discovered many other sources of detrimental energy and learned to clear them.

We've been blessed to do space clearings long distance in many countries around the world, and we've encountered a lot of strange energies. Our experience has enabled us to formulate simple and effective means of space clearing.

The earth is not inherently a dangerous place. But because every species requires a particular kind of energy to thrive, there are a wide range of energies.

Energy, as we explain in another article, is not innately good or bad, but is judged by how it affects humans. But what's bad for you can be healthy or even required for your cat to thrive. Since every species has its place in the ecosystem, all the different energies are needed, and they are all good…for the right species.

Your mission is to find and create environmental energy supportive of your goals. As you may have guessed, dowsing is the best way to identify energies, choose a clearing method and check up on your space. In this training, you will learn the basics of how to use dowsing for space clearing.

How Do You Know Whether Your Environment is Healthy or Not?

Dowsing helps you determine the level in effects (meaning the overall effects) of the environment on you. You can even dowse about its effect on particular aspects of your life.

A good question to start with is to ask about your living space:

On a +10 to -10 scale, with negative numbers being detrimental to my health, what is the level in effects on me of the most noxious energy in my house at this time?

If you aren't yet comfortable dowsing with scales, you can ask:

Are there any energies in my house at this time that have a -8 or worse effect on my overall health?

If you haven't been doing regular space clearing, you will have negative energies in your house. Anything over -8 has a very harmful effect, but don't panic yet. What's the next question to ask?

If there is -10 energy present in your house, but it's in a closet you hardly use, what harm is it doing? On the other hand, if it's in your bed, you need to clear it pronto.

You can find out where the energies are by using map dowsing techniques to check a sketch of your house's floor plan. We have a training on map dowsing in this chapter. But if you want a quick 'cheat,' you can just write a list of all the rooms in your house and list dowse what the worst energy is in each room.

Obviously, places you spend the most time are most critical. You must keep them clear. Your bed is most important, and then maybe your favorite chair. Or at your computer.

You don't really need to know the type or source of noxious energies in order to clear them in most cases.

So, you've found out what the worst energy in your house is. You've found out what areas are most affected by noxious energies. Now you can go on to clearing them.

How Can You Fix It?

Harmonizing your space to make it supportive of your goals is usually pretty easy, though in 20 years of space clearing, we did run into a few situations that we could not clear from a distance. We felt if we'd been on location, we could have succeeded at those. Our experience is almost any space can be cleared via long distance. We've never failed to clear a space in person. We're pretty sure you can succeed in most cases using these simple steps.

Step 1: Find a Method

Having a toolkit with a lot of clearing methods is very helpful here. You are basically using intention to harmonize the space for good health and happiness, and you will use something physical to anchor that frequency. Crystals, symbols, colors, fragrance, sound, even numbers can be used for clearing.

Use dowsing to select which method in your toolkit is the most effective for the goal of creating healthy, harmonious space for all who live there. Be flexible.

Step 2: Apply the Method

You're going to use a statement of intention followed by anchoring it with whatever you dowsed would be the best anchor. It's also helpful to ask your spiritual helpers, like your guardian angel or guides, to help with the clearing.

Any good general statement that reflects your positive goal will work. Here is an example:

Please harmonize the energies of my house and property to align with good health, prosperity and happiness for me, my family, pets and all who live, work or visit here. Please send any misplaced beings to their right and perfect place in the right and perfect way. Please clear or disempower any conscious energies currently having a negative effect on the people, pets and plants living here.

You can change the wording to reflect your belief system. Of course, you could even dowse on a 0-10 scale to see how effective the method and statement you intend to use will be, and tweak them as needed to get a 10 out of 10.

Step 3: Check Your Work

When you complete the clearing, ask the same question you did in the beginning to find what the strongest detrimental energy now is. If the clearing has worked, 0 should be the worst energy, and there will likely be a lot of positive energy. Energy usually clears immediately, but some stubborn energies may take up to 72 hours to completely dissipate. So if you find there is still noxious energy, dowse if it will be gone within 72 hours.

You will always improve your space by doing a clearing. If you find something you cannot shift, our *Busy Person's Guide to Space Clearing* is an inexpensive course, or you can hire a professional.

Is a Clearing Permanent?

Don't we all wish that! But no. Energies are constantly changing. Your environment is a reflection of you, so your home is a reflection of everyone who lives there and their stresses and beliefs. When there is a lot of stress, frequent clearing will be needed.

We have found that monthly clearing is needed when great stress is present. Quarterly clearing is optimal in normal conditions. Just like your house needs dusting and vacuuming, it needs regular energy clearing. Aren't you glad it's so simple to do when you can dowse?

Different Types of Noxious Energies

For advanced space clearing, it is vital to understand the sources of different noxious energies, as that often helps you better remedy them. The three categories we use are geopathic (from the earth), manmade (humans are the source), and cosmic (coming from outside the earth).

Among these categories, most of the energies just simply 'are,' but some of the energies come from conscious sources. Some are 'things' like lines of energy, while others are beings in spirit form. If you choose to learn more advanced techniques, it will help you to understand the different sources of noxious energy so you can more easily resolve them.

Once you acknowledge the invisible aspects of your environment and the effects they have on you, it changes your view of the world. You want to live a happy, healthy, safe life, and by paying attention to environmental energy, you make a conscious choice to support yourself energetically. You have the power of dowsing to help you identify and transform energies to beneficial for you, your family, your pets. So use it!

THE SUBCONSCIOUS & HOW TO DOWSE IT

If you are experiencing a negative pattern in your life, there is a reason. One major cause of unwanted patterns of experience is faulty subconscious beliefs. You cannot know what your subconscious believes by using your conscious mind. That's the definition of 'sub-conscious'. So how do you discover what the subconscious believes? Dowsing is the easiest way.

The Role of the Subconscious

Whether you realize it or not, you are living a life based on your subconscious beliefs. The most important fact you need to know is that you cannot know what the subconscious thinks by using your conscious mind. By definition, what is subconscious is not accessible to the conscious mind. Herein lies the biggest part of the problem.

You consciously want to be:

- Healthy
- Happy
- well-off
- Loved

- Successful
- Trim and fit

…and a lot of others things.

How many of the above do you consider yourself? If there is even one that you don't have, you have to admit that the conscious mind is not running the show. If it were, you would have what you want.

The sad news is that people don't realize that. So then they have to find something or someone to blame for why they don't have the experiences they want. Of course, because they are unaware that the subconscious is running the show, they look outside of themselves for answers. Most of them will decide that the following are the culprits:

- Family members
- Spouse
- The government
- Their boss
- Society
- God

This unfortunate decision then causes them to see themselves as helpless victims. And victims cannot be victors. This locks in a pattern of unhappiness and unfulfilled dreams.

A small percentage of people discover spirituality and become seekers of fulfillment and happiness. They try all kinds of methods to change their lives for the better. For example, they use affirmations. Yet affirmations don't work for most people.

Affirmations are simply statements that contradict what your subconscious mind believes. Since the subconscious is in charge, it doesn't care what you are saying. It doesn't care what you consciously believe.

Why is the subconscious so powerful? Its only job is to keep you alive. It is a more primitive operative than the conscious. It doesn't weigh pros and cons. It acts.

Your survival is its priority. So it doesn't care if you are healthy, happy and wealthy. As long as you are alive, it is successful.

The conscious mind wants the frills of living. The subconscious wants survival. And the subconscious is in charge.

It is normal for the subconscious and the conscious to disagree on fundamental issues. If that happens, the subconscious wins out. Survival takes priority over health, happiness and wealth.

Your feeble conscious attempts to change your life don't work unless you address the very real concerns of your subconscious. But you can't know what they are by using the conscious mind.

Dowsing: A Key to the Subconscious

It is vital to know what your subconscious is up to. You need to harmonize the beliefs of both the conscious and subconscious to manifest the life you want. So how do you find out? You can't just ask or think or guess.

Since the subconscious is hidden from the conscious, you must take an indirect approach to find out what it believes. There are two main ways that we have found helpful to detect the beliefs of your subconscious mind.

One way that anyone can use is an ancient tool: learning to read the signs around you. Cultures that live in closer harmony to Nature use this method naturally. They understand the connection between all things, and they are in harmony with the adage 'as above, so below.'

We use this method in our lives and also in the past to help our clients. It is based on the understanding that everything around you is a reflection of your beliefs. You just need to learn how to decode what you see and get the message. Your subconscious talks to you through the signs all around you.

For example, water leaks represent overflowing emotions. Where and how the leaks occur often can give further details of what is going on at the subconscious level. If you have a plumbing leak in your basement, knowing that the basement represents your subconscious can help you understand that you have buried emotions that are needing to be released, and they have gotten out of control.

The people closest to you are also conduits of information that allow you insights into your subconscious beliefs. The way people interact with you is a reflection of those beliefs, whether you like that or not.

Reading the signs takes a good bit of practice and some good reference books, but it can help you understand the messages from your subconscious.

Far and away the easiest way to learn what your subconscious believes, however, is through dowsing. Dowsing the subconscious requires detachment, because you are going to find out some silly and incredible beliefs in your subconscious.

Try It Yourself: Dowsing the Subconscious

With dowsing, you can quickly find out what your subconscious believes and just as quickly transform those beliefs that aren't in alignment with what you consciously want to experience. It's a wonderful exercise in detachment, plus we guarantee it will give you surprising answers, which is proof that you are dowsing and not just providing the answers you expect.

The subconscious has one big priority: to keep you alive. Everything else is secondary. It doesn't really care if you are sick, poor and miserable. It just wants you alive. Sad, isn't it?

Understanding that helps you to get started on dowsing your subconscious blocks. Think about something in your life that you really want to change. Something that you believe you truly want.

The more specific it is, the better. The longer you have tried to change it unsuccessfully, the better. Can you think of a topic? Some ideas that might work are:

- I always get passed over for promotion to management, even though I qualify.
- No one ever notices me.
- I can't seem to make as much money as I want (think of an amount).
- I can't get any respect from my family.
- My significant other cheats on me all the time.

So, think of your topic. The first thing we are going to check is safety issues at the subconscious level. Remember, that is the main job of the subconscious, so that is the best place to start. We have found that safety issues are the most powerful blocks you can have. It doesn't matter how illogical they are, they take precedence over what your conscious mind wants.

Think of your topic. Now, dowse the following question:

At the subconscious level, do I believe it is safe for me to _____.
(Fill in the blank with what you want to experience, but aren't. For example: get promoted to manager, have a faithful spouse, etc.)

You must be detached and allow whatever the answer is to come through. If you are not experiencing what you want, more than likely you have safety issues. If you get that it is safe, then check the following at the subconscious level by filling in the blanks with what you consciously want to experience:

- *I want to* _____. (This tests desire.)
- *I am able to* _____. (This tests capability.)
- *I have chosen to* _____. (This tests commitment.)
- *I have chosen to* _____*now*. (This tests for procrastination.)

Notice the above are statements rather than questions. Either work with dowsing. For statements, 'yes' is 'true' and 'no' is 'false.' If you get positive answers to all of the above, and you have no safety issues, then you should be experiencing what you want. If you are not experiencing what you want, then there may be some more complex issues impinging on it, but most people will find that they have one or more of the above active. The more negatives you have, the stronger the block.

Avoid Common Pitfalls

Before we go on to the clearing part, let's address pitfalls. The usual ones apply. Your polarity can shift instantly when you strike an emotional issue. Oftentimes, it is a way of misleading you. Check your polarity during the session to make sure it hasn't flipped.

The subconscious has such a strong desire to keep you alive that it will mislead you and even lie to you outright. Dowse these questions if you suspect you are not getting accurate dowsing answers (usually this is on a topic you have a lot of emotion about).

- *Am I able to get an accurate answer to this question?*
- *Am I lying?*

The nice thing about this is that if you discover you are lying, then you know what the answer is. It's the opposite of the one you got originally. You also know that you have major issues with this subject, and that it probably is a core issue with you. That can point you in the direction of other things you can look into, like past lives that might need clearing work.

Something that isn't strictly a pitfall, but can make you feel you have failed, is that as with all healing, this type of situation can come in layers. You can clear one layer, and then another one surfaces. The good news is that if there are layers, they get easier to clear each time.

Transforming Subconscious Beliefs

You can usually use a statement of intention or other simple means, like a symbol, to transform the energy of beliefs quickly, easily, comfortably and safely. Afterwards, go back and re-dowse the beliefs at the subconscious level.

Remember that some energies take up to 72 hours to shift, so test the beliefs three days into the future for best results. (You can 'cheat' and just ask whether they will be true at the subconscious level three days from today.)

What if the belief doesn't shift? Then that means that there is a powerful belief behind it that needs to be cleared. Once it is cleared, the original belief will disappear.

Here's an example:

You dowse that it is not safe for you to write a best-selling novel.

You attempt to transform the belief using various techniques, but it won't shift.

You then brainstorm and ask yourself what might change in your life if you wrote a best-seller. You come up with a list:

- I would be popular.
- I would make a lot of money.
- I would be famous.

You then test whether each of those experiences would be safe for you.

- It is safe for me to be popular.
- It is safe for me to make a lot of money.
- It is safe for me to be famous.

Then you discover two out of three are not safe.

You clear those.

You then go back and retest the original beliefs and find they are all cleared.

After the Clearing

After you have cleared the beliefs, it is wise to replace them with something that you want to believe. Otherwise, the habitual way of thinking might try to reboot in your system.

When your conscious and subconscious minds are in conflict, you will feel 'stuck,' and you will also feel anxious and sometimes fearful.

Remember, the subconscious is only trying to help you survive. But it gets its beliefs from past life experiences, and over the lifetimes, some of the coding becomes corrupted, which leads to a battle with your conscious mind.

While living a conscious life is a terrific goal, it is very, very hard to do. Until you reach that level of enlightenment, the best thing to do is to employ dowsing to discover your subconscious beliefs that need clearing, and then use intention to transform them. It's really rather simple and you'll have a laugh over some of the things your subconscious believes.

USING DOWSING IN YOUR CHOSEN CAREER

Learning to dowse can be fun, and you can quickly see benefits in your daily life. But when it comes to using dowsing at work, you might be stumped. This article will give you some suggestions for incorporating your intuition via dowsing in whatever you do as a career or job. You aren't likely to make a living with dowsing unless you are a water dowser, because dowsing is not valued conventionally. But you may be surprised how many professions benefit from the use of dowsing.

Dowsing for Health Care Professionals

The most obvious application of dowsing in a profession is in health care. If you are a chiropractor, doctor or therapist, you are aware by now that a simple 'standard of care' that tells you what to do with every patient is going to fail to give you the results you want in some cases, because not everyone is alike. Why not use your intuition to make sure each patient is guided towards their health goals?

There are immediate problems to this scenario. If you are in a traditional health care position, you may not have the freedom to treat patients as individuals and tailor your recommendations to their specific needs. There seems to be a move toward taking away discretion from health care providers and turning them into technicians for whatever corporate or government interest is overseeing their work.

If that is the position you are in, you will not be able to use dowsing as much as you might like. That might lead you to question whether you are in the right job. Just remember to act in integrity with your beliefs. At the very least, you can guide people away from anything you dowse would harm them.

Do you tell your patient about dowsing? Only you can decide if this is appropriate for your situation. Sometimes it is; sometimes it isn't. If it seems counterproductive to let folks know you use dowsing, you can use it in a stealth fashion. Just add it to your process when you make recommendations. You are not required to say **why** you suggest this or that. If you have a more conventional practice, it may be wise to let people wonder why you get better results. All they care about is the results anyway.

For those who have the freedom to consult individually with patients and create a personalized plan for them, dowsing is a natural tool for improving results. There are so many factors involved in healing, and everyone is different. You can use dowsing for just about anything your brain cannot determine. Some examples are:

- Checking the efficacy of a particular remedy, therapy or plan
- Finding out the level of side effects
- Determining whether surgery would be effective or create more problems
- Locating the place in the body or aura that is the cause of the symptom
- Determining how much the patient is in alignment with reaching their stated goal, or how much they are on board with your plan

Chiropractors use muscle testing, a form of dowsing, in their work, and they get great results. But dowsing has a much wider application than just finding subluxations. All practitioners are faced with a staggering array of remedies from vitamins and minerals to pharmaceutical drugs, and no one can keep up with the scientific progress in health care, because change is coming at such a rapid pace.

Most practitioners have little time to read all the journals or attend conferences, and even if they did, corporate interests are directing research towards their interests more and more, making findings questionable in some cases. Dowsing can guide you toward your goals, whatever they may be.

Health dowsing is a complex and valuable application for dowsing. It is also one of the most challenging to master. Whether you are a veterinarian, a naturopath or an MD, dowsing can help you help more people. If you are interested in this subject, get our book, *Dowsing for Health: Awaken Your Hidden Talent.*

But It's Life or Death!

As a health care professional, you want the best outcome for your patients. You want to do the 'right' thing. If you do not dowse, sometimes things don't turn out well. You do your best, but you cannot control outcomes.

Dowsing is never 100% accurate. Nothing is. Without dowsing, your rate of 'curing' patients is always going to be less than perfect. With dowsing, your rate should improve if you are masterful at dowsing, but you will never achieve perfection.

It is always hard when you lose a patient or someone doesn't heal. Our belief is that health dowsing increases our odds of success. But it is an individual decision, and you need to examine the professional conduct guidelines for your particular practice and think about how you feel about using dowsing. Don't just jump in; take your time and make a clear decision that aligns with your ethics and your goals.

We consulted with many clients over the years, usually long distance via phone. We found that including the client in the process gave better results. We taught them a simple deviceless dowsing technique and asked them to dowse along with us. We always went with what they got, even if our dowsing contradicted their answers, because a person's beliefs control their reality, and it doesn't matter what an outsider thinks you can do; it matters what you think.

People aren't always ready to heal, or they aren't ready to take a certain path. By including them in the process, you empower them to see positive outcomes are possible. You also get an insight into where they are at in their healing process and what they can accept.

Using Dowsing in Therapies for Personal Growth

Another area of health dowsing is consulting with clients on emotional and mental issues. Dowsing can be applied in this career the same as in physical health professions.

If you are aware of energetic causes of mental/emotional problems and blocks to progress, you can dowse to find out if any of those things are behind your client's problem. We consulted for years with people who wanted to make changes in their lives but were stuck. Often, clearing the energetic causes gave noticeable improvement. Some examples of things to dowse and clear are:

- Attached entities (especially helpful in mental/emotional issues)
- Subconscious beliefs (see the article in this chapter on that topic)
- Past life trauma (see the article on that subject in this chapter)

These are but a few things to dowse about. Clearing is usually easy with intention, and in many cases, involving the client in the process empowers them to believe they can improve. Teach them a deviceless technique for this. It works great, even over the phone.

Of course, you need to exercise discretion about whether a client is open to this, and you need to consider ethical and professional implications.

Dowsing for Coaching or Teaching

When you are working as a coach or teacher, being able to interact with your students/clients as individuals will give you better results than if you teach your program to everyone the same way. One system never works for everyone. Dowsing allows you to tailor a program for a particular student.

This is obviously going to be easier to do in high-end coaching situations. If you are teaching third grade in a public school, you have your hands full as it is. But it can still help you.

Dowsing in these cases can help you determine:

- The level of the student's talent or engagement
- How appropriate the program is for that student in order to reach particular goals
- What is blocking a student's progress and how to overcome it

Dowsing for Inspectors or for Routine Maintenance

If you are in a profession where inspection is part or all of what you do, dowsing is wonderful. Maggie used to work nondestructive inspection at NASA, and she would have loved to have dowsing in her kit along with the fancy tests and equipment she had. Nigel tells the story of a dowsing teacher he had who worked quality control in a factory and successfully used dowsing to pull products off the line that were defective.

As with all dowsing used in careers, this type of dowsing is only recommended for dowsers who have mastered dowsing technique and have confidence in their answers.

You might not be a full-time inspector, but there are many jobs where being able to identify a defective part, machine or product can come in helpful. Mechanics would love dowsing. In fact, anyone who works with machines can benefit.

When Things Break Down: Dowsing to Interpret Intuitive Messages

Maggie has always been tuned in to sound. When a machine starts making a new sound, she hears it. Before she knew dowsing, she didn't know what to do with that information. She felt kind of crazy sharing what she knew.

She'd say the washing machine is making a new sound, or the car is making a new sound, and a week later, the machine would break down. She was so good at it, that when she said 'the film processor is making a new sound' at the Radiography lab at NASA, they called in a technician to look at it; it was getting ready to break down, and a breakdown would have been crippling to production.

If you can dowse, you can ask questions about whether that new sound means something bad and whether it would be beneficial to call a repair person and what person to contact. And if you aren't tuned in to sound, dowsing can tell you how well a machine is functioning on a scale of 0-10 and also how beneficial it would be to call in someone for maintenance or to do a particular upgrade.

Most people are in jobs that rely on machines, whether it is a computer and printer or a car or a lathe, and we need machines to function well to help us perform tasks. Using dowsing will help you head off breakdowns and maintain your equipment and machines in top form. People will be amazed at how you are a 'machine whisperer' with dowsing.

Dowsing for Financial Advisors

If money dowsing is a specialty of yours, it will help you invest wisely, but if you have a career in finance, it could really help you get amazing results. We have observed that most people have issues with money that make financial dowsing tricky. You have to overcome any bad money energy you have to use dowsing effectively about money. But it would be worth the effort if your profession is finance.

Knowing that a person's energy around wealth is the most important factor in their success with money gives you insight into why one investment strategy doesn't work for everyone. If you are guiding someone, you will be more effective if you can work with whatever their beliefs and energy are, rather than giving them a one-size-fits-all program.

Financial advising often takes the form of dowsing the future. See our article in this chapter on that tricky subject. Dowsing money is hard enough for most people, but dowsing the future of a financial choice is even more challenging. But it can theoretically be done, and if you master this, you will certainly make your clients wealthy (if they really want to be on all levels).

As with other professions, in financial dowsing you might choose not to reveal to investors that you use dowsing, as they might not see it the way you do. But when you get good results for them, they will be happy. Your methods in this are like a trade secret, and they won't expect you to share.

Do You See the Pattern?

No matter whether you work at a burger joint or are doing high finance, there will always be ways that you can do a better job and get better results if you focus your intuition with dowsing. The applications are limitless.

You may get a feeling when flipping burgers that that batch of meat is 'off,' and dowsing confirms it, so you save people from food poisoning. Or you may use dowsing to discover a traditional drug would have fatal results for a patient, so you switch to one that dowses better. Perhaps you use dowsing to find out that you need to service the company car, printer or whatever machine or it will break down.

Summary

Think about your job or career. How could dowsing help you do a better job? How could focusing your intuition save you hassles? Living more intuitively always improves life. You will need to adapt it realistically, as most people don't accept the validity of dowsing. But you don't have to tell them that's how you figured something out.

WATER DOWSING

In the desert, water is a priceless commodity. If you live in a city, you probably don't think about how lucky you are to always have enough water. In the desert, water is called a 'limiting factor.' If there isn't enough water, you can't live in a place.

We were asked to dowse for a spot to drill a water well on a residential property in a part of the desert where many people failed to find water. The property owner had to find water on his few-acre parcel so that he could live there. He was concerned, because he had been told that the area was noted for not having water, and many people told horror stories of paying big bucks to drill dry holes.

We dowsed, found a site and he drilled and struck water. He was pleased with the output of the well. He and his wife invited us to come see their home when it was finished and decorated. It was quite lovely.

Dowsing is a natural ability we all have. As long as there have been humans, there have been humans dowsing. Historically, dowsing for water is one of the consistent uses of dowsing that has not been suppressed. This is probably because water is such a vital commodity for life. As a result, many people think of an old guy carrying a forked willow branch looking for water as a definition of 'dowser.'

In this mini-training, you will find out a number of ways you can use dowsing to find, evaluate or change water. So don't skip this training just because you don't intend to dowse for water wells. We've made sure there's something for everyone, because we all need water to live well.

Water Wells

Because city dwellers take water for granted, water dowsing is not that commonly known, and it is becoming a dying art. As more people take to the cities, there is less need for that talent. But even in modern times, the ability to dowse underground water can be a valuable skill.

If you have an interest in this type of dowsing, it is a skill that you can use professionally that will help people and make you money. Unlike dowsing for healing, dowsing for underground water has no 'New Age' stigma. Many well companies like to partner with a water dowser, as it is win/win. Fewer dry holes means more profit and a better reputation.

Another advantage to mastering water dowsing is it's very simple and straightforward. When dowsing for one thing, as water, oil and mineral dowsers do, you generally are using the same question every time you dowse, so you will master it quickly. Perhaps this is another reason water dowsing has survived so long. It's simple and gives measurable results.

Veteran water witchers (as water dowsers are sometimes called) can have amazing success rates. As quantum physics reveals the nature of the web of life, people have begun to ask how water dowsers are so successful. In researching records of water witchers, they found that the dowsers always seemed to find what they were looking for in the place they were looking for it.

It seemed odd that they would site a 50 gallon per minute well as requested within 500 feet of the house, and then go back to the same property 10 years later and find another site for a 100 gallon per minute well within 200 feet of the house. This led to the question of whether they were finding the water or creating it via intention.

Dowsers also frequently will relocate underground water to remove energetic issues. If you can divert water, why not call it in to a place?

Because of the ability to peruse records, this is one area of dowsing where there are actual statistics to support the theory that reality is being created via focused intention.

Before we teach you the steps to locating a well site, let's look at things anyone can dowse about water anytime, anywhere so you can get some practice.

Try It Yourself: Check the Quality of Your Water

Most people don't have the opportunity to go site a well and then hire someone to drill to prove them right or wrong. So how can you dowse about water in a meaningful way that you can confirm your results? It's easy!

Dowsing can be used to evaluate water quality.

In most areas, it is possible to submit a sample of water for testing of certain minerals, pH, contaminants, etc. Find out what you can test for in water for the lowest price. Or go online and buy a home water test kit. Some are very inexpensive.

Normally, we say don't dowse something you can find out rationally. And it's true you can pay for a water test for these things. But if you master dowsing water quality, you won't need to buy tests, which will save you time and money. More importantly, if you master this process, you can dowse for substances that are not included in any test for any price, but that matter to you.

Get samples of water from more than one source. Tap water is a very good one. Bottled or filtered water is another. If you have a pond or natural source of water outdoors, that makes a good third sample. Put a small amount of water in a glass vial that may be sealed tightly. Label the vials with numbers or letters and keep a record of which sample is which. If you number or letter them, you can distance yourself a bit from the results.

Now formulate dowsing questions related to water quality. Some that you might ask are:

On a scale of 0-10, with 10 being the most contaminated, how contaminated is this sample with bacteria? With viruses? With heavy metals? With plastics or plasticizers? With prescription drug or chemical residue? With arsenic? With E.coli? Do not be surprised if they are all higher than 0. But you should get a spread of numbers if your samples are different enough.

On a scale of +10 to -10, how healthy overall is this water for me to drink at this time? Bear in mind that a small amount of contamination in your water might be harmless, but drinking it daily could be detrimental to your health. We would expect you to see differences between the samples.

Make a note of your results. If you have labeled the vials with numbers randomly assigned by another person, that will keep you from being prejudiced about results. Then go back and see which vial is which water.

Do the answers make sense to you? How can you explain them so that they **do** make sense to you?

You can send the water samples for testing and compare the results of the lab with your results. Before sending the vials out, make sure you have dowsed for whatever factor the lab will be testing them for. Make a clear dowsing question and record your results. If the lab results are reported in parts per million, ppm, then dowse ppm of whatever it is you are asking about.

If you have purchased a home test kit, then dowse for the factors the test kit will dowse using the same terms and units of measurement. Record your dowsing results. Use the test kit to then test the samples. Compare your results with those of the test kit.

Try It Yourself: Charge Water with Intention

It's pretty exciting to dowse for a water well and have confirmation that you were right. But most dowsers never get a chance to dowse for water that way. Something that you can easily dowse for using water is related to health and healing.

Dr. Emoto in *Messages from Water* made people aware of water's ability to hold energies. Many dowsers have been aware of this property for years. In fact, one of the problems with underground water is the ability of water to carry noxious energies. But Dr. Emoto brought this subject to the forefront by taking photomicrographs of water that proved beyond any doubt that the structure of water can be changed by the energies of emotion to which it is exposed.

His photographs show that the energy of love, peace and forgiveness give water a beautiful structure, while anger, hate and judgment make the structure of water ugly and disorganized. It has recently been shown that water in your body is structured in a unique way that aids the healthy function of your body. It is believed by some experts that certain environmental factors are harmful because they break down this structured water. Others believe that your thoughts and emotions affect the structure of your body's water. So that health is not only determined by hydration, but by how your water is structured.

You can evaluate your water source using dowsing. Use a scale of +10 to -10, with negative numbers being detrimental and positive ones being beneficial. Ask for the overall rating of your drinking water for your health. Ask the same question for each member of your family and each pet. If you have horses, it is wise to test their water as well. Note that the same water does not have the same effect on everyone.

Water is vital to health. We advise against using tap water to cook with or drink. We advise using a filter on your bath or shower to remove chlorine if you are on city water. But even if you are using filtered water, it may not be a +10.

If you have an R/O system, do you maintain it regularly, having a professional change the filters and check the membrane? If you are using bottled water, what type of container are you using? If you reuse it, such as when you put water in a barrel for your horses, how often are you cleaning the container and what do you use to clean it? Pure water can grow bacteria quite easily, which is why city water has chlorine in it. But chlorine is bad for your health. There are many considerations, and dowsing can help you work your way through them satisfactorily.

Once you have gotten the best water you can, you can use intention to raise the healing properties and healthfulness of the water. Dowse the healing properties of your water. Or dowse how beneficial it is for raising your level of health overall. Use a scale of +10 to -10. Make a note of the result.

Now focus your intention and send love to the water. Send gratitude that it is so pure and healthful. Send appreciation that it helps you heal and restore your physical body. Send it whatever positive energies you wish.

Now dowse the same exact question again of that water sample. In most cases, you will see the number improve dramatically. Doing this intention before using your water will help your health and well-being.

Please be aware, however, that just because you used your intention, it might not have made any change. Dowsing the result of this experiment is a very good exercise in detachment from the results! Don't be disappointed, but be determined to try again and do better.

Because our bodies are mostly water, we have a tendency to carry energies that we are exposed to, pick up or have directed at us. Therefore, true positive thinking and focused intention to create positive outcomes is very important for health.

The locations you frequent and the people you hang out with all have an effect on you, as they resonate with energies, and your body picks the energies up or at least is affected by them. Associating with positive people and places therefore makes sense as a good health choice.

How to Find a Well Site

This may be done using a detailed map of a property or on site in person. If done on site, L-rods or a Y-rod are usually the tool of choice for the job.

As with all dowsing, accuracy will depend with how good a question you ask.

Here is the question our acquaintance the professional water dowser used, filling in the values for the depth and flow-rate based on what the client wanted:

Please show me the electromagnetic energy from only a legal, drillable, pumpable, potable, palatable, free-flowing underground source of primary replenishing water at a depth of less than x feet which will deliver y gallons a minute or more at the surface in my time now with a real pump installed and with electric power wired, and which will not go dry in drought years.

Remember how we said a good dowsing question is usually long and contains who, what, where, when, how and why? This is an excellent example of that.

Ask if there is a source in the area you are dowsing that fits the specifications in the question. Sometimes there isn't, so you don't want to waste time.

If there is at least one location that meets the requirements, you want to find the best, given the criteria of the person asking you to dowse. Within the area indicated by the person who requested the dowsing, focus on your question, looking for the best place that fits and walk a pattern over that area until you get a 'yes' answer. Ask the question again at that spot to make sure you are getting the answer to that question.

The nice thing about water dowsing is that you get confirmation of what you dowsed. Keep a good written record of your dowsing so that you can see how you are doing.

Even if you have difficulty arranging to locate a well in your neighborhood, you can still develop and refine the two essential skills of well-dowsing: flow-rate and depth.

You can practice this relatively simply by using a hosepipe. Start the water flowing through the hose and dowse what the flow rate is. You can vary the flow through the pipe. Simply ask whether it is flowing at a rate of, say, 3 gallons a minute, or 4, and so on. Or, you could ask if it flowing at a rate of less then 10 gallons a minute, or twenty, and so on. If you use the latter method, then your questioning might be along the lines of, *Is this water flowing at rate of under 10 gallons a minute? No, Under 20? Yes, Under 15? No, Is it 16 gallons per minute? No, 17? Yes.*

The beauty of this is that you can measure your results with a bucket and stopwatch. That way, you will learn to become more accurate.

There are various ways you can dowse the depth. All of them rely on getting a 'yes' response to the correct depth. You can either ask for the depth a foot at a time, which is not recommended if you are over a 500 foot deep aquifer, or you can become more and more precise in your questioning.

So, for example, you can start off by asking if the depth to the top of the water is less than 100 feet. If you get 'no,' then ask if it is under 200 feet. Keep asking until you get a 'yes.' Let's say that you get a hit that it's somewhere between 300 and 400 feet. In that case you switch to asking in units of ten. *Is it less than 310? Less than 320? Less than 330?* and so on. When you get another hit, you ask for the units. That way you can quickly find out the depth is, say, 373 feet to the top of the water.

Another, old method of finding the depth is called 'The Bishop's Rule.' Basically, you find the center of the stream of underground water, mark the location and then walk away from it at right angles until you get another 'hit.' The distance on the surface between the center of the stream and the second hit is the same as depth from the surface to the top of the water.

In all cases, wherever possible, check your results against the physical evidence if you are going to develop water-witching as one of your skills.

Pitfalls to Avoid

As with any type of dowsing, there are pitfalls when dowsing about water. Here are some of the most common you want to look out for and guard against:

- Never dowse about anything you have strong emotions about.
- Make sure your polarity is correct before dowsing, and check it now and then during your dowsing to make sure it has not 'flipped.'
- Do your best to detach and remove your ego from any dowsing exercise.
- Make sure you are properly hydrated when dowsing.

Dehydration can reverse your polarity and give you incorrect dowsing answers.

Summary

Water plays an important part in our lives and in our health and well-being. As a dowser, you can use your dowsing skills to find water, to move water to a new location, to evaluate water, to heal water and to infuse it with healing properties for those who drink it. Expand your thoughts and applications of water dowsing and watch how it promotes balance and harmony in your life.

6

CONGRATULATIONS! YOU'RE DOWSING!

You made it! Okay, maybe you didn't do all the advanced dowsing trainings. That's all right, because you aren't interested in every dowsing application. The main thing is that you explored the ones that attract you, and you gave them a try, and you now feel motivated to start using dowsing even more in your life.

You've seen for yourself how powerful dowsing is, how amazing it can be. We've given you a peek into how dowsing can reduce stress, save money, add fun to your life and improve your health, relationships and finances.

Dowsing is the most powerful tool we ever learned for personal growth and life improvement. Thanks for letting us share it with you.

We hope you had fun learning dowsing from us. Dowsing has done so much for us, we want to share it with everyone we meet. Thanks for letting us into your life for this brief time so we could share with you.

Happy Dowsing!

Maggie and Nigel

APPENDIX: DEVICELESS DOWSING TECHNIQUES

In all of the following, you should always check your 'base' question, about where you were born in this lifetime. That way you will know which is your 'yes' and which is your 'no' response. Also, remember that 'yes' and 'no' also means 'true' and 'false.'

Blink

Consciously hold your eyes open and think your question. Soft focus the eyes and look at a neutral area. This helps you to stop focusing. After you become used to this, you can blink dowse pretty much anywhere. A blink occurring against your will signifies a 'yes.' When learning, it can sometimes help to point at the possible answers. Some people have two blinks for 'no', one for 'yes.'

Finger-thumb

Rub your finger and thumb together and think your question. A rough feeling signifies 'yes'. A smooth feeling would be 'no.'

An alternative to this could be that you can have a second opinion on the finger behind (the middle finger), giving a rough for 'no' if you are not sure about the first response. This form of dowsing can be done with your hand in your pocket.

Hand rub

Use the fingertip of one hand to rub the back of the other hand. This is similar to the one above where stickiness or roughness = 'yes' and smoothness = 'no.' It is very simple to do.

Table rub

This is very much the same as for the previous two, except you rub a table top with the fingertip of one hand. The top of the table must be clean for this to work well. In fact, you can use this on pretty much any smooth surface such as a glass window, a drinking glass, enamel and porcelain and some types of tile.

Double pinch

Gently pinch your right thumb and first finger together and then enclose them in a similar left-handed pinch, so that you are sort of encircling the first pinch with the second. Now ask your question and try and open your right pinch (the encircled one) against the left one. Success signifies 'yes,' failure = 'no.'

Remember that this version looks like you are sticking the first pinch through the second one and then trying to open it. It might seem a little ungainly or awkward at first, but it very soon becomes easier to do.

Two-ring

This is a variation of the above one. To perform this one you pinch one thumb and finger together and then, with the other hand, you pinch the thumb and finger together, but the two links are like a chain, so that as you gently part your hands, keeping the links intact, they pull on each other, just as a chain would. Now you ask your question and try to pull them apart. Success = 'yes'; if the link won't open = 'no.'

For some people, the reverse is true; hold fast for 'yes' and open for 'no.'

Squash-pinch

This is a single-handed variation on the pinch theme. Gently close your forefinger and thumb together and ask your question. Be aware of what happens to the pinch. If the pinch intensifies, or becomes stronger or seems or feels more stable, that's a 'yes.' No movement after asking, or maybe the pinch even opens just a little = 'no.'

Pinch-and-Strike

Gently pinch thumb and forefinger of non-dominant hand to form a circle, like in the earlier double-pinch example. Now use the forefinger of the other, non-dominant, hand to strike the pinch where the finger and thumb meet. If you break the pinch = 'yes,' if you fail and the pinch holds firm ='no.'

Opposed thumbs

Place your hands palms-in in front of you as though sheltering your stomach, with the eight fingers hanging down almost parallel and the two thumbs upwards, pressing hard against one another in an upside-down V.

This might take a little practice at first, but you are really trying to press the thumbs together while the fingers are loose. By keeping the thumbs under pressure, you are making it easy for them to either flick towards your stomach or away from it.

Now ask your question and the two thumbs flick away from you for 'yes' and towards you for 'no.' For this to work well, you must have sufficient pressure on the thumbs to allow them to flick forwards or back easily.

A variation of this method could be for getting numbers. The higher the number, the further out your thumbs flick. You could, for example, get rough numbers out of 10 immediately, if the thumb movements are graduated over a 90 degree range.

Hand jab

Ask your question and thrust your right or left hand down sharply as though trapping a bouncing tennis ball. The hand closing spontaneously means 'no,' opening out, 'yes.' The key here is to not think about what the hand might be doing, just to perform the action quickly directly after the question.

Slinky

A 'Slinky' is one of those machined spiral metal coils which if you place one at the top of a staircase and push it over, will somersault slowly down the stairs. Imagine you are holding one upright in your right palm, place your left palm next to it but lower, like a stair, and ask your question.

If you feel the 'slinky' arriving in your left palm (and/or your hands rising/lowering to match the change in weight) that signifies 'yes.' This can be really quite noticeable when it works!

Whole body (also called the Body Sway)

For this to work, you must stand straight with your knees relaxed, shoulder-width apart, and ask your question. A slight bow/twist/bend ='yes'; other way = 'no.'

This really can be quite slight to begin with. It helps if you have your eyes closed when you first try this as you will then be able to sense any movement more easily. Then, when you are more confident about it, you can do this with your eyes open.

Wrist twist

Reach out with either hand as though you are about to shake hands with someone. Ask your question. If your hand twists clockwise = 'yes'; anti-clockwise ='no.'

Again, the rotation does not have to be a large one, but enough of a one for you to see.

Tongue rub

Run your tongue over the roof of your mouth and ask your question. Rough= 'yes.'

In essence, this is like the finger rub (above) except you are using your tongue as the guide. This can also be very unobtrusive to do, but do beware that, if you do this a lot, you can make the roof of your mouth quite tender! Remember that you are not pressing the tongue hard up against the roof, only allowing it to rub over it gently.

Signal arm

Have you upper arm relaxed by your side, with the forearm horizontal and pointing ahead. (From the side your arm would make an 'L' shape). If when you ask your question your hand swings in to touch your body, that's a hard 'yes'; if only part-way, a partial 'yes.'

The action of this one is rather like using an L-rod in that you are using the pivoting action to indicate the answer.

You can use the angle to give you numbers or percentages, as in 'clock' dowsing (below). If your arm swings outwards, that will be the start of a 'no' reaction and you can either switch it mentally to give a graduated 'no,' swinging inwards, or use the other arm.

As in clock dowsing, you also get a 'more-yes-than-yes' indication if your hand presses your stomach hard. This signifies a 'yes' stronger than the terms of your question have allowed. If say you had asked 'has she passed her exam ?' this might mean 'she came top.' Likewise a 'no-beyond-no' if you're in 'no' mode. (In the above example, a 'no- beyond-no' might mean she never turned up for the exam. Another example might be asking if the plane has arrived on time, and 'no-beyond-no' could indicate that the flight was canceled.)

Thumbs up

Extend your arm and make a thumbs-down with your hand. Ask your question and rotate your hand to a thumbs-up position. If your thumb goes beyond the vertical, that is 'yes,' if it does not reach the vertical, that's a 'no.' Again, the trick here is to rotate the hand smartly as you ask, and not get trapped into thinking about it.

If the wrist-twist (above) does not work for you, then this one probably will. It's basically the same motion, only the thumb will give a clearer indication of the answer.

Finger wiggle

Hold your hands limply and ask your question. If the fingers of one hand flutter like a curtain in breeze = 'yes.' If it is the other hand = 'no.' This can be a very subtle movement to begin with and you will have to learn which of your hands is used for 'yes' and which for 'no.'

Nod

Hold head straight as weakly as will just keep it from flopping. Ask your question. Involuntary nod = 'yes.' 'No' might be a shake sideways or a jerk backwards.

I've always thought of this action like the moment you fall asleep in a chair and your head flops forward and you wake up. It's that sort of delicate balance you are after with this one.

To find your body response: ask your question and just remain alert to any noticeable sensation or body part twitch or movement. You may get a sensation of cold or hot or a breeze, but more than 50% of people have a hand reaction of some kind - two fingers moving apart or together, or a clenching or opening (see hand-jab).

The point about this one is that there is invariably something happening in your body as a response, the trick is noticing it!

Point-and-Sense

This is a variation of the Body Response one. Either have an actual hand-written list of possible answers, or give each finger of the non-dominant hand a possible answer (like 'less than one hour,' 'between 1 and six hours,' ''this evening,' 'tomorrow,' 'never.' Or it could be numbers as in 'between 1and 25%,' '25 to 50%,' '50 to 75%,' '75 to 100%,' 'none of these.' You can think of similar types of answers.)

Ask your question and point at the possible answers, which you have attributed mentally to the fingers of the non-pointing hand or point at the written list. A distinctive sensation (a sting in the neck or ear lobe is common) signifies 'yes.'

Some people will have a different response for a 'no.' You will have to make sure you ask both types of questions to get the baseline response for this one.

Invisible balloon

Use one hand to sense with and the other (or the wall itself) as a wall. Ask your question and move your hand towards the 'wall.' An invisible balloon (or prickly ball, a cold area, etc.) getting in the way signifies 'yes.' The bigger and harder the response, the surer the 'yes.'

You can play around with this a lot - e.g. have balloons signifying 'no' and no balloon signifying 'yes,' or have different areas on the wall for diagnostic balloons giving you choices, numbers, times, etc. The 'balloon' idea is used a lot to sense auras and energy bodies.

Robot nose (field of view + blink)

As in the 'Nod' version (above) but keep your eyes looking ahead and ask your question which will be answered by something in your field of view (*'Which melon tastes best ?'*, for example.). Allow your nose to point to the answer. Another way of describing this might be:

Move your eyes across the scene from left to right, imagining a vertical line. An involuntary blink means: the sought after goodie is on this line. Hold eyes on the line and scan up and down it. A blink means: you are looking at it. This is especially good when picking stones or shells off a beach. You keep a reserve blink for something which is hidden underneath the top layer(s). This can be very good in supermarkets where the best fruit and vegetables are some way down in the pile. Rummage on the chosen coordinates until you get a blink. Users of this system are apt to look like a robot, however!!

General Notes 'Switching'

In all these cases, the significance can be reversed for some individuals, or by willpower, or against your will when you get tired (this is sometimes called 'switching'). You have to find out which is which by asking questions such as 'which is my yes ?' before you start. After a while, you will begin to get a feel for whether or not you are balanced and able to dowse without having to worry about whether you are 'switched' or not.

The 'Clock' system

Established dowsers will be able to make most of these modes work. But beginners can also usually get at least one to work, which is immensely heartening. The clock system is a useful indicator system with and without tools and perfect when driving, with the steering wheel handy.

Using an actual or visualized clock face, you can have degrees of 'yes' and 'no' starting at twelve o'clock and moving clock- or anti-clockwise until you get a 'stop' reaction. You probably have a natural direction for 'yes' - it's not always clockwise - so find that out first with 'show me my yes.' If, say, your 'full yes' is three o'clock which is usual, you will find some answers are at four o'clock - this is the 'more-yes-than-yes' reaction (see 'Signal Arm' above).

The clock can be changed in a flash to have whatever meanings are useful to the quest. Water diviners are now using it to establish the depth of water in a logarithmic sense - that is, one o'clock means 10 ft, two means 100, three means 1000. You don't have to wonder what half past one means, because you can switch the clock to 'tens of feet' and start again. The area between five and seven o'clock can be used for the 'idiot' response: 'that was not the right question to ask.'

You can also use the steering wheel when driving to get directions simply by moving your hand down the wheel to check left, right, straight ahead or behind you. Useful for checking where the cheapest gas station is! (Don't forget to ask how far!!!)

Your Own Method

The key to making anything work well for you is to make the necessary changes which make sense to your system. For example, you might find that deviceless dowsing works really well for you with numbers, or distance or better with food or some other area of investigation. In which case, you will doubtless develop useful shortcuts or tricks to help you get better or quicker answers. Always be on the look-out for ways in which you can accelerate things without losing accuracy. It is a sure-fire way of developing your dowsing skills!

Everyone Has This Simple Skill!

Anyone can learn to use their natural intuitive sensing ability using these techniques. There are endless applications!

-Original list compiled by Dan Wilson

RESOURCES

Dowsing Charts

Nita Ott at Mirrorwaters makes a variety of charts for dowsing. You might prefer getting just the charts you'll need from her instead of investing in a book of charts, many of which you won't use.

See what she has at www.mirrorwaters.com.

Other Valuable Offerings

Dr Patrick MacManaway (who contributed the Foreward of this book) is a third-generation dowser and Past President of the British Society of Dowsers, teaching and working with clients in the UK, USA and Australia.

See his work, courses, books and CDs at www.patrickmacmanaway.com & www.simplygoodco.com. *We have personally enjoyed his books, meditations and teleclasses and highly recommend all that he offers.*

More Books You Might Enjoy

Our other books dive deeper into topics and applications of interest to dowsers. The titles tend to say it all, as in *The Dowsing State, Ask the Right Question,* and *Dowsing for Health,* a few of the 20 books we've written.

Our *Busy Person's Guides* to energy clearing give you everything you need to know to clear all kinds of detrimental energies.

You can get copies at your favorite online retailer and see the full list on our author pages at each site.

Our Free Ebook

Don't forget to download your free digital copy of *101 Amazing Things You Can Do With Dowsing.*

ABOUT THE AUTHORS

 Nigel and Maggie Percy met online in a dowsing group in 2000 and quickly noticed a strong attraction existed between them. It was so strong that Maggie quit her job, stored her belongings, put her Reiki practice on hold and went from Arizona to the UK to meet Nigel. Several months later, they were married, and a few months afterwards, they returned to America to begin their business, which was based on dowsing, of course.

Over the years, they worked with a global human and animal clientele in space clearing, health dowsing and dowsing for personal growth. They made numerous presentations at dowsing conferences and chapter meetings. Their Discovering Dowsing website had 200 pages of free material for dowsers. Nigel created 50 You Tube videos on common dowsing questions.

Empowering people by teaching them to dowse was always their favorite thing to do. In 2012, 2013 and 2014 they hosted the online Dowsing World Summit to inform and attract people to dowsing. They created many courses on dowsing and related subjects in a variety of formats.

Together they have written over 25 books, mostly about dowsing, as writing has been a lifelong passion for them both.

Nigel and Maggie lived in Arizona for 20 years before moving to the Appalachian Mountains of northern Georgia. They are lifelong animal lovers and at one time had 12 rescue animals, including a rescued chicken. As of this writing, they have one pet, a cat named Sugar.

They don't know how the future will unfold, but they are confident their intuition will guide them to be in the perfect place at the perfect time for their goals. And they will always use dowsing.